Other Titles in the Northwest Readers Series

Series Editor: Robert J. Frank

Badger and Coyote Were Neighbors: Melville Jacobs on Northwest Indian Myths and Tales, edited by William R. Seaburg and Pamela T. Amoss

The Collected Poems of Hazel Hall, edited by John Witte

Nature's Justice: Writings of William O. Douglas, edited by James M. O'Fallon

A Richer Harvest: The Literature of Work in the Pacific Northwest, edited by Craig Wollner and W. Tracy Dillon

Wood Works: The Life and Writings of Charles Erskine Scott Wood, edited by Edwin Bingham and Tim Barnes

Fishing the Northwest

An Angler's Reader

Glen Love, editor

Oregon State University Press
Corvallis Oregon

The paper in this book meets the guidelines for permanence and durability of the Committee on Production Guidelines for Book Longevity of the Council on Library Resources and the minimum requirements of the American National Standard for Permanence of Paper for Printed Library Materials Z39.48-1984.

Library of Congress Cataloging-in-Publication Data
Fishing the Northwest : an angler's reader / Glen A. Love, editor.
    p.   cm.—(Northwest readers)
ISBN 0-87071-481-3 (alk. paper)
1. Fishing—Northwest, Pacific. I. Love, Glen A., 1932-   II. Series.
SH464.N6 F57 2000
799.1'09795—dc21

                                                                00-008388

Oregon State University Press
101 Waldo Hall
Corvallis OR 97331-6407
541-737-3166 • fax 541-737-3170
http://osu.orst.edu/dept/press

OREGON STATE
UNIVERSITY

Preface

In 1990 the Oregon State University Press issued its first two books in the Northwest Reprint Series, *Oregon Detour* by Nard Jones, and *Nehalem Tillamook Tales,* edited by Melville Jacobs. Since then, the series has reissued a range of books by Northwest writers, both fiction and nonfiction, making available again works of well-known and lesser-known writers.

As the series developed, we realized that we did not always want to reissue a complete work; instead we wanted to present selections from the works of a single author or selections from a number of writers organized around a unifying theme. Oregon State University Press, then, has decided to start a new series, the Northwest Readers Series.

The reasons for the Northwest Readers Series are the same as for the Northwest Reprint Series: "In works by Northwest writers, we get to know about the place where we live, about each other, about our history and culture, and about our flora and fauna."

RJF

To all my fishing friends,

to Gavin and Alex, tomorrow's anglers,

and to the memory of Stoddard Malarkey and Ernie King

Table of Contents

Introduction

"You can't say enough about fishing," says Thomas McGuane in Russell Chatham's book, *Silent Seasons*. "Though the sport of kings, it's just what the deadbeat ordered. Water is as mysterious as fire: we stare into it for hours, a tendril of drool at the corner of the mouth. ... You can't say enough about fishing; but that won't stop me."

You can't say enough about fishing. Herman Melville proved that in *Moby Dick,* the biggest and best book about pursuing watery creatures ever written. Melville wrote and wrote, and still ended up thinking that he couldn't dive deep enough to fathom it all. We seem to be mesmerized not so much by the chance of catching a fish as by the certainty of our attraction to water.

Our bodies, we are told by those who know, are more than eighty percent water. We take shape in the womb encased in a watery membrane. Our evolutionary past tells us that the earliest forms of life came ashore from warm oceans. Hunters and fishers in our prehistory, we've got fishing deep in our bones. Water laps and laves our imagination. If Niagara Falls were a cataract of sand, Melville asks in the opening chapter of *Moby Dick,* would anybody come to see it? "Why did the old Persians hold the sea holy?" Melville continues. "Why did the Greeks give it a separate deity and make him the own brother of Jove? Surely all this is not without meaning. And still deeper that story of Narcissus, who because he could not grasp the tormenting, mild image he saw in the fountain, plunged into it and was drowned. But that same image we ourselves see in all rivers and oceans. It is the image of the ungraspable phantom of life, and this is the key to it all."

Norman Maclean ends *A River Runs Through It* with the sentence, " 'I am haunted by waters.' " So are we all. You can't say enough about water. Or fishing. But that won't stop writers from trying to

2 Fishing the Northwest

hook the ungraspable phantom. And it won't stop another book on fishing, like this one.

Considering that the Pacific Northwest is water country, a collection of writing on Northwest angling comes as no surprise. Rivers like those that drain the great Columbia, Snake, and Fraser watersheds, streams, lakes, ponds, reservoirs, estuaries, the Pacific Ocean, Puget Sound, Vancouver Island, the Inland Passage through British Columbia to Alaska—water is what defines and distinguishes this corner of the world. Where there is so much water, there's fishing. And where there's fishing, there is writing about fishing. Because you can't say enough about it.

In an earlier day, Arnold Gingrich, the founding editor of *Esquire* magazine and a certified easterner, would claim of the New York Anglers Club that the books and articles written by its members would serve pretty much as the angling literature of its time. Today, though, much of the angling has moved west, and so have many of the angling writers. The fish are bigger and more plentiful out here, a Northwesterner can hardly be restrained from saying, not to mention the rivers and mountains and trees. That's what draws a captive easterner like Howell Raines, author of *Flyfishing Through the Midlife Crisis,* to confess to all the money he spends to fly to Montana and hire a high-priced guide in order to float down a famous trout river waving an expensive fly-rod in the air.

Then, too, many of the fishing writers have moved west because the East is no longer the cultural and publishing arbiter of the nation. Americans no longer wait for New York—or any other historical seat of authority—to tell them what to think. In this day and age, any place can become THE place. One could make a pretty good argument for Missoula, Montana, as the new literary center of America, emitting the defining cultural beeps—at least for fishing and outdoor writing—that used to be limited to New York City's editorial offices. Today, all places are equally real. All a region needs is a good writer or two to put it on the cultural map. Real places like Missoula and Corvallis and Campbell River and Astoria and the Deschutes and Seattle and West Yellowstone are making their own waves with their writers and publishers. And readers are carried along, because nothing makes a place so real as what is written about it.

At first glance, all of this westward migration of angling literature may seem to be the result of the phenomenal success and influence of Missoulan Norman Maclean's book, *A River Runs Through It*, first published in 1976. A word-of-mouth bestseller, the first work of fiction published by the scholarly press of the University of Chicago, where Maclean was a legendary teacher for many years, *A River Runs Through It* spawned a new generation of flyfishers, while reminding the oldsters of what they didn't know they knew about their sport. The movie version extended that influence even more widely to audiences in the U.S. and abroad.

There is a kind of sweet western justice in all this success, for as Maclean recalls his book was first rejected as "western" by several eastern editors, one of whom included in his rejection letter, "These stories have trees in them." Later, after the book had finally been published by the press of Maclean's own university and had become famous, the same editor, conveniently ignoring his previous dismissal of the work, wrote Maclean a fawning letter, praising the book and obsequiously suggesting that Maclean give them first chance at his *next* book! To which Maclean responded, "If the time should ever come when you are the last publisher in the world and I am the last author, then that will be the end of books, as we know them."

The truth is, though, that the movement of great angling writing westward began some years before *A River Runs Through It* with a British Columbia fisherman-writer whose work deserves to be more widely known. Before Maclean, there was Roderick Haig-Brown, who is the true founder of memorable angling literature in the Northwest. Although Haig-Brown was actually a few years younger than Maclean—born in 1908 to Maclean's 1902—Haig-Brown published his first fishing book at the age of twenty-four in 1931, at a time when Maclean was just beginning his teaching career at Chicago, and when writing fishing stories about his Montana youth was something far off in his future..

Haig-Brown came to the Northwest from England at the age of nineteen. He worked as a logger, trapper, and fisherman in Washington and British Columbia before settling in a home on the banks of the Campbell River on Vancouver Island. By the end of his career, he had written a total of thirty-one books. He died in

1976, the year Maclean published *A River Runs Through It*. Haig-Brown's work is held in highest esteem by literary fisher-folk, including Arnold Gingrich, who said in 1974 that Haig-Brown's work was the surest contribution that recent times had made to the main tradition of angling literature. Add to this Russell Chatham's more recent claim that Haig-Brown ought to be required reading in every school, and Harmon Henkin's statement that Haig-Brown was the best fishing writer that North America has produced, despite his being born and raised in England. Among Haig-Brown's best books are *A River Never Sleeps, Return to the River, Measure of the Year*, and his sequence of the fishing year, *Fisherman's Spring, Fisherman's Summer, Fisherman's Fall*, and *Fisherman's Winter*.

I fish for pleasure, as I suppose we all do. We read for the same reason. And part of the pleasure of reading, as C. S. Lewis said, is in knowing that we are not alone. I hope that the selections included here will bring you as much enjoyment as they have brought me. Acknowledged masters of the field of fishing writing, like Haig-Brown and Maclean and Zane Grey, are joined in the following pages by a number of less well known but noteworthy newer writers whose works are sure to give pleasure to Northwesterners and readers everywhere who value good fishing and good prose. I am sorry that there was not more room to include other notable Northwest fishing writers, especially from among the newer ones.

All good fishing writing carries an implicit message of conservation. With the ever-increasing threats to fish and to the beautiful places where they live, everyone who fishes must become a guardian of home waters. Because this book is a labor of love, and a chance to give back something to the sport that has given me so much pleasure, all author/editor profits it earns will be donated to the Pacific Rivers Council, a nonprofit conservation organization dedicated to restoring, protecting, and enhancing American rivers.

Long years ago, I sold my half-interest in a McKenzie driftboat that I owned with a friend. Why? Because I found I had more pleasure being *in* the water, wading a river or fishing a lake out of a float tube, than I did being *on* the water. I could give practical reasons for my choice: I could rightly claim that I could be stealthier, that I could get closer to the fish by wading or float-tubing. But the most important reason, looking at it honestly, was the pleasurable feeling of immersion. Of becoming something more like a fish myself, with the press of water against me, with the full, satisfying force of all that delight.

I can see myself ending up like Haig-Brown who, in his later years, often pulled on a wet suit and a snorkel to go swimming through the pools of the Campbell River which flowed by his home, content to just watch the same fish he had angled for and caught all his life. "I find," said Haig-Brown in one of his last books, *Fisherman's Fall,* "that I have practically no desire to go out and catch the fish I have seen when diving; I would rather go back and have another look at them. By the time I have watched the same fish twice, he is an old friend and I wouldn't dream of going out to kill him; I would even hesitate to disturb him by catching him and putting him back." Perhaps this experience is the ultimate baptism in nature that we all seek when we go fishing.

"We need the tonic of wildness," said the old master, Henry David Thoreau, in *Walden.* "We can never have enough of nature." Thoreau, a sometimes fisherman himself, had it figured out a hundred and fifty years ago, like Melville. The same attraction to the ungraspable phantom of life. In this spirit we take our fishing pleasure so seriously. Ourself, with a fishing rod, on one end, the wildness of a watery nature on the other end, and a pulsing line connecting the two. Maybe that is why we can't have enough of fishing. Or of writing—and reading—about it.

Glen Love

Part One: New Voices

This anthology begins with the work of those who have written most recently—in the 1980s and 1990s—about fishing in the Northwest. I need to justify this affront to chronological order. First of all, there has been, in the last couple of decades, a virtual explosion of good writing about fishing. This has been especially true of angling stories and essays from the Northwest. So, right off the bat, here is fishing prose that is not only new, but news.

It is news because so many new fishing books, essays, and stories have reached a high level of excellence that they have become a rapidly growing branch of literature. For example, Mark Browning, in his new book, *Haunted By Waters*, makes a strong case for the literary value of North American fly-fishing prose. Many of the contributors in "New Voices" help to make Browning's case. Browning admires Corvallis author Ted Leeson, who leads off this first section, so much that he quotes Leeson more than any other writer he studies.

For some reasons which Browning explores, fly fishing has seemed to attract the best writers, like Ted Leeson and most of the authors included here. On the other hand, it is worth remembering that Isaac Walton, author of the seventeenth-century fishing classic, *The Compleat Angler, or the Contemplative Man's Recreation*, was a bait fisherman. (This is a fact which irritates young Paul Maclean, brother of Norman Maclean, who wrote *A River Runs Through It.* "The bastard doesn't even know how to spell 'complete,'" complains Paul.) And if I had to choose my favorite fishing story of all time, it would be Ernest Hemingway's "Big Two-Hearted River," which is about trout-fishing with grasshoppers for bait. Still, the recent growth of fly fishing as a literary field is a notable and newsworthy event, as this volume will show.

Newsworthy too, in recent fishing writing, is the emergence of memorable work by women anglers. Historically, fishing for sport has been primarily a male pursuit. True, women can point to a fifteenth-century noblewoman, Dame Juliana Berners, as the first author of a work on fly fishing, although her treatise was directed to men, as the acknowledged fishing class at that time, just as Walton's was, and as was another treatise of Dame Juliana's (on hunting). Today, though, there is no doubt that women are entering the sport in increasing numbers, as the work of writers like Mallory Burton, Lorian Hemingway, Jessica Maxwell, and the other fisherwomen included here demonstrates. From them, we get what Holly Morris calls "a different angle," the title of her book of fishing stories by women. Women writers on fishing, as Morris notes, often plumb the waters of self-discovery and renewal in their work. With their entry into the field, the fishing books of the future, like this one, will have a little different look.

It seems clear that we can no longer refer to everyone who fishes as a *fisherman* or a *he*. I've belonged for years to a club that has been called the McKenzie Fly*fishers* ever since it was formed in 1964. It started out all-male, but now has women and men members. *Fishers* no longer seems an awkward term for me, but we have throughout the anthology retained the author's chosen terminology.

Starting with the new writers also makes sense as an attractor, a lure for today's readers. We come at fishing, as do these writers, from a quickened pace of living, from times when the wilderness is a little less wild, when environmental and conservation issues have become a more insistent part of our thinking, when catch and release, instead of catching a limit, is the norm, when our fishing is tied more closely than ever to the sorts of lives that send us fishing in the first place.

So, with these contemporary writers, these kindred new spirits who also still have the old magic powers of creating and entertaining, this book begins.

Ted Leeson

Ted Leeson immediately broke into the the top rank of fishing writers in 1994 with his first book, *The Habit of Rivers: Reflections on Trout Streams and Fly Fishing*. It has been called brilliant, consistently wonderful, and eloquent. It is also ruefully comic, as revealed by the following adventure, a too-early Spring trip for a too-anxious Northwest fisherman. Ted Leeson is a contributing editor of *Fly Rod & Reel* magazine. He is the editor of *The Gift of Trout*, and the co-author of *The Fly Tier's Benchside Reference*. He lives in Corvallis, Oregon, where he teaches at Oregon State University.

The Farthest Distance
Between Two Points

A good traveler has no fixed plans and is not intent upon
arriving.
— Lao-tzu, *Tao Te Ching*

We know by experience it selfe, that it is a marvelous
paine, to finde oute but a short waie, by long wandering.
— Roger Ascham, *The Scholemaster*

April may indeed be the cruellest month. In the tight tongue-
and groove of the angling year, it seems somehow to have
slipped between the cracks. The season seems out of sync
with itself. Under warm rains and mild air, the land greens up with
promise and propels you forward. But the water holds you back, a
brown and roily disappointment, the lagtime of altitude. Some time
zones are vertical, and the rivers answer to their origins on mountain
peaks still packed in snow, melting with glacial slowness. Remote
winters drain into the valley in icy, turbid water, running between
grassy banks.

April is a jagged seam, a fault line of the year where the massive
plate of winter grinds against the immensity of summer, and the
force of occlusion erupts in freak winds, warm deluges, and berserk
barometers. The months appear to me as places, fitted like flagstones
in a year. Except for April. April is not a place-it is a behavior, the
irascible shucking of an itchy skin.

Last month's clocklike hatches of March Browns on the big valley
rivers have wound down and with them the first foretaste of a
summer's dry-fly fishing. Now you might fish all afternoon for a

small flurry of mayflies that comes and goes in fifteen minutes and a rise of trout that lasts half as long. Just as often, there's nothing at all. Still six weeks away, the Deschutes stonefly hatch is just beyond the range of fruitful anticipation. The winter steelhead have spawned and gone and the first swell of summer fish is Just now gathering off the coast. A few shad have arrived, but not yet in numbers worth troubling about. You can cobble together only odds and ends: a few hours nymphing whitefish; casting at midnight off jetties on the coast for black rockfish; taking a beating in the afternoon surf, fishing perch; half a morning indulging the eternal vanity of taking a spring chinook on a fly. But it's hard to find a mainstay in these acrobatics. They don't even feel much like fishing, just something to do with your hands.

This year is especially bad. The El Niño Current in the Pacific made for an unusually mild winter, bringing balmy air and relatively little rain. The rivers, ordinarily swollen beyond hope, remained perfectly fishable, and the fishing was exceptional. Though trout season closes in winter, taking whitefish is still perrmitted, and this technicality gives rise to a benign annual charade in which the serious fly fisherman breaks out his tackle and takes to the water. He'll catch trout after trout for hours, pretending to astonishment and disappointment that they are not whitefish, while the Fish and Wildlife people pretend to believe him. The deception is harmless enough, and this year it went on and on.

In April, the party was raided. The year caught up with itself and stalled out in a series of storm systems over the Pacific. On the nightly satellite photos, thick spirals of clouds like Crab Nebulae squatted on the Gulf of Alaska, spinning slowly counterclockwise, wheeling the year back to winter and sweeping wave after wave of December weather over the coast and valley.

Driven indoors, I tied flies by the pound, tore down reels and oiled them, built leaders, cleaned out my vest, patched waders, and organized my rods (first by length, then line size, and finally by degrees of affection). I spent a couple weeks in this methadone fishing, a substitute less important for what it does than for what it prevents from happening. Outside my window, a white camellia bloomed feebly; and from a rusted gutter left unrepaired during sea- run cutthroat season, rain leaked down to a concrete block and tapped impatiently. Having only so much tackle to fuss with, I eventually tinkered myself into a corner—all dressed up and no place to go.

But at certain times, in certain moods, it simply feels better to be moving than standing still. And rather than go no place, I decided to go no place in particular, on the kind of trip defined only by its impelling energy. You don't go somewhere, you just go. Instead of seeking a place that conforms to the shape of your desire, you allow desire to shape itself around whatever places happen to present themselves.

After a winter of good fishing, focused tightly on a few stretches of a few rivers, April came as an abrupt dislocation, and primed me for just such a trip. In a season when everything rejuvenates by taking root, there can be a kind of renewal in rootlessness too. The novelist Don DeLillo once observed, "Plots carry their own logic. There is a tendency of plots to move toward death." Plans and plots are inertial, with an order and direction governed by the inexorable gravity of an endpoint. They imply patterns of inevitability which, from forceps to headstone, are the shortest distance between two points. The kind of trip I had in mind, on the other hand—unprescribed, directionless, and entropic—is the farthest.

If just about anywhere is possible, just about anything may be necessary. I packed up trout rods from 3- to 6-weight and a vest with everything from big streamers to midges. The prospect of lake fishing occurred to me, and I tossed in another rod, a long 7-weight; a few reels with assorted sinking lines; a float tube and fins; a pump to blow it up. There was a separate vest, a rod, and two reels for steelhead, along with a wading staff and cleats. Rain gear, a fly-tying kit, extra flies, hatch books, neoprene waders and lightweight ones, and boots. On impulse, I added a huge eleven-and-a-half-foot surf rod and a big spinning reel to the growing pile, and then took them out. No point in overdoing it.

I headed north for the simple reason that the nearest gas station lay in that direction. Along the highway, I began seeing unusual numbers of hawks and counted eleven of them in less than ten miles, perched on fence posts, utility poles, and billboards, hunched against the drizzle. Sometimes it's hard not to look for omens and signs. My knowledge of birds is only middling, but I knew at once these were rough-legged hawks. I'd seen them featured in countless miles of raptor footage that aired on public television in the last decade, when legions of sleekly groomed Reagan-youth fueled a national fascination with handsome predators. I weighed the various interpretations of the omen, inconclusively.

When I began to hit the Portland traffic, I veered east toward the mountains, and eventually stopped some time later at a sagging little diner near the Clackamas River for coffee and information. Behind the counter, tiny red lights flashed silently in sequence on a police scanner, and an amber power lamp glowed on the front of a CB base unit. The only sound, however, issued from the tinny speaker of a transistor radio hung on a nail, a drone I recognized at once as the National Weather Service broadcast. Parked on a counter stool, an aged waitress in a peach uniform and white Adidas poured coffee without getting up. The fishing was slow, she said, "maybe some winter fish below the dam." She put on a pair of half-moon reading glasses and leaned over to a handwritten chart taped to the cash register.

"Six-point-three feet. That's last night. Radio man," she nodded vaguely behind her, "says more weather's moving in. River's blowed out as it is. Get caught in that and you won't stop floatin' till the Japs fish you out." She looked meaningfully over the tops of her glasses, "A Jap'll eat fish eyes, you know."

I drove to see the river anyway. It was empty except for two bait plunkers; huddled like a pair of hams by a damp, smoky fire. I watched for a time, waiting for something in the scene to lure me past the effort of unpacking my gear, and in the end moved higher up the river, away from any fishing. The season closed here three weeks ago, but there were fish in the river. Getting out to stretch my legs, I walked along a little tributary and found a pair of spawning steelhead, finning over the gravel, looking bushed. Disjunctions in scale have a way of magnifying things that is rare in the natural world, and the sight of big fish in small water is a magnetic spectacle. You couldn't help but wonder how, through the gauntlet of seals, gill nets, dams, and fishermen, they ever made it up here, if they were somehow better than other fish or just got the breaks.

Their stretch of holding water was formed by a beaver dam, which is what first caught my attention. Some years ago, I spent part of a day on a spawning tributary of a coastal river, tearing apart logjams and beaver dams that, in those less-enlightened times, were presumed to inhibit the upstream passage of fish. Even a small beaver dam is a remarkably tough structure and can take two men an hour to dislodge. What struck me most, though, was not how strongly they were built, but how they were started in the first place. This one was typical—on the bank, I counted eleven smallish Douglas fir stumps, each rising from a pile of cuttings, the fallen trunks scattered randomly on the forest floor. Some fell away from the stream, some parallel to its banks, others with the uppermost branches just touching the water. Each was a shot in the dark and a clean miss. Apparently, the eleventh one at last fell across to the other bank and got things moving. The much vaunted efficiency of nature's little creatures notwithstanding, the beavers, like the pair of steelhead, just plugged away, played like they knew how, and waited for lucky accidents—a fallen tree to start a dam, a dam to make a little spawning run, a guy who hadn't come to ruin them both. It occurred to me only later that my own method was not substantially different.

The radio man, as it turned out, didn't lie. Late in the day, a squall-like storm moved in, dropping sheets of rain that turned to clots of heavy, wet snow near Blue Box Pass, and finally thinned to a drizzle east of the Cascades when I pulled into Maupin at nightfall.

Flanking the Deschutes River, Maupin is the last major boat landing before the near-certain fatality of Sherars Falls. In six weeks, the first packs of summer rafters would arrive and the town would come alive, renting equipment, selling beer and groceries, frying burgers, running shuttles, and generally laying on some fat against the long, unprosperous winter. But now, in April, the place just waited, lean, vacant, and cheerless. Some time during the night, the rain stopped. I fished an hour in the raw, wintry morning, and left.

You don't take a trip like this. It takes you. It is indeterminate, open-ended, almost a succession of tangents except that there is no main line of navigation and so nothing is really tangential. A small body in space, I understand—an asteroid, a meteor, a particle of dust—may travel in just this way. Drawn by some distant star or planet, it bends around the gravitational field, and momentum carries it in a new direction, toward some other star or planet that diverts it yet again. A chunk of matter zigzags through space in a trajectory largely defined by things other than itself. There is, at certain times, the same inertness to being, when what you sense most clearly are the currents outside yourself, shifting forces of uncertain direction. And in such moments, what's needed most is to throw up a sail, pull in the keelboard, and just see where the drift takes you.

Still, traveling like this with no destination and no steam of your own takes some getting used to. It is difficult not to look ahead, not to see yourself on the way to somewhere. The whole thrust bucks a lifetime of habit by inverting the accustomed relation of destination and desire. Even temporary dislocations are unsettling— which is exactly why they're good for you—and for the first few days, I reluctantly picked at the trip like a plate of existential vegetables. I missed my wife, worried about the weather, about work left undone, about where to go next.

My notes record only fragments. Half a sentence for a river, a highway in an aside, a parenthetical stopping place. Spot-fishing the John Day River for hungry eight-inch smallmouth. Up the gulches and dry washes near Dayville, hunting for thunder-egg geodes. On the Crooked River, a handful of aquatic weeds squirming with hundreds of shrimplike scuds, a tantalizing fact I was unable to translate into trout. And driving, long, long, textureless miles of greening desert. All of these felt somehow preliminary. I waited, bored by my own company, and considered turning back. There seemed to be no point, which was true, and was also precisely the point.

But unpatterned time and routineless days tug at you with a sly, seductive insistence; bit by bit, they persuade you to themselves and begin to win you over. The ordinary formulae of daily life give way to pleasantly odd private jags, eating when the mood strikes, sleeping when it suits you, fishing or not, abruptly deciding to move on or content to linger, keeping irregular hours. I stopped taking notes. As always, change began with the rivers. Strangely (or not so strangely as I discovered later), I ran into no other fishermen over the course of nearly a week. I could work the best water without hurry, move when I wished, humor any whim of technique or method, and generally indulge the luxury of a man who has a trout stream entirely to himself. Inevitably, the tone and timbre of the fishing rippled back into the trip and subsumed it. According to Jung, crossing a river represents a fundamental change of attitude. Pity he didn't fish; he would have recognized that rivers are far more powerful as agents of transformation than symbols for it.

The turning point came one day along the Deschutes. I'm still not quite sure what led me back there—habit, accident, the simple consequence of unchecked momentum. I just found myself there one overcast afternoon standing on Lower Bridge, seventy-five miles above Maupin, scanning the water for rises. Against the cattails and willow thickets, a few trout dimpled sporadically. In late winter, big browns feed on the surface, first to a hatch of small black stoneflies and, later, March Browns. The odds of hitting a fish four pounds or better on a dry fly suddenly fall into betting range. But in a place like this, I care less for the stakes than for the game, for sight-fishing to individual risers on glassy, unforgiving currents. So I whittled an afternoon down to evening, sitting on the banks, marking rises, and fishing among flooded tule and current-swept brush to shy, jittery trout, one at a time.

This is a tough, technical kind of fishing, careful, deliberate, and intensely absorbing; that I'm not very good at it doesn't diminish its particular satisfactions. In fishing (among other things) style and technique are important only insofar as they define the shape of one's appreciation. Alter the style, and you change as well the nature of your pleasure. In blind fishing, for instance, say in searching a riffle with a floating fly or nymphing pocket water, you prospect for the unknown, wondering always where the trout might lie, what fly might tempt it, what cast it might come on. You fish, in essence, for surprise out of nowhere, for an instant in which you suddenly become aware that you're attached to a heartbeat. Fishing a heavy hatch—in most other respects the antithesis of blindcasting—nonetheless holds much the same appeal. I think it's fair to say that most anglers are apt to flock shoot a good rise of fish, picking out a density of rings, dropping a fly in the middle of them, and trusting to the numbers. Here, too, we fish for that moment of uncertainty, that tiny interval of unresolvedness in which we strain to assess what it is we have hold of, how big it might be, and what will happen next. As in blind fishing, much of the thrill lies in seeing what you come up with.

But the deliberate, studied fishing to a single rising trout reverses the circumstances and kindles an altogether different type of engagement. Here, the fish is the given. You know its precise location, the form and pattern of rises, often the size, and quite possibly the insect it's feeding on. With the endpoint defined, getting there becomes the question. From the particularities there emerges a kind of abstract problem, almost geometric in design—a calculation of drift lines, curve casts, and angles of presentation, superimposed on the tempo of the rise, and predicated on the caginess of your own surmise. Alternatives must be weighed; small adaptations undertaken; adjustments made one at a time; a solution converged upon; and, sometimes, the final luxury of knowing exactly when you got it right. You want to catch the fish, but you want more to figure it out, and the particular satisfactions stem less from the eventuality than the process by which the whole thing unfolds.

I doubt that I cast to more than ten or twelve fish that day and hooked only a few of them. But I did, at last, catch the rhythm of the trip.

From the road map, Bend, Oregon, rose up as an enormous hot shower. Finding one proved little trouble. Once an unassuming little town at the edge of the desert, Bend suffered the irreparable misfortune, some years back, of being "discovered." Now it sprawls in random ugliness, a casualty of too much money too fast. The old center of town is ringed with lowslung motels, fast-food huts, strange extraterrestrial boutiques, minimalls, and inflatable subdivisions, and overall, looks like something you might find if Dante had been a real estate developer. I had to see it all, touring the place two or three times when I got lost looking for a fly shop. It turned out to be three blocks from the motel.

I needed only some tippet material, which I asked for in a strange glottal croak, far too loud and edged with the faint inflection of hysteria. For the past six days, it suddenly occurred to me, I hadn't spoken to a soul. I also discovered something else—general trout season had opened only the day before. In a number of places, I'd unknowingly fished on closed water, which went a long way toward explaining why I'd seen no one else. This doesn't seem the kind of detail that's easily overlooked, but if you habitually fly fish with barbless hooks and release all your trout—that is, uniformly abide by the most restrictive legal provisions—you get remarkably cavalier about matters like size and bag limits, and sometimes seasons, because they so rarely impinge on your fishing. In most cases, you're already doing far more than the law requires, and in time it comes to seem impossible that you could do anything illegal. Then too, I suppose, deep down you hang from that last, shady loophole— to claim you're after whitefish—though only an angler with the soul of a personal-injury lawyer could trot this out with any conviction.

I should have been relieved at not being caught; instead I felt only like an idiot—a lucky idiot at that, which is the most ridiculous kind. I'd hoped to summon the spirit of Thoreau in the Maine woods or Pirsig on his motorcycle. Instead I got Mister Magoo.

I told the fly-shop clerk nothing of this and made only the usual inquiries. He said that the fishing had been "only fair," a revelation that surprised me. A fly shop is the only place I know of where the fishing is always "excellent," since there's no reason to provide a customer with less than best. As a result, any fly-shop report must be adjusted for inflation, which in this case meant fishing was lousy. We talked a bit, he suggesting a few places I might try, when our conversation drew the attention of a customer who seemed to browse the shop solely for the opportunity. He leaned an elbow on the glass counter, beamed an indulgent smile, and introduced himself: "Can I tell you a little something about fly fishing?" Statistically, my chances of running into someone who can "tell me a little something about fly fishing" are pretty good, so I had to wonder how this person so soundly whipped the odds. The type is regrettably familiar—polar fleece and a haircut stretched over a hideous bubble of gas. They never brag. It is too merciful. Instead, they insist upon "explaining" things to you, benevolently strolling among the worldlings and torturing them with little lectures. This one was particularly insufferable, droning at length about the previous weekend spent on a two-hundred-dollar-a day fee-lake, hitting fish after fish on midges, modestly subordinating his own Olympian achievements to more general proclamations on the proper way to fish *Chironomids* on still water and play large trout on light tippets. It was amply clear that his actual knowledge of midge fishing was dwarfed even by my own pale understanding of the subject. Worst of all, he repeatedly referred to the insects as "Geronimos" and each authoritative mispronunciation seemed like a tiny pellet expelled solely for my irritation. I left, and forgot my tippet material.

But it's an ill windbag that blows nobody any good, and if nothing else, he did remind me about stillwater fishing, which is sometimes obscured by my overly rigid association of trout with rivers. The fee-lake held little attraction. I still carry around enough populist baggage to be put off by the idea of paying to fish. The overtones of elitism don't bother me so much (after all, *not* paying for fishing is perhaps itself a form of elitism). Rather, fee- fishing seems somehow rigged, artificial, too contrary to the spirit of the thing. It's commonly remarked among many anglers (particularly those who can't afford it) that paying for fishing—not for tackle, or travel, or licenses, but simply for someone's consent—is a lot like paying for sex. Ethics aside, such arrangements, businesslike as they may be, nonetheless hinge on a pretty unflattering species of indolence. But in a world steaming full-throttle toward privatization, this attitude may eventually become a little too precious.

I left Bend in a pounding rainstorm, looping southeast toward drier skies (which I eventually caught up with) and a rumored pond (which I never found). Another day and a half of continuous prospecting turned up nothing, and I was well into the second of the truck's two twenty-three-gallon fuel tanks. In the eerie moonscape of the Warner Valley, I spread a map on the dust and pinned the corners with rocks. Unchecked, the prevailing momentum would bring me south to Pyramid Lake in Nevada by the next day. The road to the nearest gas station ran north. I debated, then took it.

There's little to say about long drives that hasn't already been said. They dislocate your sense of reality, and the outside world becomes less a place than a medium through which you vaguely move. Whatever is real is contained within the jarring shell of a pickup cab, and the landscape rolls by like a long, plotless movie projected from all sides. After a while, you can't remember a time when you weren't driving, and what you might have seen or done seem like things told to you by someone else.

More than anything, though, is the weird introspection that it induces. On a small tape recorder, I started taking notes again. I dictated replies to long-neglected correspondence, made lists of various kinds, pondered out loud the big questions. I composed a letter of resignation from my job, a churlish and huffy little speech (never delivered) that trailed off into a rambling indictment of the American university, which gleefully split the atom while solemnly guarding the integrity of the infinitive. For a time, I just let the tape run—recording the road vibration and wind noise, the gargle of a perforated exhaust, John Hiatt singing about a band of Indians— to remind me of the traveling (I am listening to it now). Seized by some morbidity, I made out my will.

The gas station at Brothers came just in time, right at the point when it occurred to me that I wasn't really taking notes. I was talking to myself. In a dingy little restroom, I stripped to the waist, washed up in the sink and shaved, and got my bearings again. Half an hour away lay a small reservoir I'd heard about. An astonishing number of these impoundments are scattered about this arid, unremittingly exposed landscape. People call them "lakes," though this is an insult to real lakes everywhere. Most are manmade, little more than shallow depressions with a bulldozed earthen dam just high enough to trap a thin film of turbid, ugly water. Some are seasonal, some more or less permanent, and of those, a few manage one deeply redeeming quality—they grow trout at a phenomenal rate. The one I made camp on had this reputation.

In the morning, for the first time since setting out, the sun rose in a cloudless sky. It woke me early. A few fishermen were already on the water; offshore, a guy in a float tube netted a trout. I raised my rod and pointed with exaggerated gestures at the fly on my hook keeper. He cupped a hand to his mouth and shouted, "Nimps!" I walked on, led much of the way by a horned lark hopping through sagebrush in a highly convincing crippled-wing performance. On a small arm of the lake where I could get the morning sun to my back and the glare from my eyes, I tried nimp after nimp. Big dragonfly nymphs on sink-tips, olive marabou damsels on intermediate lines, and finally, by luck, a floating line and a # 14 Prince. That one rang the bell.

In a rare inversion of the normal order, the catching was comparatively brisk, although the fishing itself was slow. I made maybe twenty casts an hour. There was the long delivery, an even longer pause to let the fly sink, followed by an agonizingly deliberate, inching retrieve almost to the rod tip. Then, just the smallest resistance. Not a tug, only the faint feeling of a little extra weight. I missed the first few fish, assuming that the take would be more decisive and palpable, but eventually got the hang of it. None of the trout jumped; in the cold water, they dogged the bottom amid the flooded sagebrush; by noon, I'd taken seven thick rainbows, and lost as many more.

The fishing held up well for the next couple of days, predictable enough to require only a single box of flies and a minimum of gear. One morning, I set about emptying my vest of extraneous baggage (of which there was an enormous quantity). I have never quite made peace with my vest and envy the angler for whom it is a settled matter. He may try a new gadget here or there, or carry a few new fly patterns now and then, but for the most part the character, the gestalt of the vest is a formed and recognizable thing. My own vest, though, has always been restless and dynamic, a pendulum oscillating between a profligate Neronian excess that knows no limits and a lean Spartanism that admits no frills. My flyfishing life, in fact, has wandered between these same extremes, at times reflecting the conviction that the world is entirely contingent and is best met by covering all the bases. Gradually this gives way to its opposite—trusting to a few wisely chosen things and recognizing that a larger number of alternatives merely increases the likelihood, in any given circumstance, of resorting to the wrong one. Although a rod or reel may embody a general taste, or specific predilection, or even an aesthetic, it is finally just a piece of gear. But a vest is a philosophy, and paring mine down was overdue.

The weather continued to moderate—cool, sunny days, cold and clear nights—and time passed in the kind of pleasant rhythm that comes easily when you are alone. Yet at the same time I became aware again of a vague feeling I'd had off and on since the beginning. It was more inkling than idea, a vague perception that something, was hovering on the perimeter of this trip. I sensed it only as an indistinct significance, possibly a place or a direction, something to find or be found by, or perhaps only a reason for coming. It didn't drive the trip, but seemed to accumulate along with it, and though I now understand what it was, at the time it remained at the edge of intuition and would not be thought or coaxed into the open, or snuck up on and surprised. Nor would it quite go away.

The trip through Hines was a strange hallucination. A gas station attendant discovered a grotesque swelling on the sidewall of a rear tire. I was sent to a specialist who diagnosed the bulge as terminal, indicating as well that the other tire, to all appearances in good health, was in fact rapidly failing. Skeptical but helpless, I surrendered the keys and walked a few blocks to a diner. For reasons that became abundantly clear, it announced itself with a handlettered sign—no name, just a message: "The Worst Food in Oregon." This, I discovered, was no joke. The coffee might just have been the worst in the world. I ordered up the breakfast special (recorded in my notes as "Toast-and-Eggs Regret"), and under the circumstances, found it difficult to complain about the result, the cook having lived up so fully to his end of the agreement. The place itself was scarcely larger than a Fotomat, with a few picnic tables inside, and walls covered in graffiti of a spooky and unvarying "Go Jesus!" type. The management apparently encouraged the practice, which seemed appropriate to an establishment where mere matters of the flesh, like food, commanded so little regard.

Outside the tire dealer, my pickup awaited as promised. I paid the bill, and the clerk handed over a receipt along with a package wrapped neatly in white paper and hard as a brick, a promotional bonus, I was told, for the new radials. I asked what was in it. "Seven pounds of ground beef," he said, walking off. One might have expected a stainless-steel tire gauge or a Naugahyde litter bag. Instead, burger—the national solvent. Only in America.

It wasn't over. A few miles from town, I pulled into one of those convenience market/hardware store/gas station/bait shop/video rental places, the kind of fully self-contained retail ecosystem that flourishes only in thinly populated areas. I hoped to get some information about the fishing. The clerk was pleasant, an inexhaustible talker more than eager to help. In the course of a few minutes, he found out where I was from—he had people there—and established to his satisfaction that although we had no friends in common, his friends almost certainly knew my friends, which made us friends of a sort. The discovery pleased him enormously, for he was bursting with some news about the fishing, but obviously regarded the intelligence as so valuable that he wouldn't want it to fall into the wrong hands, and by god wasn't it lucky and *pretty incredible* to boot that such a good friend should happen by because he just had to tell *somebody*.

He drew close, took a quick glance around the empty shop just to be safe, and addressed me in tones I hadn't heard since *The Graduate*. Dustin Hoffman got one word: "Plastics." I got four—*Pautzke's Balls of Fire*.

My face must have betrayed the meaninglessness of this revelation, and so he launched into a light-speed paean to the Balls of Fire as I listened impatiently for more specific information about what I concluded must be some very local fly pattern and, of course, waited for him to produce a Ball of Fire for my inspection.

The truth dawned gradually. After each invocation of the name, he gestured vaguely behind him, where my eyes finally rested on several rows of glass jars entombing garishly dyed individual salmon eggs—hot orange, electric red, neon pink—each bottle burning a hundred eternal flames in the memory of Pautzke.

The clerk would not be reined in. He explicated the theory of the Balls of Fire, furnished corroborating examples of their efficacy, and moved on to discourse in general about the genius of Pautzke. I interrupted to ask him if the pink ones tasted any different from the orange ones or if it was just a matter of color. He paused for the first time, conceded that it was an interesting question that he couldn't answer, but assured me it could not have escaped the notice of one such as Pautzke and that the whole matter had undoubtedly been worked out.

The entire exchange—edited substantially for brevity—took place less than two feet from a plastic display case housing several hundred reasonably decent trout flies. Of these, the clerk never once made mention even when I reminded him that I would be fly fishing, a comment that met with a second pause, as though he were trying to determine any conceivable relevance of my remark to the Balls of Fire. He apparently concluded there was none, and though I declined his offers, we parted friends, sensing perhaps some deeper kinship.

An hour south, the Steens first appeared, an isolated mountain range in remote country riven with geological fault lines. Ten million years ago, the area was a broad basalt plateau; over time, stresses along the faults fractured the sheet of rock into immense blocks. Some of the blocks sank, like the ones to the east in the Alvord Valley. Others pushed upward in abrupt, sheared escarpments, forming the Steens that rise a mile above the valley floor and 10,000 feet above sea level. The western approach to the Steens rim, near Frenchglen, is a gradual rise, cut intermittently by deep glacial valleys. At the foot of the mountains runs the Blitzen River. Moving water again.

The Blitzen, I've been told repeatedly, holds some large rainbows, though I've never hooked one or seen one or been in the presence of anyone who has. Rumors take on a life of their own whenever big fish are involved. But it is a hard, jagged, beautiful place, and in past years I've hiked upstream for the small native redbands, a subspecies of rainbow trout that long ago adapted to the desert. Mostly, they inhabit the steep canyon of the upper river, and I wouldn't go there on this trip. The jeep trail is tenuous enough in the best weather; at this time of year, it would be five miles of thigh-deep mudholes.

I worked the lower river, where it levels out onto a marshy plain that, in a month or so, would breed a quantity of mosquitoes impossible to believe in this dry landscape. Again, only the small fish were willing, though plenty of those.

Nothing gnaws like a detail, and comfortably encamped with fishing enough to satisfy, I became strangely consumed with the burger question. A windfall, even a small one, is not to be taken lightly. Thawing in the cooler, the package had bled on the beer and stained the water a thin, milky pink. I weighed the options against its obviously accelerating halflife, and the next night mashed the whole lump into a big cast-iron skillet over a white- gas stove, and for the better part of an hour tended the largest hamburger with which I've ever personally come into contact. Out of duty, I ate as much as I could, wrapped a few cold wedges in a plastic bag, and laid the remainder on a stump near camp. In the morning it was gone, a second windfall for some other creature and an occasion for musing: a bad tire was transformed into a hunk of ground beef, which in turn became a skunk or porcupine, which might eventually meet its own fate beneath a careless tire. "Burger to burger, dust to dust." Clearly, it was time to move on.

Down the Catlow Valley, the flatland was already greening and the hillside sprouted shoots of monkey flower that would soon line the seeps and springs with their absurdly pure yellow flowers. On the long grade between the Steens and Pueblos, I coasted into Fields and another one of the oddest little eateries on the planet, a low-ceilinged white-enamel cubicle, like the inside of a refrigerator, heavy with the smell of grilling hamburgers. I ordered the fish.

By early evening I was headed back north on the Fields-Denio Road, a fifty-mile stretch of washboard gravel that follows the eastern base of the Steens. Twenty minutes out of Fields, I stopped at a hot springs that bubbled through fissures in the hillside. Someone, some time ago, had cozied it up with a cement basin and a corrugated steel windbreak, and it's become a regular stopping point for the few travelers on this road. Sitting and soaking, I watched the water steam in the cool air and trickle down to the Alvord Desert spread out before me, sixty square miles of dust, sand, and baked dirt, flat as a griddle and almost completely devoid of vegetation. Over the desert floor, columns of soil swirled in dust devils, coalescing suddenly, traveling a random spin over the flats, and settling back into powder when the wind quieted.

With the mountains to your back and Tule Springs Rim on the far side of the valley, you get the distinct and accurate impression that you're sitting at the bottom of a lake. By the time of the last ice age, the Alvord Basin was filled with water, forming a lake nearly a hundred miles long, though still dwarfed by the huge inland seas of Lake Bonneville and Lake Lahontan to the south. Long cut off from any connection with other waters, the cutthroat in the Alvord Basin evolved into a distinct subspecies that, like the redband, adapted to tolerate the increasingly harsh conditions of the region— burning cold winters; frigid runoff; the splintering heat of high summer; streams that almost disappear in rainless spells; and warm slackwater creeks so saturated with dissolved minerals that the water leaves a white film on waders when it evaporates.

About 8,000 years ago, the lake dried up completely and the trout retreated to the small mountain streams, their numbers dwindling until, in this century, they were thought to have become extinct. In spite of their evolutionary handstands, the cutthroats couldn't compete with cattle herds and irrigators for habitat and were too willing to interbreed with introduced trout to maintain an undiluted wild gene pool. But in recent years, a handful of fish believed to be the Alvord strain were discovered toughing it out in a remote creek, a remarkable fact that holds only the grimmest reassurances.

But this ancient lakebed validates the overwhelming sense of this desert as a world of its own. Even now, the streams that head in the mountains are part of no larger river system. Willow Creek, Whitehorse Creek, Trout Creek, Indian, Pike, and Alvord Creeks are their own watersheds. They simply flow out of the mountains to a dish in the dust, as if nothing had changed in 10,000 years, though now the waters simply sink into nothingness or evaporate in alkaline sumps. Few sights can affect a fisherman more profoundly than to walk downstream along one of these creeks and watch it, in just a few yards, disappear into the desert floor. You know you are in a different place, self-enclosed, with its own rules.

As always, some people just don't get it. One morning, a few years back, the handful of residents here awoke to find an enormous geometric design carved into the hard desert flat. It immediately occasioned the usual titillating speculation about extra-terrestrial beings that, in the twentieth century, have become technology's way of accommodating the persistent human need for a metaphysic. I strongly suspect that should such a visitation ever occur, it would run a disappointing second to the expectation, like meeting the Buddha and discovering he had hemorrhoids and a short temper. On the other hand, no spacemen have so far appeared, which at least argues for superior intelligence.

As it turned out, a certain "artist" stepped forward to take credit for the design, explaining that when no one was looking (which could be almost any time out here), he and a few accomplices laid out the pattern with stakes and string and harrowed it into the dirt with a hand plow. The figure, he patiently elaborated, reproduced an ancient, mystical pattern, meditating upon which would heal the aura, grow hair on a bald soul, cure existential dyspepsia, and administer karmic medicaments of various sorts, of which a misty, Miss America-like version of peace on earth was the very least to be expected.

In an unrelated incident, Bill Witherspoon, a name terminally associated with frauds of this type, erected a similar monument to himself—several hundred three-story logs stuck upright over sixty acres of desert to form a "cosmic transducer." (It is my great hope that a real visionary will come along and plant a giant, stuffed coyote by each pole, a hind leg lifted in salute to Witherspoon's achievement.) The cosmic transducer was erected, he said, to make contact with nature, because "to make contact with nature is to make contact with the most intimate part of oneself." Personally, I prefer that he just went somewhere in private and made contact with the most intimate part of himself in an essentially similar, but less obtrusive, fashion. The arrogance and obtuseness of spirit are staggering, as though the place somehow needed these portraits of the artist to invest it with significance.

It was after dark when I pulled off on the rutted two-track leading to Mann Lake. I made camp in the light of a half-moon. Despite the clear sky, the surest sign of a cold night in the desert, the air was inexplicably mild.

At certain moments, this can be a deeply serene place, one of those landscapes in which you feel a kind of reparative and healing power, even when you don't believe yourself to be in need of these things. In part, I think, it is a consequence of perspective. To the west, two miles off but feeling much closer, the white peaks of the Steens rise a mile high. In saddles between angular summits, snow and ice linger into summer. Below them, the mountains fall away in a steep, smooth arc, sloping more gradually at the foot, and finally leveling down to the shore of the lake, forming one of the most beautiful curves of landscape I've ever seen. The scale is impossible to hold out against; the land coaxes you into a kind of equilibrium with itself.

At other times, however, it simply beats you into submission, and five or six days out here can leave you feeling pretty worked over. The high-summer sun will simmer your brain in its own juice, and there is no shade anywhere; in winter, eyes ache from the cold and the hair in your nose crackles like icicles. The distance from one extreme to the other is sometimes a matter of minutes. With mountains so close on the west, you can never see the change coming. The weather is on top of you in an instant. I've fished the far shore of the lake in shirtsleeves, bolted for camp when I felt the first waves of cold air rolling down the mountain, and jogged the last hundred yards in snow.

Mostly, it's the wind, the most difficult element to convey because people think they understand it already. They know windy days and believe they can imagine one after another after another. Yet they still have no idea of a place where the wind doesn't die down, not at evening, not in early morning. It rocks a tent all night long. There is nothing to block or blunt the incessant tunnel of moving air and all that goes with it—alkalai dust, cinders, bits of dry grass and sage bark; the lip-cracking dryness; and perhaps in the end, most inescapable of all, the noise rushing ceaselessly past your ears like traffic, so unremitting that it finally seems to be coming from inside your head.

On a windy afternoon, every angler on the lake will be lined up on the lee shore, hunched against the weather, with forty feet of fly line held stiffly horizontal over the water. You must dip the rod tip in the lake to set down a fly. And most of the fish are on the other side of the lake anyway, feeding on the drift and churn of the windward shore.

Still, it can be worth the trouble. The Lahontan cutthroats here— another ice-age subspecies genetically groomed for desert life—are remarkably handsome fish and grow to a size that seems impossible in this thin pan of water. They can sometimes be caught on big woolly buggers or leeches, sometimes on damsel or *Callibaetis* nymphs, sometimes on nothing at all. Day-in and day-out, though, the staple is *Chironomid* pupae, midges, Geronimos. They flourish here in unimaginable abundance, and on a warm summer evening, enormous numbers of adults collect along the shore, swarming about, clinging to grasses or to one another, vibrating in the wind. From some distance away, you can hear their collective sound, a continuous low-level whine, everywhere in general but nowhere in particular, nearly subsonic, like the hum of a power plant.

When I finished making camp, I walked down to the lake and there, for the first time, noticed something strange. There was no wind. It was absolutely still.

There is, I'm convinced, an innate human predisposition toward patternmaking. From three random dots on a blank page, the mind's eye constructs a triangle. We find familiar outlines in the night sky and transform clouds into recognizable shapes. We discern as well geometries of experience and order them in narrative. History, to us, has a structure and we read it like a long, untidy novel. Our own life stretches behind us as a story told, and ahead like a plot unfolding around a hero named after ourselves.

At home in the Willamette Valley, looking back on the trip and tracing on a map where I had been, I saw just such a pattern unexpectedly emerge from a route that seemed at the time shapeless and undesigned. Though I had deliberately taken a trip with no particular direction, it now seemed to have a particular indirection, which can be just as certain, and sometimes truer. I'd driven wide, looping curves, wandering back and forth, zigzagging across a hypothetical line that marked the shortest distance from my doorstep to the shore of Mann Lake. And whether drawn or impelled, I still can't say.

That first morning I awoke, about as far away from home as I could get and still find trout, in a landscape as capricious and as little to be counted on as any I know, and discovered what couldn't be seen the night before. A vast expanse of purple lupine on the desert floor tinted the landscape with a deep amethyst, supped between broken ridges. The air, still calm, was spiced with the odor of rabbitbrush blooming in a million tiny yellow blossoms. Bees worked in the morning nectar flow, and the calls of meadowlarks chimed off the rimrock. And I remember standing there and thinking that back home in the valley, it must be spring now, too.

Robin Carey

Robin Carey's 1998 book, *North Bank: Claiming a Place on the Rogue*, recounts his experiences while putting down roots in the country near the mouth of the Rogue River, where he and his wife have bought an old cabin. It's a book about coming to know a place, about getting familiar with the surrounding woods, with new neighbors, both human and animal, with the well-worn cabin, and above all with a new home river and its fishing. Carey's writing reminds us of how thoroughly we are creatures of place. We spend our lives looking for the right place, always near trees and water. The fishing is a bonus. Carey is also the author of *Baja Journey: Reveries of a Sea Kayaker.*

Building with Bones

When my wife, Catharine, and I first aspired to be coastals, we lived in a rented cottage with its own short path down to the sand and the breakers of the Pacific. That was in a little community called Nesika Beach about midway between Gold Beach and Ophir, Oregon. But at the end of our first year there, the dresser drawers all swollen one inch out from flush and the clothes dank, we turned inland again and bought a place along the Rogue River. This new place wasn't far inland, only three miles from the coast by road, less than that on a straight line. But our move put the hump of Geisel Hill between ourselves and the Pacific.

The eastern slope of Geisel Hill felt calm and welcoming, out of the fog and the sea wind. It felt like inland places we had known before. Wind, at the right moments, howls very romantically, of course; but the wind at Nesika Beach had grown too commonly abusive for our sensibilities. It blew salt-slurry over our windows, and whipped rain into our faces at a near-horizontal slant. Looking at the new place as prospective buyers, we didn't think it mattered just how much cat hair had packed into the baseboard heaters of that cabin, how much water stain had spread across the fiberboard ceilings, or how much glaze had whitened the leaky thermalpanes, just so long as the place was out of the wind, someplace where we could regularly pull-to a door without a struggle.

There was, then, a sense of shelter to this Rogue cabin from the start, a home-quality. That was the idea—to make it home. This was in June. I watched red-tailed hawks circle in the thermals above the cabin. I felt at home with hawks.

I went out circling, as the hawks did, scouting out in arcs across the back hills to discover any paths we could use. It was rough going back there on the east slope of Geisel Hill behind the cabin, lots of slash. But the idea of home for me means knowing a place.

Learning the territory is a process I don't fully understand, but one that tugs at me with a feeling like necessity. Once beyond the stumbling beginnings of it, the process makes me feel nested and solidly on home ground. Anybody who cares about the land and who has gotten knocked from place to place in the transient society we call ours, knows about this process of re-creating the familiar, of remaking and reclaiming the landmarks. Because the North Bank is river country, the process out here starts with river pull-offs and river trails.

When the family lived in Wisconsin for a time, it was grouse hunting that led me out over the hills to the places that needed knowing, out to where the old farms tilted between hillsides, where the gray buildings sagged and fell, where the old harrows and wheels lay in the grasses, and the abandoned orchards put forth wormy apples for the grouse to feed on in the warm afternoons of Indian summer. In the upper Rogue Valley of other years, it was mountain quail that served the same purpose as those Wisconsin grouse.

But out here along the coast, the trees and brush grow too thick for much cross-country wanderings. Here the rivers were always the sites of settlement and travel. The old homesteads and schools stood near the rivers, the paths ran along the rivers, and what places I want to discover hold there, along the rivers, though I have not yet found so many of those places as to be dead certain just what they'll look like when I come upon them.

The inland cabin that we bought stands near this river world, on the north bank of a wide Rogue meander. The location could not be more convenient for my wanderings. From this point I can explore upstream toward Lobster Creek and beyond, or downstream toward the Wedderburn Bridge and the Rogue's mouth. South of us, and north of us, other coastal streams and creeks run their courses to the Pacific.

There will be different smells to these rivers than I have known elsewhere, different bird cries, and different beetles under different stones. There will be secrets at each bend, roadside secrets and trailside secrets. Gathering these will be my pastime. Learning these will be my study, as will the subtle ways that the strange turns known and then, at last, familiar.

Below our cabin, separating it from the Rogue, runs old U.S. Highway 101. New Highway 101, a straighter shot along the coast, renders this curve of old 101 mainly a local-access road. The locals call the old road simply "North Bank." The post office would have us add "Rogue" to distinguish this North Bank from North Bank Pistol, North Bank Chetco, North Bank Winchuck, North Bank Smith. I glimpsed the full name once on a rusted signpost: "North Bank Rogue River Road." Most of the local rivers have north bank roads, popular residential roads, too, because the sun in a south sky slants down to them and warms them. The sun ripens up the tomatoes in the sag-fenced garden patches and discourages moss on the rooftops. The south bank, for its part, mostly languishes in shadow.

From our cabin we couldn't see the Rogue at first. Myrtlewoods and pines screened the front of the place. We could see the air corridor above the river, though, that corridor where the gulls and the terns flew. Kingfishers dipped and chattered there. Mergansers wheeled in flocks upstream. An occasional eagle floated high in the thermals. After a rain, swallows glided delicately back and forth above the river. At dawn, sometimes, the clouds hanging low over the river corridor rose almost vertically with some thermal upthrust of river air. Then, too, we could hear the Mail Boats go by, and could hear the drone of the Mail Boat drivers' voices intoning information. They all stop their boats somewhere out front of the place and spout for awhile. Something monumental around here inspires these speeches, but I don't know what, unless it's the way the main river channel has moved clear over to the south leaving only a residual back-channel here on the north side, known locally as "The Snag Patch. "

Four acres of fir stand on the back slope behind our cabin, a few more down in the seasonal-creek draw, mixed with some enormous tan oaks, rotted on the uphill side ("cat-faced" the locals say), and a maze of myrtlewoods, pines, and holly in the front. Despite the corridor of river birds, the uprising clouds, and the summer sounds of Mail Boats, we hardly realized at first how close the Rogue River ran by us. Not until I asked our new neighbor, Neighbor S., if I could cross his land, not until I had crossed the North Bank Road, cut a swath through Neighbor S.'s blackberries, walked a plank across Edson Creek, waded the Snag Patch channel, and crossed a stretch of willow-thicket island, did I find that stretch of river called Johns Riffle, named for a fisherman, Jacob Johns. I turned there to look north and west, and saw then how the bend of river above me ran not so very far at all from the tall firs of our side border.

Various local chain saw specialists advertise in the *Curry County Reporter* their skills at dropping trees and cutting "windows" through blocking foliage, accommodating the viewing passion. The faller who showed up at our door for an estimate had sly-looking eyes, bulky shoulders, a pointed nose, a thin brown beard. It happened we knew in common a teacher, this timber faller one of her former students. As he told me stories of how she had thrown chalk and erasers at various uncooperative students, of how she had once pulled her hair in a rage of frustrated pedagogy, he took evident pleasure in bouncing his shoulders up and around in their sockets, and hooking his thumbs under his suspenders.

"Yup. Old Sara. I surely do remember her."

His partner, the topper, when he came, laced his climbing-pacs with a deft weaving of one hand, and carved a small glimpse of river for us, out to the south, between the limbed trunks of two girthy firs, a glimpse sufficient for me to peer past a post on the front stoop and see "the view."

It is not "the view" that particularly interests me, however, but rather just where the winter water level runs. The naked eye manages that task in pleasant weather, but when rain or fog is blowing, binoculars help. What I see through those dusty optics, additional to the river itself and the occasional winging mallard or merganser, is a slanting gravel road on the far south bank, and below it a straggly line of brush cross-woven with high water flotsam, mostly dead leaves wrapped and pressed to those brush stalks like rags to a yard pipe. This brush line is my marker, my point of reference. If the river runs below brush line, then I can wade the Snag Patch channel, and Johns Riffle is low enough, and clear enough, for a fly.

Our cabin sits perhaps one hundred feet above the river, the angle of view too oblique to make out the river's color. Generally the river-glint turns even muddy water to silver. It's mostly true that low water translates to clear water, but not always. The other day, having finished some new casements and brushed on the first coat of varnish, I pulled into my waders, laced my wading boots, grabbed my fly rod, and headed down the driveway. Three red-tails screamed at me from above. I wondered if the odd one out was an interloper or a hang-about juvenile. Down at the road, I put an outgoing letter in the mailbox, cut down through the blackberries, crossed Edson Creek, pushed through some myrtlewood, slid down a clay bank, and slogged across the Snag Patch. The usual flock of ducks—mallards this time—got up below me as I reached Johns. Watching them, I took four steps into the river before seeing that the water ran thick brown. Some fellow up by Galice, I learned later, someone deaf to regulation, had drained a mining pond into the Wild and Scenic Rogue.

Nonetheless, the view helps gauge the river, and gauges more than the Rogue. At midbrush level the smaller coastal streams will be running green through their canyons. Some fall mornings, however, I gauge fishing sentiment without the view at all, and easily, for a heavy droning at dawn of fishing boats headed up from the Port is always a sign of promise.

My father would have loved this place, would have sat in the summer sun on the stoop, Johns Riffle glinting over his right shoulder, the violet-green swallows darting in and out of their nesting hole under the eaves, the blue herons flapping low over the house from their Snag Patch fishing to their rookery in Neighbor H.'s back pines, uttering somber rasps and rattles to their young. That sound fills the summer air here as constantly as the winter's is filled with a gushing of seasonal creeks. And the strung-along jibber my father uttered after his stroke, his raspy oddities, almost as baffling and strange as the speech of herons, maybe said this to me: "I've saved a little money. Take it, when I die, and buy some place where you can see a river."

I suppose, in the certain ways I live, the certain habits I lean to, my father has his presence, and I don't begrudge it, particularly that tendency of mine to fish seriously. Then, too, there are those foxed and faded first editions of his scattered around our bookshelves, and his old tackle box in the garage full of tooth-raked wooden plugs. Those leavings add their qualities to the character of this place.

When I think of my father, I remember those stormy days he favored for his fishing. He knew how walleyes fed when heavy waves churned up the shallows. The winds of those fishing days blew up some intimidating waves under us on some big Minnesota lakes, but those winds never lasted too long. Get winds of that kind in youth, and they seem like the right winds. They blow, and then they stop, and they make the incessant Nesika Beach winds seem wrong. On the North Bank we sometimes get a howling, tree-bending wind that pounds pinecones into our windows. But after a few hours it stops. It feels right, and sets me to remembering Minnesota thunder and that yellow, tornado-coming storm-light of certain summer afternoons.

The wraith of my father, puffing his pipe on the North Bank stoop, knows all about these winds, and about fishing compulsions, that excitement in the belly. He'll probably not stay on the stoop for long, but drag himself down to the river, crawl or roll if necessary, land a fish at all costs, and keep his pipe lighted through the whole process. The ghost image of him, there on the stoop, gives this North Bank cabin a familiar and homey quality, something like the feeling cast by those clan portraits hanging on the interior walls.

It is late February now. We've seen some good rains. The Edson Creek Frog Chorus has begun a nightly rehearsal, a single monotonic fluting that sometimes quiets on an instant, some coon hushing them down with its hunt. Herons are flying steadily back and forth from the Snag Patch to the back pines. I can't see what they're doing back there, but it must be nest improvements occupying them, home building.

They're working on their floors, probably, maybe their edgings, and building with flotsam. I'm working on the long-neglected cabin walls, building with memories of how a cabin should look, memories of northern Minnesota cabins, and of Wisconsin sand-country cabins. And the ambiance of this place feels right. When the big North Bank myrtlewoods wave in the yard, and across the road, they remind me of those midwestern cottonwoods I watched from my bedroom window as a boy. One myrtlewood, down on the northeast corner of the lot, is so large in the bole that I could put a chair up there between the first branchings. The coons know the place; it is always filled with their sign and with a faint odor of coon. These are different trees from the cottonwoods, of course, these myrtlewoods, evergreen, and with their own perfumed smell, but their tops blow properly in winds, and the distant emotions they generate in me make this North Bank place feel true and right, what the Swedes and Norwegians must have felt when they found Minnesota, what my distant Hollander kin must have felt when they found Lake Michigan and remembered the North Sea. Such memories, dim though they are, yet take hold of my hands with the plane and the saw, guide the hammer strokes against the boards, and I build with this flotsam, these memories, these bones.

Steelhead runs are spotty. Yesterday on a slick I ran into a giant fellow with a full brown beard and a front tooth missing. He carried a shoulder bag and a spinning rod, some pencil-weight dangling from the arced tip of the rod. "Nothing gives," he said. "But they should be in there. They should be in there." A kind of bewilderment showed in his repetition. He shrugged and wandered on past me. "I'll just try it down here," he said over his shoulder.

I'd fished all morning, myself, over some pretty good drifts, a two-inch rain just clearing away. One half-pounder was all I'd touched, wild and jumpy, but not one of those freight train chromers of February. The rancher who'd let me fish his place drove up. His black Stetson knocked the pickup roof when he turned to ask how I'd done, and his look turned perplexed when I told him. He pushed back his hat. "Should be good now with that rain," he said. "Wonder how the professionals are doing, Milt and Earl."

That rancher had about twenty sheep climbing the back end of his pickup, trying to get at the hay bales. "Well, I better get to work," he said, checked the rearview mirror, and backed his truck around. He nudged a couple ewes out of the way with his fender, dropped down off the road into the grassy field toward the white humped ribs of a winterkill, and let me pass by.

It's an empty, wistful wonderment inside that goes with the phrase, "They ought be in there." But a couple months ago I drove up to Cape Sebastian with my binoculars and watched gray whales spouting all along the sea's horizon. They're in there now in a way they haven't been for years, come back from endangerment to abundance. And the next day an Oregon Department of Fish & Wildlife (ODFW) staffer, Dave Harris, told me, all smiles, "There's a great run of steelhead coming into the Chetco, big and bright. We got some in our nets." Another ODFW man, the local director, Tim Unterwegner, told me of the Rogue this winter, "We're doing about as well as anybody in the state."

Last winter I got a call from a commercial fisherman I know, John Wilson, who asked if I'd help him with some hatch boxes up on Coy Creek, a creek not far at all from the North Bank place.

John and I beat through blackberries all one morning unearthing old PVC piping, fixing the breaks. By noon we had water, cold and beautiful. I'd worn work gloves. John hadn't, and wore a couple dozen stickers in his sea-weathered, salt-cured hands. When John trucked down ten thousand eyed chinook eggs from Elk River Hatchery, and the water started perking through them in their hatch boxes on the platform above Coy Creek, we both felt pretty good. We stood there on the freshly swept platform, newly cleaned and rocked hatch boxes at our feet, fresh water gurgling in the scrubbed-out storage tank, purple eggs rocking in a gentle wash, and felt a fatherly expansiveness run through our veins.

Coy Creek is a feeder stream of Euchre Creek, and wild-stock salmon have been all but extinct in Euchre Creek for some years now. A decade back the watershed streambeds got used as skid roads in logging operations, and the banks scalped to the stream edges. Step out into Euchre Creek today, years after the logging, and you sink down a foot at each step. The creek is still cleaning itself of the accumulated silt of that period, washing it a few more yards downstream with each winter flooding.

Not so many years ago there were salmon in Euchre Creek so thick that up at that old cabin above the forks they'd kick one out for the dogs to eat whenever one was needed. Sometimes they'd cook it and sometimes they wouldn't, just toss it into the dog run. The going was easy along the creek back then, too, because the timber was big and the bears made fishing paths, wide, and well trampled. These things I learned yesterday from Neighbor S., seventy-six years old, not looking it, I told him, honestly. "But I goddamn feel it," he said.

Last week I hiked a cross-country slant from a high contouring logging road down into the roadless upstream canyon of Euchre Creek, followed thorny seeps and elk trails, and hit the stream several miles up from the last road. Three brown humps moved in the water, otter backs. I watched them through the thick new-growth alder until they porpoised around the bend. Then I stepped out into the water. The gravel was firm and crunchy. The pool below was deep and clean. Two small fish held in the current, smolts I thought. I crisscrossed the bends back to the road, climbed over and under blow downs, and saw new-scoured pools. The old wounds are healing.

It's not always a blessing to have known the earlier days the way Neighbor S. knew them, not an easily evident blessing anyway. Memories of plenty carry with them a pressing nostalgia. My own West Coast nostalgias need looking at some because they shape the paradigms of plenty that I live with and build upon, a plenty diminished a little from Neighbor S.'s early days, but still a plenty. Those memories began on the Quinalt River of the Olympic Peninsula. I waded out into that first morning, with leaky hip boots and a couple of spinners. Before I'd worked down past the first bend, I'd hooked one enormous salmon, two steelhead, and a sea-run cutthroat. I decided maybe the West would be a place I'd like to stay, to make home.

A long-muscled old man in a neighboring campsite told us we should have some high-bush cranberries to go with the one steelhead I'd kept, and showed us where to find them. He was right about the mix.

"One other thing," he said as he left the next morning. "Always hunt your elk uphill from your rig. Remember that." And he drove away with an unspoken certainty on his face that I would stay in those parts and need his advice. He was right about that, too. We settled in Oregon.

Ashland, Oregon, was a sleepy little town when we moved there, not yet the destination theater town of present times. I found a couple of fishing friends at the state college. We'd drive up to the upper portion of the Rogue River any afternoon we could get free, and wade out at Casey Park, or upstream from there at McCloud Bridge.

The first time we drove up to fish the upper Rogue, its famous name buzzed in my head as I rode along, two of us new to the place, tenderfeet, riding in back, two river veterans riding in front, talking the language. At the river, then, the veterans went their ways, wading off through spawning salmon in the shallows. We two new fellows, slow at gear-rigging, finally waded out to cast. Dave, below me, cranked partway into another long sentence about

Ohio, then went half-cocked silent. I looked downstream in time to see his rod tip slide beneath the surface and a torrent of bubbles rising.

The Rogue is a deep and ledgy river It can get skittish with unwary immigrants.

We'd park at the McCloud Bridge, myself growing gradually familiar with that stretch of the Rogue, and walk down through the dry grass to the top of a half-moon drift, about a hundred yards of riffle filled with planted rainbow and the occasional Rogue summer-run steelhead. Almost always some slack and hook-jawed salmon carcass lay wrapped on a log, another drying on the beach, emitting elemental perfumes. I'd cast a saggy line and a knotty leader, hook a steelhead, and lose the fish with a snap. It happened over and over that summer, my casts not worth putty, my blood-knots worse. Sometimes there was a skinny-dipper or two around the bend, a man with bony white shoulders and flaring black beard, a woman with hair down to her bare bum. "Don't bother us if it don't bother you," he'd say, and I'd fish on by them, extra careful with my backcasts.

Those are my nostalgias—days of plenty, days of high-bush cranberries, days of learning my knots. These days on the North Bank I sit at the oak table under the kitchen swag-lamp, the Edson Creek frogs droning, a territorial cat- hiss now and again sounding behind the cabin, and I tie elegant leaders with good, solid bloodknots. Deer chew under the apple trees, tame as cattle, eyes gleaming out of the darkness, and the rolling loop of running line in my hands turns perfectly over the shooting head, pulls tight, and holds. Nylon circles between my thumb and finger, circles again, pulls through, and the perfection loop draws tight exactly to its name. I use micrometer and measuring tape, consult my log of experiments, and run elementary calculations of weights and diameters. Last month I devised a flyline by splicing a high-density tip to an old braided belly, then the belly to a new plastic-coated running line. Tying the splices, I peeled off coating down to the nylon core, divided strands with a needle, stroked and twisted the fuzz of each end to three prongs, waxed and interlaced those, twisted them tight, wrapped them smooth with a gyrated bobbin, then coated them with a mixture of Goop and Meek. The splices slide through my rod guides like eels, hardly a touch of resistance.

The whole process reminds me a little of the way I've put together my life in different sections of the country, of the way most of us have put together our lives, smoothing together the transitions, testing the splices. There's a backing line out of Minnesota, a running line out of Seattle, a belly-section out of Ashland, and now these delicate gradations of North Bank tippet. With my micrometer I could measure the years.

An old fellow up at Lobster Creek the other day nudged his Labrador out of the way with one muddy boot and allowed as how he'd done some fly-fishing. He'd seen me returning from fishing on the south-bank riffle and come out of his camper to chat, the Lab prancing around with a raised ruff and uncertain bark.

"Oh Christ yes," he said. "Christ, absolutely. Hardly a California river I haven't fished with a fly. Always could do better with a fly than anything else. Tied my own, too."

He said this last as though it were the true touchstone of the fishing breed, looked over the Street Walker variant on my line, just eyed it without my intending to show it to him in any particular way, and said, "Hummmmm."

I was wet from a hard winter wade, and remembering the perfect form of an egret that had sailed off the far-side gravel bar ahead of me.

The old fellow talked about the Klamath, how he'd fished that river years back for steelhead, down low somewhere, what was the name of that town?

"Weitchpec? Orleans?" I said, unlacing my boots, remembering Weitchpec, and Orleans, and the Yurok toughs, and the old road down to Pecwan.

"No," he said. Then, "Orleans. Orleans. That's it."

"Nice canyon below town, down to Bluff Creek."

"Absolutely," he said, brightening. "Caught a lot of fish down there. Used to tie up a Silver Hilton, good little fly on the Klamath."

It was a good fly on the Rogue as well. I'd tied them, fished them, lost them at McCloud, at Casey, heavy hooks on thin leader, a foolish combination, and said so.

The old fellow and I stood there remembering in the cold river wind, reworking landscapes, shaping our Rogue scene with Klamath parts, the Labrador sniffing at my leg, maybe scenting the dig-it-up method. I scratched the dog's ears, and wondered, as I had wondered some times before, just who was remembering what, reinventing what, in naming a bark-sided boondocks Klamath River place like that Orleans.

Could be some displaced kin of mine, I suppose, hammering with dreams, building with bones, taking some cross-the-sea remembered place upcurrent past the sea winds of Requa, past Kenek and Weitchpec, to that wide, sand-spitted, inland bar at the river curve. Whoever it was, I'd guess, sat down to lunch somewhere along that tangled Klamath riverbank, imagined himself back on a remembered curve of the Loire, and called the place Orleans. And he did so, I think, simply because of some familiar scent in the air, or because a prompting turn of sky blew into view, or because a bird sat a branch just so in silhouette, or because of any of a hundred-odd other possible reasons for memory, from the cut of his bread to the lace of his shoe.

I was learning at the North Bank place just how that all worked, that home-claiming process, how the memories of family and landscape and former homesteads prompted recollection. The more I thought about the matter, the more I understood that French fellow, whoever he was, down there on the Klamath River, and how he came to name that wild river bar Orleans.

Jessica Maxwell

Jessica Maxwell will try anything, when it comes to sports and adventure travel. She has written for *Esquire, Sports Afield, Audubon, Pacific Northwest,* and other magazines. Her book, *Femme d'Adventure*, collects her "travel tales from inner Montana to outer Mongolia." Her career as a flyfisher is the subject of *I Don't Know Why I Swallowed the Fly*, from which the following selection is taken. A new book on golf and the neophyte, *Driving Myself Crazy,* is her most recent sporting adventure. A lively sense of humor, a keen ear for fresh language, and a sharp eye for detail mark Jessica Maxwell's work. She lives in Eugene, and fishes the nearby McKenzie River.

River Deep, Mountain High

A million gallons of water pressed hard against my thighs. Ancient rock cliffs soul-kissed the sky above me. Every move I made had distinct dinosaurean qualities. Every step I took seemed to take eons. I felt like Tina Turner trapped in a Paleozoic music video. What was I doing on the wrong side of Oregon standing in the middle of the Deschutes River with nothing to hold onto but the butt-end of a fly rod?

Trying to learn to fly fish, that's what. Which was why my fishing coach had parked me here in this flamboyant piece of fast water. Somehow I was supposed to complete the entomologically correct assessment of an invisible insect hatch, tie the appropriate caddis-whatever to the end of an invisible fly line, and make my linguini of a fly rod cast with impeccable accuracy to the waiting mouth of the invisible trout I had managed to spot in the Mount Vesuvius current blasting along in front of me. And I was expected to do all this without getting knocked on my neoprened derriere. But the truth was that nothing in my fishing life had prepared me for the relentlessness of rivers.

I grew up surf fishing in Southern California on the deckled edge of the American left coast, and became by default a person of oceanic rhythms. Waves build and crest and break with a one-two-three waltzing grace. The spaces between them let you breathe, little aquatic mezzanines where your mind can sit back, put its feet up, smoke a cigar.

Rivers offer anglers no such luxury. They hit the ground running, and run nonstop, twenty-four hours a day, year after panting year, and you are expected to keep up with them. This, I think, explains the inherent hyperactivity of fly fishing, the merciless casting, the endless exchange of one perfectly good fishing hole for another, the chronic wading, when sitting on the dock of the bay, so to speak, would do just fine. This was not the peaceful sport I grew up with. Fly fishing was some kind of Attention Deficit Disorder ... with hooks!

I missed the briny serenity of my youth. In general, West Coast water doesn't do anything fast on a regular basis. Waves continue their usual impersonation of western civilization (build, rise, fall), tides shift gears imperceptibly within the Pacific motor, and most of the time the water itself just sits there and does a slow, Jell-O hula. So, when you step into the surf and cast a baited hook out beyond the breakers, you can count on a long, easy tour of duty. You stand facing the horizon like the Queen of the Beach, eyes filled with the blue plane of the sea that spreads out before you like an anonymous, magnificent future. You stand and take stock approvingly of this your saline kingdom, enjoying a watery leg massage calibrated to match your resting heartbeat while the surf sucks lazily on your line—often for hours—until it all finally ends with the climactic burst of a big fish taking your sardine to China.

To a novice fly-fisher ocean person, river rhythms feel manic. You cannot, for instance, go down to your local hardware store and buy a river tide table. Rivers don't make predictable changes; they are immune to the moon. This, I think, is why they felt unknowable to me, a foreign kingdom ruled by a force so distracted there was clearly no chance to have a real relationship with them.

Given the tumult of the situation, I reckoned the explosion of a fish hitting my fly would just seem like part of the scenery. I knew I'd miss it. Of course, that attitude might have had something to do with the fact that the only fish I'd ever hooked and landed in a river so far was a Mongolian lenok about the size of your average banana. As I recall, it wiggled at precisely the same velocity as both the riffle from whence it came and the alder leaves shimmying above it, obfuscating the entire experience, which was already blurred by the weirdness of its having occurred on the steppes of Outer Mongolia, of all places.

It was there, in the shallows of Mongolia's Sharlon River, on the green, leafy fringe of the Siberian border, that my heart first thrilled to the high art of fly fishing. I was, after all, witnessing an artist: Guido Reinhardt Rahr III of Portland, Oregon, one of the most gifted young anglers in the Pacific Northwest.

Though we'd never met, Guido (pronounced "Gheedough," not "Gwee-dough") and I had both signed up for something called The First Western Fishing Expedition to Outer Mongolia. Under the auspices of a Seattle outfitter, fourteen of us fishing fanatics were going after the biggest "salmon" on earth—the species *Hucho hucho taimen,* which are actually giant trout that can weigh up to two hundred pounds.

At that point I had been an impassioned salmon fisherwoman in my own right for years, favoring an old British Columbia version of the sport called tyee fishing. It's done out of a rowboat and instead of bait uses classic Northwest tackle, such as wooden Lucky Louie plugs and metal "spoons." But, like the saltwater live-sardine bait fishing my father had taught me, when you're tyee fishing you just toss your lure into the water and wait. It was a far cry from the frenetic cast-and-step activity of fly fishing.

I was familiar with fly fishing back then. I'd had a few lessons and I liked fooling around with feathers and hooks, if only to make scary earrings. But the triumph of masterful angling was unknown to me until I saw Guido draw his delicate scrimshaw on the ivory underbelly of the arcing Mongolian sky. He stood there in the shallows of that exotic water, broad-shouldered, narrow-hipped, square-jawed, and tan. The bright Mongolian sun only amplified the male grace of his form. When he moved, gold flashed both from his cropped yellow hair and the metal rim of his glasses. But when he talked he sounded as though he were on TV.

"We're standing here on the far edge of farthest Outer Mongolia," he announced suddenly, punching out every syllable, "fishing for the BIGGEST salmonids on earth."

There wasn't a hint of farce in his voice, not a trace of irony, and no sign of self-consciousness anywhere. The young man was serious, and, as it turned out, he *was* on TV He was talking into a video camera whose operator remained hidden behind a tree until I stepped a little closer and saw him.

"We're using giant Marabou Muddlers with spun deerhair heads," Guido continued. Little coronas of spit now followed each word. "Because these fish are CARNIVORES known to feed on mice and muskrats ... even small dogs!"

With that he turned and, still on camera, resumed his exuberant, powerful casting, laying down one perfectly straight line after another with the precision of a French pastry chef. Never had a Mongolian river received such a lavish decoration. Never had a *National Geographic* scouting video inspired such a bravura performance. And never had I beheld such an act of aerial finesse.

Until that moment, fly fishing remained a distant distraction, a rarefied adjunct to the broader sport I'd loved all my life. But when I saw the way Guido's line moved, its impossible lengths suspended for whole moments above the surface of the river before its business-end dropped its fly exactly where he wanted it—well, I knew then that I knew nothing of the soul of this sport I had taken so lightly. Like the African tribe that has no word for God other than the blowy sound of "whew," I said as much myself, sat down on the ancient Mongolian earth, and watched for all I was worth.

Observing Guido cast gave me an uncomfortable sense of comfort. For a moment I couldn't figure out why. Then it hit me: my father. As a child I had spent hours watching my father cast. Not the fore-and-aft continuum of fly casting, the single long-bomb forward action of big saltwater reels. But my father's rod cut the air the same way, and his line always shot out to kingdom come, just like Guido's. Even their postures were similar: the strongly planted feet, the athlete's hips, the rocking right shoulder, the sure brown hands, the eyes that never left the far end of the rod. I knew that posture as well as I knew anything about my father. It must have imprinted itself deeply on my mind during the early years from piers, from beaches, from the uneven granite plates of coastal outcroppings. It was as if all the love and all the pain between fathers and daughters were locked into that form—its sweet familiarity, and its distance. When Daddy fished he was happy, but he was also always Over There. It was, I think, his therapy in those pre-therapist days. My mother is a cultured woman, nourished wholly by art, literature, and a beautiful home. But the only thing that gave my father peace of mind was the thing that cut him off from me: the solitude of fishing.

In any weather, any season, if he were staring at the tip of a fishing rod, my father was happy. The heavens could unleash pit-bull monsoons that sent saner campers to their tents, and my father would still be fishing. The fiercest wind could send those tents cartwheeling down the beach, and my father would still be fishing. The truth is, while we had fished together throughout my childhood, by the time I took up the rod again as an adult, my father was too infirm to go fishing with me, racked as he was by emphysema. On fishing trips I took along instead my most powerful memory of him: his lone form standing on the end of an old rock jetty, casting over and over into the wild blue California yonder.

I was raised in a beach town when they were still beach towns and not the suburbs of Los Angeles. It was the late fifties, and the air did not yet sit on the ocean like yellow grease. On Sundays our father often walked my sister and me down the long Manhattan Beach pier and claimed a spot in the clear blue air around the strange roundhouse snack bar-bait shop at the pier's western end, from which we caught mackerel or barracuda or banjo shark with live sardines that cost the same as a Big Hunk, except that you had to catch them yourself, which my sister and I thought was the best fishing of all. We picked out the fish we wanted, and, being the eldest, I chased it around with a dip net until my eyes lost it when it passed other sardines that looked suspiciously like itself. Then my sister said, "No, *that* one," and got me back on track until, finally, we proudly offered our catch to our father in a white Chinese food container filled with salt water. And that was always the end of our intimacy with it, because he never expected us to poke a hook through the nose of a pet sardine.

Our father was very clear on that. Had we been sons instead of daughters, his chivalry might have transmuted into a gory education. But it was still the fifties, and we were girls, and I'm sure he reckoned that our squeals would have disturbed the other fishermen who, like himself, were there to stare with complete concentration at the tips of their rods while the ashes of their cigarettes grew longer and longer until they crash-landed in purified piles on the dried sardine blood and ossified fish guts that laminated the cement surface of the old Manhattan Beach pier. In the summer we abandoned pier fishing and drove south to the hillside town of Palos Verdes where we hiked down a certain cliff, which was the color of Dijon mustard, not green. The cliff path ended at Bluff Cove, an off-center half- moon of water whose right curve rose onto a pocked plateau that shot straight into the ocean.

When the tide was out, the plateau became a landscape of child-sized saltwater lakes. That was when our father lit a cigarette, stationed himself on the sight of that granite gun barrel, and held his particular piece of the Pacific ransom. He wanted its rockfish, its coppers and cow cod, and he would stand out there all day firing his baited bullets into the boiling target while the surf fired back at him, encircling his form again and again with frothy shrapnel.

While our father fished, my sister and I played in the tidepools, a sport we never tired of. Our father had taught us the secret: move too fast and you miss things; pay attention and everything comes to life. It remains to this day my own First Law of Fishing ... of everything.

It was riveting work, peering like God into whole worlds you did not create, watching for diminutive sculpin and baby octopus. But every so often I looked up to check on our father standing out there on his private peninsula while the white hands of the surf tried again and again to drag him under. They always failed and fell back in despair, leaving him with salty haloes around his head, as if he were an angel for having daughters, not sons, and not regretting it.

It was our good fortune that he just went ahead and treated us like sons, teaching us to do the things he himself had learned to love as a kid growing up in New Zealand—camping, hunting, and most especially, fishing. Like Guido's angling, our father's was a sight to behold. When he fished, all his nervous energy drained out his hands, and, traveling at the speed of thought, ran up his fishing rod, transferred to the geometry of his line, and was simply thrown away. All of his pain—his own father's early death, the orphanage, the war, the divorce—all of it vanished and left him stilled, freed even, for whole hours at a time. Witnessing my father finally at home in his own body is, I think, what made me fall in love with fishing at such a young age. It is, I know, what brought me back to it as an adult.

For vacations we took long driving trips, heading north always, camping and fishing as we went. Maybe we made it to the redwoods. Maybe the Oregon coast. Twice we got all the way to Vancouver Island, and it was on those trips that I first was charmed by the Pacific Northwest's malachite beauty. Later I chose the region as my home, settling on one of the little green islands in Puget Sound I had seen and loved from the ferry so many years before.

On that island the world outside my door is utterly different from the tawny open beaches of my childhood. It is self-contained and dense and very difficult to know. Its remnant forests are still threaded with silver stitches of water; indeed, water rules this boreal universe—lakes, fjords, rivers, the inland sea that surrounds my own island like a protective arm. And, of course, the rain.

When I left California in the seventies to go to school in Oregon, I fell madly in love with the rain. When I left California again in the eighties to move permanently to the Northwest, I was like a person dying of thirst and reaching for water. To this day my fixation on water borders on dementia. Some people carry a Saint Christopher's medal or a dolphin pendant as a talisman. I carry water. Always. Full liters in my car, a little bottle in my purse, even a tiny silver flask in evening bags that draws snorts of disbelief and disappointment when I say, "It's only water."

I never touch any of it. It Is not for drinking. It's for having. Keeping. Because nothing sends me into a panic faster than running out of water. I can't explain it, really. It would be easy to say it has something to do with security or health, as the world continues to poison its supply of drinking water, but I suspect something a lot closer to home. I am convinced that water is the key to understanding a landscape on which the sky weeps nine months of the year.

Here in the Northwest, water feels charged with the possibilities of birth fluid. In the half-light of winter, dark and wet as a womb, fish emerge from our rivers and streams as if just born. They look, and feel to the touch, more like congealed water than the animals they are. Their link to the land is inescapable. They evolved with it, surviving ice age after ice age, riding the geographic changes as they came, colonizing and recolonizing streams and rivers as they charted and recharted their courses. Fish grew up with the place, and ever since I myself arrived, I have not been able to divine a better way of understanding this piece of watery earth than to fish it.

Like the finest umbilicus, casting your line into water joins you to it. The currents speak to your bones in iced tongues. The loam perfume of conifer rot and mud attunes your nose to the local biology. You taste its chemistry, wash your ears in its sweet white noise, let it take you back to a time before words and teach you things language never could.

My father was a bait fisherman, a man of salt and surf. The ocean still has a powerful hold on me, and always will. But when I saw the cursive grace of Guido Rahr's fly line writing prayers I couldn't read to the river gods of Outer Mongolia, I knew my name was written there too. Fly fishing was going to be my version of my father's sport, my nod to my Scottish ancestors and to myself, and to the fish-crazed part of America I had claimed as my own. That night, when the campfire smoke sent its own cryptic messages heavenward, I asked Guido if he would teach me how to fly fish once we were back in the Northwest. Like the brother I never had, he said yes.

Of course I had no idea how much effort went into serious fly fishing. And knowledge. Raw skill, and instinct, balance, strength and undiluted concentration. Not to mention equipment: waders, wading boots, fly vests, shortie rain jackets, several sizes of rods, reels with several sizes of line, all kinds of tools, Polaroid glasses, a hundred kinds of flies, and a thousand kinds of feathers and fur if you dare to tie your own. No wonder Daddy stuck to one-rod/one-reel saltwater fishing with sardines. Learning how to fly fish was going to take years!

What a joke. I'd taken up this crazy sport specifically to get to know the grand, green Pacific Northwest, and there I was on the inland side of the mountains floundering around in a skinny spit of water in country that looked like the reason the Okies left Oklahoma. Fortunately I'm not one for depressions, great or small, so I tried to find something good about the place. Well, I thought, it's … not raining. Now that was depressing. it's dry here, my mind warned. Real dry. I reached for my water bottle.

Then I remembered that I was standing in water. Well, that's a plus, I thought: you've always got enough water when you're standing in a river. This piece of radical intelligence cheered me considerably—until Guido showed up again and ordered me out of the water.

"Time for Master's Eddy," he said, and made me hike downstream with him another quarter mile, a real trick if you're wearing a pair of clunkoid too-big sopping wet wading boots. But I clomped along behind him like a trained brontosaurus until he stopped short above a slowly undulating elbow of the river.

"There it is," Guido announced. "Master's Eddy."

From above, the place looked like a giant hurricane.

"It's one of the Deschutes' classic fishing holes," Guido advised me. "See all those little pink dots? Those are rising trout mouths. Master's Eddy is like a giant rotating insect buffet. The bugs get trapped in the currents there and just go around and around, and the fish just hang out and stuff themselves. So," he said with a courtly sweep of his hand, "start casting."

Good idea, I thought. But first I have to get down there. The bank above Master's Eddy is at almost a ninety- degree angle to the river and it's made largely of loose rock. So, while Guido stomped off to go fish somewhere by himself, I slowly worked my way downhill, feeling like Lucy trying to sneak up on Ricky's fishing party. An avalanche of stones telegraphed my progress to every fish within a two-mile radius. Soon I started skidding and ended up going the rest of the way sitting down. Then I virtually belly-flopped smack into the eye of the hurricane, scattering trout in all directions.

That done, I stopped to take a look around. I must say, the place had a style all its own. Unlike the bright turquoise plate of the Pacific, the basalt cradle that holds the Deschutes River looked spent, a beleaguered husk of a landscape that couldn't help but show its age: four million years and counting. Rushing hard out of the middle Cascade Mountains, the river drains the entire escarpment of central Eastern Oregon, but its mute palette of ochers and taupes is relieved only by silver bolls of sage and darker fans of juniper. Oaks hold forth stoically in the desiccated lowlands, but alders quake at the water's edge like refugees dying for a drink. Only the most sophisticated of designers would find inspiration in the Deschutes' monochromatic, mineralized dust. In the dry light of an autumn afternoon, standing in water again seemed like a very good place to be, especially in the shadow of the volcanic upheaval that cut the region off from water-bearing Pacific storms in the first place. Though it's hardly the powerful presence of the Pacific, the mere existence of that youthful blue line of river in that arid terrain seemed miraculous.

Encouraged, I tried to cast. But Master's Eddy is deep. I couldn't wade out very far, and without much room for backcasting, casting itself seemed impossible. I raised my rod and carefully lowered it behind me, but its tip collided with the bank. Guido had warned me that Master's Eddy was a tough place to fish, but he blamed it on the currents, "which are always changing and you never know when or how," he had said. The problem was that the river pushes against the rock wall there and sends the water into ever-shifting spirals. And that makes it difficult to get a good drift, according to Guido, "because the water tends to push away from you without warning and make your fly drag—a sure sign to a trout that what appears to be a bug is really something weird."

All in all, it takes a master to master Master's Eddy, and despite my supra-neophyte status, for some reason Guido thought the practice would do me good. Probably because that's where he himself had learned to fly fish decades before.

While the rest of the Deschutes continued its mad dash north, I tried to figure out where I could position myself in that watery sidewinder of a fishing hole so that I could cast without floating away like a giant mayfly. My borrowed men's boots swam around on the rocks and my feet swam around in my boots—sort of a swim/swim situation. More than once I almost went swimming myself, but Master's Eddy moves slowly, so you tend to fall in quietly and thus avoid disturbing the dozens of kissy pink trout mouths that do indeed stipple this merry smorbugasbord.

Having waded as deeply as I dared, I procured a precarious balance and cast. Sort of. I really still didn't know how to do it. So I tried to imitate my mental image of Guido's beautiful cast: I carefully lifted my line off the water, pulled my rod back to ten o'clock ... and—zing!—became profoundly hung up in the brush behind me.

I slopped over to the bank and scuttled uphill, clinging to the falling-apart terrain like a neoprene leech. When I finally found my fly, I marveled at the shish kebob of leaf and branch I had made with one flick of a novice's wrist. Then I scrambled back down, slid into the water, and popped up like a breath mint, scattering the fish again.

Giving the ancient basalt a forty-mile stare, I waited until the greedy little trout mouths reappeared. Then I decided to try to execute a roll cast, which I didn't know how to do either. Again mimicking Guido, I drew my rod up until it pointed directly overhead, then slammed it down like a sledgehammer and ended up hooking my chin.

"Yeow!"

I slipped again. Holding my rod high in some bizarre half-reflex from my early salmon-fishing training, I began a slow, floating orbit around Master's Eddy like a narcissistic Statue of Liberty hooked only on herself.

Now, of course, is when Guido decided to come check on me. Somehow missing the compromised position of my mandible, he explained that the real action was to be found at Lunker Haven, the stretch of boulder water just around the bend. "I'll meet you there in about fifteen minutes," he said, "now that you've mastered Master's Eddy."

What I'd actually mastered is Fly Fishing Safety Rule #1: "Remove all hooks from soft tissue under water, where near-freezing temperatures anesthetize exposed nerve endings and you can't hear your fellow anglers' hyena laughter." Which at the moment was ricocheting off the Deschutes' old canyon walls like the ghostly voices of fly fishermen past, begging me to take up stamp collecting.

Frank Soos

Frank Soos grew up in Southwest Virginia, and began fishing for bass and bluegill at about age six. He started flyfishing when he was twelve. In 1986 he moved to Alaska, where he teaches English and creative writing at the University of Alaska in Fairbanks. He has published two collections of short stories, *Early Yet* and *Unified Field Theory,* as well as a book on fishing, *Bamboo Fly Rod Suite,* whose last chapter is reprinted here. Frank Soos is co-editing a new collection of essays and artwork from Alaska, *Under Northern Lights.*

Obituary With Bamboo Fly Rod

Here's a story Dave Stark told me. Once he and another guy drove over Murphy Dome to do some fishing on the lower Chatanika. On the west side of the dome the road drops down into a permafrost bog. That's where they got balled up in the mud on that one-lane road too skinny to turn around in. Equipped with nothing but an axe and a come-along, they spent the better part of an Alaska summer day pulling themselves out of the muck and yanking the truck around in the road for the trip back over the dome. I'm not sure if they did any fishing at all.

I used to teach high school English in a little town in piedmont Carolina, a little town that lies along the road from the Charlotte airport to my parents' home in Virginia. There, in my very first year of teaching, I taught a boy who was clearly smarter than I was. I saw his quickness instantly, the way he probed a short story and came out with things, made connections that none of the other kids quite saw, that I saw but had to admit I wouldn't have thought of myself. Because I was a new teacher, I didn't have the self-assurance or presence of mind to see that at least I had the edge in simple knowledge. I taught this young man for three years, coached him in cross-country, led him on hikes with the outing club. When I moved on to graduate school, I started a short list, the kind of list I wonder if all teachers don't secretly keep, of the truly gifted, of those marked for some future distinction. For a few years he remained the only one on that list, and I waited for his name to turn up in the newspaper, maybe in the book reviews or academic journals. I was sure it would turn up somewhere so that even way over in Alaska I would detect the ripple.

That's the kind of information I'm on the lookout for when I read the paper, the little connections that assure me that through a messy web of tangles the world is held together. Everybody scans the paper for the big stuff—who's bombing whom, further proof of what scoundrels we've elected to high office—but I want to get around that to the revelations of the human heart also to be found right there in the daily newspaper. For this reason I must read both "Dear Abby" and "Ann Landers"; the features on outstanding local schoolchildren; the sports page, with particular emphasis on the compiled statistics of hometown leagues and results of local foot, dog sled, and automobile races; the announcements of engagements, weddings, and births; the letters to the editor; the court judgments; and the police blotter.

There in the police blotter on a dark day deep in the bottom of winter, among the requisite petty thieveries, DWIs, and collisions, I saw a report of a man found dead in his apartment, dead of a gunshot wound. Foul play was not suspected, but I wasn't mystified. I know how to read the evasive language of the police report.

I know the spot on the lower Chatanika that Dave Stark was headed for. I know the road up the Fairbanks side of Murphy Dome. The road leads to my house, but to get to the river you'd go past my turn and on up the dome. Toward the top, the road flattens out and you can see you're pretty much above the tree line and into tundra. Some willow shoots line the road, but behind them are big patches of blueberries and low bush cranberries. In the late summer we come here to pick those berries, especially in the fields just below the Air Force radar installation. And if that place is too crowded or over-picked, we will go out the road onto the saddle below the dome. From there the road drops off toward the Chatanika River and Minto Flats beyond. Which is why, they say, this road to almost nowhere exists. A state senator wanted a quicker way to get out to the Flats for his bird hunting, his moose hunting, his pike fishing, than driving all the way around to the far side, to New Minto Village off the Elliot Highway

This state was rich then. Putting a rough road through with a couple of Caterpillar tractors and a heavy road grader so a senator and his buddies could more conveniently slip away to the real Alaska was no big deal. Alaska isn't so rich now, and that senator is dead. The road has deteriorated. I wouldn't try it except in a truck with four- wheel drive. I always remember to carry a come-along and an axe too.

I found the rest of the story of the dead man a few days later when I read another part of the paper I read daily without fail, the obituaries. A modern obituary is often a stingy bit of reportage; nobody wants to get too close to revealing the cause of their grief. This one was more forthcoming than most. The dead man was older than I was, though not by much. He would have been a senior in high school when I was a freshman, one of the big guys who punched freshmen in the arm, who smoked behind the gym, had a girl and his own car. And he was one who wound up in Vietnam whether he intended to or not.

It might be too easy to imagine that nothing went right from there. He had a string of jobs—policeman in two states, sold cars and was good at it, mined gold, worked for the Bureau of Land Management. Left a couple of wives, a couple of kids in different states. Most recently he lived with yet another woman. Maybe he gave up on the durability promised by a ceremony. And maybe at the end as he died of cancer, as death became more inevitable and life more painful, neither she nor anybody else could do anything to help him

The obituary says he owned a bamboo fly rod, his grandfather's old rod, his grandfather from back in Missouri. I lived down in Arkansas for a while where the runoff from the fertilizer and chicken litter had ruined the fish for eating. So maybe I envied the people up in Missouri where the water ran cold and clear out from the bottoms of hydroelectric dams and made the fishing for trout good year-round. I wondered how it was then, when his grandfather must have caught rainbows as long as your arm fishing the tailwaters down from the sluice gates. That would have been before the editors of fishing magazines started running feature stories, the kind where a fisherman in waders kneels before the camera offering up a subdued and weighty fish in his outstretched arms. And I wondered what it was to come to own such a fine fishing rod, a rod that had some fishing in it, and I considered why, in the end, it wasn't enough.

Sometimes a thing comes into your hands without its history attached. Sometimes you have to figure it out by yourself. After it's been used a while, a bamboo rod can take a set, a noticeable bend in the tip section of the rod. A casting set, its tip bending upward, is an indication of many more casts than fish taken, and a fighting set means a rod took its share of big fish, fish that took something out of the rod. My own bamboo rod arrived without a casting or a fighting set. It said very little of who had owned it except that perhaps one day he put it up wet and stored it carelessly. The steel guides rusted through their wraps; the varnish crazed.

Shouldn't it be otherwise? Shouldn't the elegant old thing come dragging the past behind it? When I am on the riverbank with my bamboo rod in hand, I want to stand in the present and look back into a past that leads not only inevitably to this moment, but to the rightness of this moment. Norman Maclean might think so, too. I've read in *A River Runs Through It* where he says nobody ought be allowed to catch a fish off a bad cast. To think such a thing is to believe in the rightness of nature, or in the case of Mr. Maclean, to believe in the complicity of God with nature, God lurking in the background to make sure things come out right.

And I think, what about accidents? Accidents, for example, like the one where I overshoot my cast and it flips up around a twig hanging over the river, swinging just a minute before it slithers off and into a river. Maybe a fish has caught a glint off the hook and is rising to take the fly even as it falls. And I think if we're going to disallow that catch, then what about fish caught on poorly tied flies, caught on flies tied in Third World countries by underpaid peasants? Fish caught on cheap outfits that are an insult to the art of fishing or fish caught on overpriced ones bought by the vainglorious who think a brand name says something about their human worth. If you took those reasons into account, who among us has caught many fish worth mentioning?

Among the stories I took up with my high school students was Joseph Conrad's "Heart of Darkness." It is not a particularly easy story to get across in a high school classroom. I found myself taking my students through it one sentence at a time in places, feeling a little like the narrator Marlow himself chugging up an unknown river—always against the current—in his steamer. It was a worthwhile trip for me, if only because I taught myself something I'd managed never to see clearly in four years as an English major at a pretty good school. Here were great paragraphs. Here were paragraphs that ran sentences by the reader like rivers of words, sometimes rushing, sometimes majestic and barely seeming to move at all. Here was a skill you could spend your life trying to grab onto.

And my student, the smart one on my very short list, saw Conrad's genius too, though he thought for a minute it might be me. "The man really knows how to read this stuff," he told a bunch of other kids as one class pushed out the door against the next one coming in. Still, I was relieved. I thought I had taught him something useful.

There is a need in all of us, I think, to believe the world is somehow ordered. In the river there are fish. Even if our eyes are good, we rarely see them, yet we cast into the pools to the spots where we expect them to be holding. The flies we use are often the flies we used the last time the light was like this, the water this high, the season right about now. Often this method works. We cast, and sure enough, just like last year, there's a fish rising, revealing itself.

One afternoon, driving my brother's car home to see the folks, I took the exit off the interstate, drove into town and up the main street divided by the little-used railroad tracks, took the right on Center Street, and parked in front of the school where I had taught. Maybe it was ten years, maybe fifteen. But everything was just as it was, the same school secretary, my friend the physics teacher still in his same room, still at his desk grading some tests or lab reports. I sat down in a student desk and pretty soon many of the other teachers I had known came by. My ex-uncle- in-law was there and so the talk turned to my other ex-in-laws and where they were and how they were doing. Which saddened and embarrassed me, to think that a whole part of my life had sheered off and drifted away from me like an iceberg. Rick came up, my ex-brother-in-law, as smart and mulish a man as I've ever known. I believe I'd like him still, though I'll bet he's gone Republican on me.

"He was our only Morehead Scholar," somebody said. And I said, no, my student had been a Morehead Scholar too.

"You know what happened to him, don't you?"

"No." And I believe I wanted to know.

"He killed himself." Nobody knew why. That's too bad, we all said; that's a shame. But we were friends who hadn't seen each other in a long time, so our talk moved on.

It's hard not to blame myself. That's another secret list I suspect most teachers have—the list of all the mistakes you make, all the things you could have done differently, said differently, or never said at all. It's one thing when the guy you sent to the principal's office once a week knocks over a gas station; it's another when it's a kid off your short list. Here was a kid with the world rolling out in front of him, just waiting for him to walk in it, to make a piece of it his own. What went wrong? And what could I have said or done that would have stopped it?

How to be? That's what Conrad really wants to know. That's what I sometimes worry that Norman Maclean wants to come at a little too easily, something having to do with his Presbyterianism. God is out there and has the whole thing planned out. Except there's the central problem of *A River Runs Through It,* the wonderfully gifted brother, dead of another kind of self-destruction. Despite the rich, assuring language of Mr. Maclean's closing paragraphs— the river has cut through the rock as ordained for ages—the brother's death stands as a senseless, unnecessary act. Death cannot be reconciled despite a wash of words. How, then, to be?

In the obituary before me, I read that our man has been awarded three Bronze Stars for valor and a Purple Heart. You'd think that would be lesson enough. You'd think that having steamed upriver with Marlow, my student would have seen the horror of a life unraveled. You'd think lessons learned at such young ages would wrap themselves around a person like a magic girdle, making these men somehow immune from failures at marriage, failures at work, from accrued disappointments. If not immune from disease, then immune from the humiliation, the degradation of constant pain and physical decline.

At its tip, a well-made bamboo fly rod is about the diameter of the lead in a wooden pencil. Six sections of split, planed, and tapered cane have been fitted together so as to appear a single piece of wood. A picture of a good fisherman caught at the end of his back cast will show the butt of the rod upright and barely passing beyond the perpendicular line made by his body. But the upper section of the rod will be well bent, trailing behind with the line almost like an elongated pennant. Despite the great force brought to bear on it, as near as I can tell, such a rod can't really be worn out.

For a while, though, that's why I thought bamboo rods came with two tips, that somehow you could fish the life out of one. But it turns out this isn't so. Most bamboo rods get their tips snapped off in car doors, against tree trunks, under the feet of careless or clumsy fishermen.

One of the most satisfying experiences you can have as a teacher is for one of your old students to look you up. Just to say hello, just so you can see he's doing OK in this world. Jeff was stubborn and absentminded. A long- distance runner and cyclist with out-of-the-way interests for a high school boy in cooking and sewing. Now he was a cowboy, a real one, and a ferrier and a saddle maker. I took a look at the pictures of his leather work, the English and western saddles, and saw in the clean sure lines that he'd grown himself a sense of style. The saddles were elegant, functional things.

Our talk turned, as I knew it would, to my student on the short list, and of course Jeff knew about the same facts I did. Maybe it was his job, maybe his marriage. We were back to saying another round of too bads. Only this time we were eating Italian food in Alaska when it was twenty below outside. "He sure is missing a lot of fun," the cowboy said.

Well, yeah. We fly-fish in the pouring rain, ski in the freezing cold, when anybody with sense would sit home by the fire. We invite pain and discomfort into our lives. And I guess I do it in part for practice. So that on the days when pain and discomfort come unbidden and won't go away, I will have somehow prepared myself.

I have no confidence this trick will work. If it did, the suasive powers of writers like Joseph Conrad and Norman Maclean would be enough to make us all look into our souls and come up better for it. We'd come to know badness for what it is and stay away from it. The fly-caster's four-count beat would be a kind of mantra for us all, suggesting a mechanism for a life of precision and control. Our ethical behavior would grow naturally from the beauty of these writers' words.

It's been a few years since I've fished the lower Chatanika, the place where Dave Stark got bogged down. I've decided I don't much like to fish that spot. You come out on the river at a long, flat pool, a good place to launch a boat, but no use to a fisherman without one. Upriver is an island and on its west side is a deep hole promising all sorts of fish. I've tried it with dry fly, wet fly, nymph, and streamer, and never taken a fish out of it. There are two hundred yards or so of good water just above that hole where big fish can be found in the late fall. And beyond that, more straight water where sometimes a fish or two can be had. But there are no compelling fishing problems here, no sweepers hanging over the river, no riffles to channel the current, no combination of tricky turns and rocky hiding places that make a spot a fishing revelation. And there is the road. That muddy track through permafrost looks to be a clean shot to the river as you approach it from the saddle above. But every year it makes itself more a pathless wood, a muddy bog that can leave you far from the river with no chance of turning back.

How to be? For that poor guy holding onto his grandpa's bamboo rod, full of bright promises of clear water and big fish, it somehow was not enough to preserve him. A mistake, maybe, to think the objects of this world have talismanic qualities. Having the old man's rod, we think we have his experience, his wisdom. Maybe we do if we look at it another way. The rod cannot say what wisdom grandpa had. It can only be a tool in your hand. You can fish with it through good days and bad. If you know how to find fish and know how to cast with it, the rod will help you catch them. You can use it, and maybe learn some things for yourself.

I take to the river in the last good days of fall. The leaves are yellow and dropping, but the river is still full of life. Bugs are rising, and the fish are following them to the surface. In the quiet, I cast and hear my line rattle through the guides as my own bug settles on the water. Soon it will be cold; the fish will regard my flies from the river's bottom with lazy suspicion. Here are days; there won't be any others.

Lorian Hemingway

Being the granddaughter of Ernest Hemingway turns out to be only one of the many life trials experienced by Lorian Hemingway. She takes her life and her fishing hard, but eventually finds her own fresh version of salvation in the streams and woods of the Pacific Northwest. She discovers that it is a world that goes its own beautiful and disregarding way, and that does us good, if we let it. Like a fictional Hemingway character, she fishes for mortal stakes, and catches herself a life. Readers who enjoy the following selection will find a fuller life story in her powerful 1998 book, *Walk On Water: A Memoir.* She is also the author of a novel, *Walking into the River.*

Walk on Water for Me

I take fish personally, the way I have my life, like a sacrament. This is my body. Eat of it. This is my blood. Drink. I imagine this reverence is what they want of me. The alchemists made an eyewash (collyrium) of fish, believing it would bring omniscience. I've tried to envision the process: cooking the fish, as the alchemists instructed, until it "yellowed," mashing it into a crumbly pulp, mixing it with water and then filling the eyes with this paste so one might gaze with as much dimension as trout in a clear stream. But as with all things in alchemy it was the process that mattered, the final result never as important as the ritual preceding it.

Knowing fish is a process. I have been acquainting myself for forty years. To know fish you have to have been intimate, the way the alchemists were. The first fish I ever caught was a baby bass netted from a deep Mississippi ravine I lived near during summer. It was my refuge, that ravine, a place of discovery, revealer of miracles, its depth filled with a heavy current of reddish-brown water during the spring floods, its clay bottom dried to a pockmarking of deep holes by mid-July. I was tirelessly curious when I was young, bound inextricably to all natural mysteries beyond four walls, nervous and jumpy if made to sit too long indoors, recalcitrant once sprung. I'd watched this particular fish for days, trapped in a pothole in the ravine, swimming in a quick panic from one side to the other, instinctively seeking a tributary leading from its footwide prison. I empathized, imagined myself locked in my room for days, dizzy and breathless from ensuing claustrophobia, frantic enough to pull up the flooring with my bare hands. I understood feeling trapped, my life then nothing more than a crash course in how to escape.

After a few days the water in the pothole had diminished by half and grew so thick with ravine mud that the fish hung motionless in the ooze, its gills laboring for the oxygen it needed. On my knees I stared into the hole, goldfish net in hand, thinking it was evil what I was about to do, snatch a living creature from its habitat and bring it, luckless, into my own. I remember the delicate, thin striping on its flanks as I lifted it, unprotesting, from the muck, and how soft and filmy the skin felt as I stroked a finger along his length. I remember, too, how my heart raced as I dropped the fish into a jar, watched him sink quickly and then just as quickly take his first breath in a new world. Within moments he was moving through the jar as manically as he had the pothole days before. I had given resurrection in a pint of water, become God to a fish. Years later I would remember that moment as one of grace.

Fish became my fascination, and began to appear in dreams, their shadows deep in dark water, cruising, fins breaking the surface from time to time, a teasing swirl of movement as I stood on shore with net or rod or hands poised to strike. In one dream I stood before a pool of monster fish with bare hands greedy, my fingertips singing the way a line does when it's pulled free from the spool. As I leaned forward, a shape would slide deliberately beneath my reach, and I would lunge into water that was dense and thick as oil, only to come up soaked and empty-handed.

I don't know now that the dreams had to do with catching fish, but rather with some unconscious, archetypal need. I have consulted Jung on this one for the obvious, loaded symbolism. I have even dreamt, in these later years, of Jung, standing atop the stone fortress of his tower at Bollingen, fly rod in hand, a wooden piscatorial carving dangling from his leader line. He smiles in the dream, proud of himself. He did say water is the unconscious and that fish are a Christ symbol. I deduce then, from these two boldly fitting pieces, that I am at times fishing for Jesus, or in some way, in recent dreams, dry-flying for Christ. I like the simplicity of it, the directness. I like that it speaks to Christian and Hedon alike.

But during those Mississippi summers I paid little attention to dreams, mesmerized then by a world filled with fish, snakes, turtles, toads, and lizards, anything remotely amphibian. I progressed from netting bass to catfishing with a bobber and worm, frittering away entire days on the banks of muddy lakes, certain, always, that the fish lived dead center in the middle of the lake, assuming the notion that the truly elusive spend their time where we can never hope to reach them. To cast where they hid became my ambition, and once mastered I understood that fish went wherever they damned well pleased, unimpressed by my clumsy form hurling hooks into their midst, immune to my need to know them.

I had patience, the sort I suspect God has with people like me. It was nothing to be skunked for days on end. I lived in perpetual hope of seeing that wayward shimmy of the bobber, then the quick dip and tug that signaled I had made contact with aliens. At that time in my life this was my social interaction. I talked to the fish hidden deep in the ponds and streams I visited, trying to imagine what they saw beneath those mirrored surfaces and reasoned it was hunger and not stupidity that made them take bait so crudely hitched to an obvious weapon. Compassion surfaced. I pictured scores of starving fish grubbing for worms only to be duped into death by my slipshod cunning. When I'd reel them to shore I'd cry at what I'd done, at the sight of the hook swallowed to the hilt, at the flat, accusing eyes of the fish, and then I'd club them with a Coke bottle, the heavy green kind with the bottling company's name on the bottom. No one ever said there was another way to do it. In Mississippi, there was the hook, the worm and the bobber, a holy trinity on a hot day in August—low-maintenance fishing I call it now. My guilt was usually pushed aside by their quick death beneath the bottle, and eating what I had caught seemed to remove the shame considerably.

My favorite fishing hole—I look back on it now as Mississippi's version of Mecca—was a place that to this day I am certain only one other knew of, the landowner who'd barbwired it off and posted a huge, hand-painted sign along the fence—Warning: SNAKES. Roaming deep in a pine woods in rural Hinds County one summer afternoon, I came upon the pond, the edges of it rising in volcanic fashion from the otherwise flat land. I was accustomed only to ponds that were slipped like sinkholes into the surrounding pastureland, and as I made my way up the slight incline of earth, hands grasping the barbwire delicately, I beheld, not a rock quarry as I had expected, but instead a perfectly black pool of water, its dimensions no greater than those of an average swimming pool. At first I could not believe the color of the fish who were pushing to the surface, dozens of them, nosing one into another, their bodies as opalescent as pearls, and huge, their lengths dissolving into the shadow of the pond. I had never seen albino catfish, had never seen any white fish, and thought for a brief, illogical moment that they had been segregated from their darker mates simply because of their color. In Mississippi, then, it fit.

To have called this pond a fishing hole is misleading. I never actually fished its waters, too mesmerized by the cloudlike shapes that moved without sound through the deep pond, believing, beyond all fishing reason, that to catch them would bring the worst sort of luck. So I watched, alone in the woods with these mutants, some days prodding their lazy bodies with a hickory stick, which they rubbed against curiously, and on others merely counting the number of laps they made around the pond in an afternoon, hypnotized by the rhythm they made tracing one circle upon another.

The fish were as truly alien as my starkest imaginings, and I became convinced they were telepathic, reading my thoughts with such ease I had no need to speak to them. I called these sojourns "visiting the fish gods," my treks to that mysterious water that had no business existing in dry woods, and took into adulthood the memory of them, as if they were a talisman, granting me privileges and luck in the fishing world others could only dream of.

As I grew older I began to think of fish as mine. I'd been in close touch with them long enough to develop something that I believed went beyond rapport and came, in time, to border on feudalism. Fishing became far more than sport or communion. It began to develop the distinct earmarkings of a life's goal. No longer content to watch and prod, no longer in command of patience, I lived to fish, becoming, in my own mind, a fishing czarina, my luck with rod, reel and bait phenomenal.

Self-taught in the simple mechanisms of spinning gear, I had perfected a bizarre way of holding the reel and rod upside down while casting and retrieving. It is something I have never been able to undo, the habit of flipping the rod over before I cast worn into my nerve pathways like my image of Christ as a skinny Caucasian. Years later someone told me I cast like a child. So what. It never marred my accuracy, and in fact I was a little pleased childhood habits had stalked me this far. I was also told "any idiot can catch fish with a dead piece of flesh and a bent nail." I *was* an idiot, but smug in my idiocy, refusing to let go of sure-fire methods I'd known as a kid in Mississippi. Holding true to my fundamentalist, country fishing ways, I began to gain a reputation for being the only person certain, on an outing, to catch fish. An attitude surfaced as rapidly as fish to my bait. Men were forced to regard me now, but warily, as I moved within their circles, trying always to outdo them. Gone was the solitary fishing of my childhood, the secret visits with fish gods. I had become competitive.

I cannot place the exact time when my fishing innocence turned streetwalker tough, when imagined power over the waters of childhood turned to a calculating game, but I suspect it was when I discovered that good-old-boy fishing and beer went hand-in-hand. I'd been drinking plenty before I became truly obsessed with bait and tackle, but now I began articles I wrote on the subject with lines like "Nothing like a cold six-pack in the morning," causing my editors to wince and accuse me of writing manuscripts "afloat in beer."

I took to drinking the way I had to in that ravine in summer, daily, and the false tough-girl attitude it fostered launched me into an arena that included the truly elusive, monsters who swim leagues deep in saltwater. Armed with the fishing world's equivalent of an elephant gun, I hunted tropical waters for marlin, shark, tuna, tarpon and barracuda, catching them all, tearing muscles and breaking blood vessels while in battle, but anesthetized to the pain because my six-pack in the morning had now become a full case in a five-hour stint.

The popular image of a fisherman sitting on the bank on a quiet Sunday afternoon, pole propped against a rock, cold beer in hand, contemplating, was about as close to what I did on the water as Andy Warhol is to Degas. On board I was a one-armed windmill in one-hundred-knot winds, my hand dipping in the cooler for a drink as fast as I hauled fish on deck. I was Macho Woman. Back off. This is the life, I told myself a lot during those days, the idea that one occasionally encounters periods of grace eluding me entirely.

Still, I was ashamed when my prey would slide alongside the boat, exhausted, beaten to near death. I'd release them, guiltily, my hand still reaching involuntarily for the Coke bottle, now a flimsy aluminum can, worthless as it turned out, for any feat of strength. People would slap me on the back and say things like, "You fish like a man. You drink like a man," offerings that in the light of what I was to become seem almost comical now. But at the time I considered it an honor, posing willingly with other people's four-hundred-pound slabs of dead marlin, beer can held aloft, grinning crookedly, a mutant now compared to that girl bent over the potholes, goldfish net in hand.

For several years I was flat-out on the gonzo stage of fishing, where any method of felling fish was acceptable. I never batted an eye at ten-pound teasers rigged to the transoms of forty-foot sportsfishermen. The anchor-sized saltwater reels looked normal to me, and fifty-pound test, what the hell. I had lost sight of that first delicate intimacy, the tiny bass swimming clearly in my seethrough jar of river water. I no longer practiced communion, but sacrilege. My life, as well as my fishing, had turned brutal.

I prefer the confessional to the cross, figuring if I own to enough treachery I will be spared in a moment of mercy, like that bass in the ravine. When I quit drinking—finally—after an eight-year period of uncommon buoyancy on sea as well as land, my liver shot, my eyes as yellowed as the fish the alchemists sought for insight—I quit the gonzo lifestyle. "Blind drunk" is not a phrase without meaning, and to me it came to mean that I had been blind, almost irrevocably, not only to the damage leveled in my own life, but to the life beneath those waters that came so frequently in dreams.

Dead cold sober now, I took up fly fishing. Not on the same day, certainly, because the shakes wrack you for a while and all you're really good for is mixing paint. I'd held a fly rod only once during my fish-killing days, off the coast of Islamorada during tarpon season, while fishing with legendary guide Jimmie Allbright. In the saltwater fishing world, *guides* and *anglers* are legendary, never the fish who serve them. After meeting enough of the old masters, I came to the conclusion that to become legendary all one needed was to catch oversized fish and not die from sunstroke or lip cancer, tie a few exotic-looking flies, cast phenomenal distances against the wind and remain steadfastly laconic when a novice is on board. What I remember most of the first fly-fishing experience is a lot of yeps and nopes directed at my questions, the fly line cinched tightly around my ankles after a bad cast, and a sunburn that bubbled the skin on the tops of my ears. It was a waste of energy, I figured. I didn't get the point. All that whipping and hauling and peering into the distance just reminded me of bad Westerns.

But something happens when you get purified, take the cure, lob your body onto another plane of perception. Without a beer in hand, fly fishing seemed far more appealing to me than it had when I'd been trolling with bait big enough to eat. Back then I'd called it effete, elitist, prissy, egg-sucking. I figured the entire state of Montana was crawling with seven million people who looked exactly like Robert Redford, all of them hefting custom fly rods. Now in a completely altered state of mind, I began to notice the grace involved in a simple cast, how the arm of a good angler was merely an extension of the fly rod. I studied the art a little, secretly, not yet ready to be labeled a wimp.

About the time I was reading Izaak Walton's *The Compleat Angler*, I got a call from Florida writer and fly fishing guide Randy Wayne White asking me to fly fish on his PBS-syndicated fishing show, "On The Water." I didn't tell the man I couldn't cast spare change into the hand of a willing Hare Krishna, much less fly cast for tarpon, which was what he had in mind.

"Sure," I told him, eager, as always, for a new opportunity to humiliate myself. "I've caught tarpon before," neglecting to mention it was with an orange Day-Glo bobber and a live mullet. I wanted to be prepared and figured with all I'd read on the subject I could learn the basics in half an hour of hands-on practice. So after taking a quick lesson in a downtown Seattle park, I flew South.

I was soon sitting anchored off a mangrove island on Florida's west coast with Randy. Randy Wayne White is what you would call a burly man, built like a fireplug with forearms the girth of oak saplings, an image that belies his physical grace, and particularly his ability with a fly rod.

"Where'd you learn to cast, Lorian?" he was asking politely as he grinned into the sun and the PBS camera, while I whizzed a live pilchard past his head. He hadn't seen me fly cast yet because I'd begged off after watching Randy sail his line eighty feet toward a school of feeding redfish. Nah, I'd told myself after watching a redfish pounce the fly, this won't do. I was out of my element entirely, beerless, baitless, naked.

"I never did learn," I told him, my back to the camera as I slung another pilchard into the mangroves. "Amazing, isn't it," I said, "what you can teach yourself." Randy nodded, his eyes losing hope. This exchange never survived the edited version of the show's tape, and in subsequent shots the camera gently panned away into the mangroves, or to the pelicans flying above, as I cast upside down and reeled backwards, dragging whole mangrove tubers boatside.

The second day out we headed in Randy's flats boat for the coast of Boca Grande where scores of tarpon were rolling on the surface of the water. Randy slapped a custom, saltwater fly rod into my hand and said, "Go for it, Lorian!"

Go for what? I remember thinking. For what, for Christ's sake. It was enough in a ten-foot chop on a three-foot-wide boat to merely right myself and stand there lurching starboard, portside, fore and aft, like one of those sand-weighted plastic clowns that lean wa-ay over but never quite go down. I viewed the wallowing tarpon at eye level and imagined offering my lunch as chum into the churning water.

"There're hundreds of them, Lorian. Hundreds. Go ahead and cast," Randy called from the stern.

I think I pulled maybe six inches of line from the reel before I noticed the particular leaden quality of the sky just north, south, east and west of us, as Randy yelled, "Two o'clock. Tarpon at two o'clock."

The sky at two o'clock looked like midnight with the occasional atomically bright lightning bolt shearing the blackness.

I'm no fan of lightning while in an open boat, no fan of lightning while wearing a rubber suit in a six-foot-deep cellar. It's a phobia of mine—call it silly—one that's rampant, unchecked, paralyzing.

"Graphite," my head said. "You're holding a goddamned graphite rod." PUT IT DOWN. What they don't tell you about fly rods is that they're superb electrical conductors, right up there with copper. I chucked the rod in Randy's direction, hit the deck and yelled "Drive!" about the time a bolt struck dead center off the bow and the air turned crispy crackly with electricity. I could feel the hair on my neck and arms rise up.

I spent the beat-your-kidneys-to-Jello ride back to shore face down in the boat, my nails tearing at Randy's left calf, hissing Hail Marys, as lightning popped in the water around us.

"Next time I see you, I'll give you a casting lesson," Randy told me the next day, as I wandered around randomly kissing the ground, his hand, the cheeks of strangers, stunned to be alive.

"Like fun," I said.

It took a while before I could look at a fly rod again without itching to buy life insurance. But the dreams returned, this time of pink speckled trout in blue streams, less threatening than tarpon in boiling, black water, and I thought, sure, that's where I belong, in a trout stream wearing waders and a nifty fly vest displaying hand-tied flies, maybe a telescoping depth wand strapped at my hip, Swiss army knife dangling from that ring on the vest pocket. That's me all right, the Orvis girl. And since I figured you don't have to be a ballerina to dance, I took up casting again, practicing in my back yard—and a one and a two—secretive and clumsy, the cat my only witness. Somewhere around my fortieth birthday my husband Jeff had given me a new rod and reel, complete with weight-forward line, and I took to the business of learning to cast as earnestly as I take to anything, which means if I don't master it on the second or third try, I quit, stick out my lower lip and glare.

I had achieved mid-beginner status (capable of placing the fly on the water by wadding the line in my fist and heaving it) when Jeff and I took a trip to the Salmon River in Idaho. I had taken fish there years before, six-pack in hand, spinning gear in the other, dragging the rocks—twenty-four trout in half a day, my finest hour, but drunk when I did it so maybe the count's off by half. I wanted to return to make amends, to take a trout clean and easy without the heavy artillery.

The Salmon is a beautiful stretch of water, clear, relatively shallow and fast, unlike the slow, clay-weighted waters of Mississippi. When I first moved to the Northwest I was amazed you could see so deeply into the water and would sit for hours on a river shore staring at the rocks beneath. Jeff, on the other hand, grew up with this purity, which may explain why it seems to be in his blood to fish these waters, and fish them well, in fact better than anyone has a right to. He has the sort of luck with a fly rod that I used to have with bait, a fact that has compelled me to accuse him of actually robbing me of fish-luck, a high crime in our marriage.

Our first day on the river I'd waded in bare-legged and was fishing generally the same area of water as Jeff, but politely upstream so the fish would get to me first, when his luck (he calls it skill) kicked in. He'd released six fish before I'd even gotten my fly damp. Normally I handled such flagrant displays with stoicism, wanting to keep my image as a good sport intact, but this day was different. I'd returned to waters that had blessed me once with uncanny luck, to waters that had kindly not swallowed me whole as I'd staggered through them, and all I wanted was that brief, immortal contact with aliens, the way I'd known it when I was a kid, new and simple. I was obsessed that day with taking a fish on fly. I'd read A.J. and Norman. I'd gone to the outdoor shows. Nothing seemed more perfect or vital than the feel of a trout on the end of that nerve-sensitive line. I'd felt how mere water current could electrify the line, transforming it to a buzzing high-voltage wire, and I wanted some of that magic.

"Yee—ha!" Jeff yelled from down river as he released another perfect form into the water.

I false cast and hooked my chin.

I could feel them all around me, the sense of them, fish moving the current in swirls around my bare ankles, fish swimming between my thighs. I inched my way in Jeff's direction, watching his fly line thread out before him and then drop like a whisper onto the water.

I got within twenty feet of the man and flung my line in an awkward sidecast right where I'd seen his last fish surface. I waited. I prayed. I watched. I peered. Nothing.

My husband is someone who takes athletic grace for granted, figuring it's something we all can achieve in time.

"Your presentation's wrong," he told me.

Had I read about this? I searched my memory.

"My what," I said, coming up blank.

"The way you're putting the fly down. It's wrong."

Well, what the hell. It was enough, I thought, to get the fly in the water. Who could resist after that. And when did fish get so picky, worrying about presentation, the particular color of a hackle. With worms there had been no guesswork. Eat this tasty sucker, you cretin, I was thinking as I fingered a rubber worm I'd stashed in my vest pocket.

"Fish are color-blind," I said with some authority, apropos of nothing.

" So," he said in that way he has that tells me he's already written a book about it.

To illustrate presentation, Jeff whipped off another perfect cast. A trout rose to his fly, and bingo, the water around us was alive. I hated him.

"Maybe it's my fly," I said.

I waded over to him and switched rods, thinking, *Okay you, give me that magic wand, we'll see who catches fish.*

"Yours casts so easily," he said as he set the line in motion.

Wham. I swear to God that fish hit the fly in mid-air.

"Nothing's wrong with your fly," he told me as he released the biggest trout of the day.

"That's it," I said, stomping toward shore as gracefully as possible in four feet of water. I'd snatched my rod from him and threw it on the bank when I emerged, soaked and cold, as pissed as I'd ever been.

"I thought you were a good sport," I heard him calling from the river.

There, I'd blown it. Years of cultivating an image, gone.

"Go to hell," I yelled. "Go straight to hell, you and your stupid fly rod, you jinx. Jinx! Ever since I've fished with you I've caught nothing. Not a goddamned thing. You took all my luck, and now you rub my nose in it. I'll never fish with you again. I swear to God."

I sat down on the bank and literally stomped my feet, hands clenched into fists at my sides, my heartbeat clearly audible in my temples. I'd heard about people like me. Poor sports. Whiners. Lunatics.

"It's just your technique." The wind carried his words so that "technique" seemed to be underlined, and I shouted back, "Eat your technique. Eat it, you hear!"—a response I thought fair at the time.

It was then I saw the naked man in the raft drifting past, fly rod poised in midair. Ordinarily, naked would have been enough, but as I watched more closely I noticed he was throwing his rod tip up to twelve o'clock and then waiting for a beat before following through with the forward cast. During that beat the line straightened out behind him, unfurling slowly from the arc it made as he brought the rod forward. Again he cast, my own personal naked instructor, oblivious to me on the bank, and again with the same hesitation. Some technique, I thought, peering in Jeff's direction to see if he'd noticed the man. Nah. Naked women could have been skydiving into a bull's-eye on his head and he'd have kept on casting. I watched the man cast another perfect length of line and discovered my arm moving, involuntarily, following his motions. I watched his wrist. Hardly a bend in it as he pointed the rod arrow- straight in the direction of the unfurling line. At that moment something settled into place, the way it did that one time I bowled a strike, and I saw the whole process, not as frantic thrashing and whipping, but as one liquid motion, seamless and intact. It was the way, I thought, I should have always fished, naked, tethered to the water by a floating umbilicus, aware.

I spent the rest of the day practicing on a dirt back road, heaving that line at first as if it were a shot-put. When it would drop in a dead puddle at the end of my rod I'd try again, remembering the vision of that man in the raft, his perfect rhythm, the way he seemed to notice nothing but his line as it spun out above the water. I kept trying against what I considered rather hefty odds until I had my line singing in the air and pulling out the slack around my feet as if it were ribbon shot from a rifle. I grew calm from the effort, a way I'd not remembered being for years. I looked at my hands, steady as rocks, as they rose above my head, left hand experimenting with a double haul. Hey, I thought, I might get good at this.

That evening at dusk I caught my first fish on a fly, a beauty I watched rise in a quick thrash, greedily, as if he'd been waiting all day for my one ratty fly, frayed and battered from the day's practice, but oddly noble. It's all I wanted, that one fish, electric on the end of my line, and, God, how I could feel him, his jumpy on-and-off current carrying all the way up my arm. How do you do, I felt like saying, it's been a long time. I wet my hand and cradled his girth in my palm. Such a nice feeling. Moist, alive, not slimy the way we're taught to think. I pulled some water through his gills and released the fly from his lip, delicately, no sweat, and watched as he fluttered and then dove in a quick zigzag, deep into the stream. For an instant I remembered the delicate feel of the baby bass as I slopped him into the jar of river water, then the fish gods, white and huge, circling the perimeter of the pond, aware, perhaps, of nothing more than the rhythm their movement created, and in that instant, I too, here in the clear water of an Idaho stream, understood rhythm, but as if it were the steady beat of childhood fascination returned.

In my new dream there is the same dark pool from childhood but its expanse reaches from the very tip of my feet to the horizon in all directions, its surface flat as undisturbed bathwater, the shapes beneath it perfectly formed now, truly fishlike and sharply defined, the tails like so many Geisha fans slapping left and then right in unison, a metronomic rhythm setting forth visible currents beneath the water that never break the calm glassiness above. I marvel at the dance, watch the fish line up, nose to tail, in a perfect circle, swimming faster and faster. I look to my empty hands and realize my husband stands to my left ready to make a cast with my new white lightning rod. I say, "Give it to me. Now," and cast a Royal Coachman out to Jesus. "Come on boy," I call across the pool, "walk on water for me." The fly taps the skin of the water, and the circle of fish shatters like beads in a kaleidoscope, bathing me in light.

David James Duncan

David James Duncan's *The River Why* was the first book of fiction published by
Sierra Club Books. It went on to become a Book-of-the-Month Club
selection and a widely read paperback. Duncan describes the book as a
"serious comedy" about a fishing family and "the ultimate meaning
of life. I was ambitious," he reflects. The family is composed
of the narrator, Gus Orviston; his fly-fishing father, Henning
Hale-Orviston (H2O); his spin-fishing mother (Ma) with her
"Sears and Roebuck crane and cable"; and his brother, Bill Bob.

Duncan's other books include *The Brothers K* and *River Teeth*. A lifelong
Oregonian, Duncan moved to Montana in sorrow and anger in the mid
1990s, after rapacious logging practices had destroyed much of the forest
habitat and salmon of his beloved Oregon coastal country.

Readers of Thoreau's *Walden* will recognize Duncan's title and his
romance with his chosen place, the Coast Range, in this selection from *The
River Why*.

Where I Lived and What I Lived For

South of the Columbia and north of California, scores of wild green rivers come tumbling down out of the evergreen, ever-wet forests of the Coast Range. These rivers are short—twenty to sixty miles, most of them—but they carry a lot of water. They like to run fast through the woods, roaring and raising hell during rainstorms and run-offs, knocking down streamside cedars and alders now and again to show they know who it is dumping trashy leaves and branches in them all the time. But when they get within a few miles of the ocean, they aren't so brash. They get cautious down there, start sidling back and forth digging letters in their valleys—C's, S's, U's, L's, and others from their secret alphabet—and they quit roaring and start mumbling to themselves, making odd sounds like jittery orators clearing their throats before addressing a mighty audience. Or sometimes they say nothing at all but just slip along in sullen silence, as though they thought that if they snuck up on the Pacific softly enough it might not notice them, might not swallow them whole the way it usually does. But when they get to the estuaries they realize they've been kidding themselves: the Ocean is *always* hungry—and no Columbia, no Mississippi, no Orinoco or Ganges can curb its appetite.... So they panic: when they taste the first salt tides rising up to greet them they turn back toward their kingdoms in the hills. They don't get far. When the overmastering tides return to the ocean, these once-brash rivers trail along behind like sad little dogs on leashes past the marshes with their mallards, the mud flats with their clams, the shallow bays with their herons, over the sandbars with their screaming gulls and riptides, away into the oblivion of the sea.

The river I lived on is on the northern half of the Oregon Coast. I promised friends there not to divulge its real name or location, so I'll call it the "Tamanawis." The cabin was situated at the feet of the last forested hills—the final brash rapids just upstream, the first cautious, curving letters just below. There were a few fishing cottages near mine, empty most of the time, and upstream nothing but rain, brush, trees, elk, ravens and coyotes. A quarter mile downstream and across the river was a dairy farm, my nearest permanent neighbor. The farmer had 120 cows to take care of; he had it pretty easy. His wife had the farmer and their six kids to take care of; she had it tough. The farmer, wife, kids, and cows had an orange and purple and black house, two red and green and yellow barns, and a clearing of tree stumps where their yard should have been. (I used to thank Fathern Heaven for the trees that blocked that place from view. Something about those stumps and colors. Made me feel I'd been living on TV, Coca-Cola and doughnuts.) Below the dairy the Tamanawis Valley got more populated—a few farms, sportsmen's shanties, here and there one of those antennaed, yarn-floored boxes poor dumb suburbanites call "contemporary homes"; then a sawmill, a huge poultry farm, and a trailer court defacing the edge of a nice little town at river's mouth. (We'll call it "Fog.") Highway 101 runs through Fog, and the chuckholed asphalted Tamanawis River Road takes off from one of the five intersections in town, running up past my cabin, turning into gravel upstream, then into mud, and dead-ending in a maze of logging and fire roads. The only people who use the River Road are fishermen, loggers, hunters and an occasional mapless tourist trying to get back to the Willamette Valley by a "scenic route." The latter folk drive by my cabin all shiny-autoed and smiley, and two or three hours later come spluttering back with mud and disgruntlement on their cars and faces, hell-bent for 101 and screw the scenery. The Coast Range Maze does that to people.

Across the road from my cabin was a huge clear-cut—hundreds of acres of massive spruce stumps interspersed with tiny Douglas firs—products of what they call "Reforestation," which I guess makes the spindly firs en masse a "Reforest," which makes an individual spindly fir a "Refir," which means you could say that Weyerhauser, who owns the joint, has Refir Madness, since they think that sawing down 200-foot-tall spruces and replacing them with puling 2-foot Refirs is no different from farming beans or corn or alfalfa. They even call the towering spires they wipe from the earth's face forever a "crop"—as if they'd planted the virgin forest! But I'm just a fisherman and may be missing some deeper significance in their strange nomenclature and stranger treatment of primordial trees.

The river side of the road had never been logged. There were a few tremendous spruces, small stands of alder, clumps of hazelnut, tree-sized ferns, fern-sized wildflowers, head-high salal, impenetrable thickets of devil's club, and, surrounding my cabin, a dense grove of cedars—huge, solemn trees with long drooping branches and a sweet smell like solitude itself. The cabin was made of fir logs squared off Scandinavian-style and joined so tightly that I could light a cooking fire on a cold winter's morning, fish all day, and find it still cozy when I came home at dark. There was only one room, but it was big—twenty-two by twenty-eight feet—with the kind of high beamed-and-jointed ceiling that made you want to just sit back and study the way it all fit together. The bedroom was an open loft above the kitchen; the kitchen was the table and chairs, stove, waterheater and sink; the refrigerator was a stone-walled cellar reached through a trap-door in the kitchen floor; the bathroom was a partitioned-off corner so small you had to stand in the shower to take aim at the toilet, and if you bumped the shower walls they boomed like a kettledrum—so I took to voiding my bladder in the devil's club outside.

The cabin was dark, thanks to the grove, but some gloom-oppressed occupant had cut one four-by-four window in the south wall overlooking the river: I set up my fly-tying desk next to it, partly for light, partly so if something swirled as I worked I could be out there with a loaded flyrod in seconds. I didn't miss electricity at all—even preferred the absence of it—but H20, convinced that I'd go blind tying flies by candlelight, left me three Coleman camp lanterns that blazed about as subtly as searchlights, and Ma, appalled by the lack of racket, bequeathed me a big battery-operated AM/FM radio: both earned an early retirement on a remote shelf. Bill Bob voiced no concern over lack of sound or light, but he seemed to have reservations about my proposed life of sheer solitary angling. Though he said nothing more than that I was "lone," upon his return to Portland he borrowed H20's electric Remington and composed the first of an erratic flow of letters; it began,

I will write and write you all the time Gus. Becase your
not a lone by your slef before. So you wont get to
lonesome, will you? Are you reading your Lone Rangers?
Remember my friend at school? From Mexico, Pedro? He
says in Mexican TONTO calls LONE RANGER kemo sabe
because it means HE WHO NOBODY KNOWS. But I
know you dont I. And don't forget it! And watch out for
TONTO, becase Pedro says in Mexican TONTO means
stupid or crazy so when your are too alone write me a
letter and I will come stay with you. But I will keep
writing anyway to̸ ke̸p̸ep you compnay....

The most outrageous housewarming gift was from H20: a
fifty-gallon aquarium. He keeps one of these monsters by his
fly-tying vise and in his books recommends them to all serious
fly-makers. The idea is to catch water bugs and larvae on fishing
trips and stick them in your tank to use as living models; you can
also test an imitation by tying it to a light leader, lowering it into
the aquarium and jerking it around among its live prototypes: if it
is attacked or raped you may conclude it a sufficiently deceptive
fly. I've always thought this more than a little extreme. Trout are
not entomologists; they don't care what your fly's Latin name is.
I've suckered summer steelhead, brookies and bluebacks on a fly I
call a "Bermuda Shorts"—an abstract imitation of a fat tourist on a
golf course in a Caribbean travel brochure; my "Headless
Hunchback" may one day be famous as a trout killer, and it imitates
a thing that attacked me in a nightmare brought on by devouring
half a box of Bill Bob's Sugar Pops just before bed. H20 and his pals
rigidly adhere to the Imitation of Natural Food School of Fly Tying,
but the truth is, trout are like coyotes, goats and people: they nibble,
chew and bite for all sorts of reasons; eating is only the most
common one. Sometimes Northwest lakes and streams are so rich
in feed that their bloated denizens would sooner bite an Alka Seltzer
than a natural imitation; sometimes a bored old whopper, like any
decadent, affluent creature, prefers gaudy titillation to more of the
mundane stonefly-mayfly-caddisfly crap. (Remember Walton's
"piece of cloth" and "dead mouse"?) Piscine ennui can arouse a
taste for the bizarre that will skunk a Purist who insists on floating
sacrosanct "name patterns" over his congregation all day. Bourgeois

trout are like bourgeois people: after a week of three dull meals a day a man will empty his wallet and risk his life bombing belly and brain with rich restaurant food and eight or ten cocktails. The corresponding mood in trout is where the Bermuda Shorts comes in handy: of course it doesn't look like food; neither does a Double Margarita; and trout don't have to drive home afterward.

For a time I stashed the tank with the lanterns and radio—but soon, as Bill Bob predicted, the unaccustomed solitude began giving me fits of melancholy. So I set up the aquarium by the south window, rigged hoses to keep a fresh flow of spring water moving through, filled it with gravel, algae, snails, sculpins, crawdads, periwinkles, the works; then I took an ultralight six-foot flyrod, tied on a barbless #28 Midge and went fishing for the smallest fish I could catch. When I had fourteen or fifteen in a bucket I selected two silver salmon, two cutthroat trout and two steelhead for my tank. I ended up watching this liquid zoo so much I gave the inmates names and soon had a favorite—Alfred the Great—a steelhead smolt of about three inches.

The little salmon and trout were straightforward fish, behaving the hungry, swimmy, nervous way one would expect. But Alfred and the other steelhead, Sigrid the Small, were very unusual minnows. Sigrid was less than two inches long—the smallest fish I ever caught on a fly—and she was frail and quiet and beautiful. All she ever did was hover on the side of the tank overlooking the Tainanawis, watching the river slide by below: I don't know if she really saw it or knew it for what it was, but her eyes were unwaveringly aimed toward the wild waters of her home—and in time the sight of her made my heart sink. She was so small, yet so full of longing. Somehow that two-inch creature made me ashamed, or maybe envious—for I, a seventy-two-inch creature, had no such discernible longing, and knew of no true home to long for. But I wouldn't release her. Not yet. She was so pretty, and she was safe in the tank, so I kept her there against her tiny, unwavering will.

As for Alfred, I've never encountered a more gregarious, high-spirited creature—ouzels, otters and chickadees included—if you take into account that he'd only a finger-length, limbless body to express his exuberance. One might think friendship with a steelhead smolt awfully dull potatoes— maybe the sort of neurotic, one-sided thing some lonely old ladies have with their poodle-dogs.

But my friendship with Alfred wasn't that kind of thing at all. Ours was a relationship founded on the truth that a fish just doesn't give a damn what you say to it and will never say anything back. It lives in the water; it has no voice box; it is encumbered with neither a large vocabulary nor a large brain, and should you shout at it loudly enough to vibrate its water, it Is unlikely to take such utterance as a sign of friendship. Neither is it the kind of pet you can ride, take on walks, set on your lap, dress in a sweater, take pheasant hunting or cuddle; it is not likely to lick your face, and if it did there are teeth in its tongue. But its compensatory virtues are overwhelming: it keeps itself exceedingly clean; it won't jump up on your Sunday suit; it won't shed, won't bark you into an asylum, won't climb onto your roof and scream bloody murder all night as it engages parades of furry gentlemen in the carnal act; it will never roll in dead-salmon rot, never scratch you, never bite the neighbor's toddler in the face; nor will it puke on your bedspread, piss in your shoes or hump the leg of an important dinner guest. A fish maintains its silent, orderly existence within the confines of its tank. All you need to do to befriend it is discover some form of interaction that will create intimacy. Obviously, the key is food.

In state hatcheries the steelhead smolts are kept in huge concrete pools and fed pellets by the bucketful. This is a necessity born of their great numbers, but it is also a great aesthetic waste—for a steelhead smolt is an artist as it feeds. Anybody who enjoys basketball knows that there are dull ways and awesome ways of putting the ball through the hoop. Alfred the Great knew that the same was true for ways of putting fish pellets in his gullet. I won't go so far as to call him the Doctor J of pellet swallowing, but it should be remembered that Doctor J has a hundred or so moveable joints to work with, and that Alfred's "hands" are his mouth: fasten Doctor J's hands to his mouth and how many points will he score in a season?

The surface of the aquarium was nine square feet. If a pellet hit in any of eight of them, Alfred beat the trout and salmon to it every time; only in Sigrid's little corner would he concede—and perhaps this was chivalry. He could see food approaching while it was still in the air; he learned to react to hand-fakes I'd make high above the surface; sometimes he'd take a floating pellet and his upward momentum would carry him six inches into the air;

sometimes he'd charge one that floated next to the glass, tucking at the last second like an Olympic swimmer on a turn, thumping the wall with his tail and vanishing in a blur to reappear motionless in the center of the tank; sometimes he faked the other fish so fast so often they began gliding around in baffled little circles; sometimes he jived them so bad they swam smack into the glass. Watching Alfred eat was a joy. He had the kind of moves that cried out for instant replays.

Marjorie Sandor

Marjorie Sandor is the author of an acclaimed new essay collection, *The Night Gardener,* from which the following selection is taken, and an earlier collection of stories, *A Night of Music.* Her work has appeared in such publications as *The New York Times Magazine* and *The Georgia Review.* She has been anthologized in *The Best American Short Stories 1985* and *1988, Twenty Under Thirty, The Pushcart Prize XIII,* and elsewhere. Like Ted Leeson and Kathleen Dean Moore, she lives in Corvallis and teaches at Oregon State University, which now seems to be supplanting Missoula, Montana, as the literary capital of Northwest fishing.

The Novitiate's Tale

At the South End of Darby, Montana, right before the speed limit goes up and the Bitterroot River comes back into view, there's a Sinclair station with a marquee that looms like wish fulfillment: all in capital letters, like the message DRINK ME on the little bottle Alice finds, this marquee reads: DIESEL, UNLEADED, FLIES.

What is it about the prospect of trout-fishing that turns the novitiate's simplest act—that of buying a couple of flies or a new leader—into a quest, a rite of passage? There was a long riffle just upstream from Darby that looked magical to me—it had to be full of rainbows—and waiting through a week of work to get there, I hungered for it as unrequitedly as I do for certain film stars and countries I'll never get to: secretly, with idiotic surges of adolescent chills -and-fever.

Practically speaking, I needed a leader. I strode to the screen-door of the Sinclair station, heavily booted like any hero, but faintly aware of my relatively small size and deep ignorance. The whole business seemed a dazzling path to certain failure: wrong fly, too hot a day, too cold, wrong spot, wrong way to fish right spot—infinite and thrilling were the ways.

In a small room beyond Wheat Thins and Jim's World-Famous Jerky, a man waited behind a glass case of flies, reading the newspaper with the tricky nonchalance of all guardians of the dream world. A few packets of hooks and spools of fishing line hung on a pegboard. The whole thing looked preposterously spare and anti-mysterious, like a false front.

The man smiled when I asked for a tapered leader. "Just startin' out, are we?" he said. "You don't need it. You'll do fine with plain old monofilament." And he brought down a spool of what looked to me like purple sewing thread.

"I'd really prefer tapered leader," I said, in the hushed, careful voice of someone asking for groceries in a foreign country, He, in his turn, waved his hand casually in the air, as if my remark were utterly irrelevant.

As I took the monofilament and two locally tied nymphs, he followed me out and told me not to go to that dumb fishing access point—the place'd be crawling with tourists. He drew a spidery, complicated map of a secret hole no out-of-towners know about, which I could only get to by trespassing on a local rancher's property. "He doesn't mind," he said, and tipped his hat. As he followed me to the screen-door he added, with a dreamy air, "You'll learn the hard way on that monofilament. Believe me, when you get back to tapered leader, it'll seem like a breeze."

Suffice it to say that though I fished the wrong spot all day, with the wrong line and the wrong fly, the Bitterroot itself, with its willow-shaded margins and islands, its riffles and runs and promising boulders all just out of reach, made failure seem both a reasonable and sublime occupation: ambition, particularly, is a sin against the abiding rush of a river. But I'll confess, I wasn't even in the water when I thought this; I was still standing in the high grass before barbed wire, preparing to crawl between its thorny knots, thinking this was no ordinary fence, but the door into the unknown world in all good stories, where spiritual journeys always start. Even the little scratch, the bit of blood on my arm, seemed a right and necessary beginning.

This feeling carried me straight through to the next day, north on the Bitterroot highway into Missoula, where in a slightly clearer but no less literary frame of mind I found a bona fide fly shop. Of course Missoula has at least a half dozen, all thriving, but this one had a proprietor who, through the big plate windows, bore a striking resemblance to a dear old friend of our family's, a man who in his lifetime had loved fishing and literature with equal passion. He'd point a finger straight up as if testing the wind, and quote somebody dead—in this case, Jean Cocteau: "The greatest beauty," he'd say, "is the beauty of failure." This made my parents nervous: it was un-American to embrace failure. But he gave me my first great books, among them *Moby Dick* and Turgenev's *Sketches from a Hunter's*

Notebook. Not until years after his death would I discover that he'd wanted to write, that all his quotes contained a secret bitter message aimed at himself.

I looked at this owner innocently eating his corned beef sandwich and saw destiny in the coincidence of his familiar bald spot, his heavy glasses, his capable, square-fingered hands. Magically, no one else was in the shop for the moment, and when he saw me, he beckoned me in and spoke in a voice as miraculously gruff and East Coast as my old mentor, and took me around to all the cases, shaking his head grimly at my plain old monofilament and box of tattered wet flies while I privately misted over with nostalgia. In real life, I was apparently staring at some little hooks tied with red and gold thread, and he waved his hand disparagingly. "Sure," he said. "That's the San Juan worm, and it works just fine, but as a beginner, what you really want is a dry fly, so you can see the trout come up for it. That's what'll knock you out."

So I bought from him a half-dozen dries, a tapered leader, and some 6X tippet, all the time feeling a kind of warmth spreading in me, a great access of trust, of *home.* He threw in an extra Parachute Adams and a map of Rock Creek with his own favorite spots circled here and there. "Don't fool around up there," he said sternly. "Just stop at the first access point you find." Now, I thought, *now* I'm on track. But as I left the counter, I saw him turn with great comic enthusiasm to two young men who had just entered the shop. To him I was no hero at all, just one more dazed novice with shaking hands and weak terminology. God only knew what he was telling them now.

Back in the car, I fought the urge to go home, to give up the quest for now. But in my hand I held the map of the next mystery: a world-class fishery I'd never seen. I had the right leader, the right flies, and only 26 miles to go. I followed my guide's directions unswervingly. I stopped at the first access point and read the water; I even got my leader a tiny way out. No hits, but it was enough just to know I had tapered leader now, and after a few hours, I was sweetly exhausted by my little progress. The day passed beautifully, uneventfully, in that narrow canyon of building clouds and slate-colored water, a cool wind coming down the valley as the summer took its own first, minute turn toward fall. I'd been there to see it go, and this felt like enough adventure for one day.

It was then, in the cool of late afternoon, in a dark little glade into which leaves dropped with a mysterious living patter, that I sat down on my tailgate and set my keys beside me where I could not possibly forget them. I had begun to eat my Wheat Thins when I heard a thrashing in the woods behind me. Into view came a short heavy-set man with a red beard, an invader lumbering toward me with spinning rod and cooler. Behind him trailed an ancient, bent woman in giant rubber boots, a long wool skirt, and a kerchief around her head—a dream-babushka straight out of Turgenev's *Sketches*. She had the look of the old crone in fairy tales, the one who delivers the crucial if cryptic message, or opens the right gate, hitherto unnoticed. But no. The babushka retreated into the forest, and the man lumbered closer. I was pulling off my hip-boots when he began to speak in a garbled voice, with an accent deeper than deep South. He wanted to know how I'd done, what I was using. Parachute Adams, I said. He smirked and sprang the latch on his cooler, where a twenty-inch Brown trout lay cramped and faded against the dirty white. He addressed me again in that ferocious accent.

"Juh bring yer bait?" he asked.

"Illegal here," I said coolly.

"It's just un expression," he replied, rolling his eyes a little. "I mean yer bait box with yer minner muddlers and yer big woolly buggers. They're only eatin' the big stuff now, and they're hidin in the troughs. Din't juh notice the eagles?"

I looked politely into the sky, took another Wheat Thin. He rocked on his heels and snapped the cooler shut with a little violence. He was, I suspect, a man who did not like mysteries, particularly.

"Yer fixin ta leave yer keys," he said, pointing down at my bumper.

I tried to make the best of it, tried to convert this dirty moment as quickly as possible into story. This would be the nadir, this the dragon and the darkest moment of the heroic cycle. But I couldn't; I was depressed as hell. Something about the fading light, the dead fish in the cooler, the reminder, smack in the middle of a lyrical analysis, of the ugly side of failure: the trout lying trapped and flatly dead between his condescending teachings and my stubborn ignorance. It was too dark to go back out into the river again, and he stood there, quite clearly waiting to see me leave, as if he'd been sent to take up the last available light. The river was aloof now, cool and secretive, no risers, not a ripple in the troughs, the eagles gone up to their roosts.

"Well, I better get goin'," he said. "Don't forget them keys."

I waited there until I could no longer hear his boots crushing the brittle leaves, until I could no longer see his white cooler, that awful beacon, floating backward through the darkening woods. When it was quiet, I got back in the car and headed out Rock Creek Road, back toward Missoula. But I couldn't believe the story was over, so bleakly, hopelessly, finished. I was starved for a better ending. And lo, as if in answer, there rose up before me the Rock Creek Fly Shop, which, in my haste to get streamside, I'd missed on the way in. At the very least, I told myself, just use the bathroom, grab a soda, ask what these guys would have used.

I stumbled in, Eve expelled from the river for not knowing that the trout were lying in the troughs because of eagles, and eatin' only minner muddlers. I nodded at the man behind the counter, and tried to look like I knew my way around, but I couldn't see a rest room door anywhere.

"Lady," he said. "If it had teeth it would jump up and bite you."

"Just tell me where it is, right now," I said tensely.

He pointed behind me.

When I came out of the rest room he smiled. "You look tired," he said. "What were you using—I hear they're pulling in the big browns like nobody's business!" I shook my head and he slapped his hands on the counter. "You were using *what*?" he said. "What joker told you to use a dry on a day like this?" He paused dramatically, hand on the phone, ready to dial 911. "It's only big stuff now, they're only eatin' big stuff." Again, the sad shake of the head, the unspoken message that if you'd only asked him first instead of The Guys in Town, you'd be rich with fish, hell, Missoula's 26 miles away, what do they know?

It occurred to me that I should stop taking advice for a while, that all advice was suspect, hopelessly rooted in some deep and complicated tangle of pride and secret regret that rose up to meet the susceptible customer with her own deep and complicated tangle of pride and secret regret.

But the proprietor had stopped talking, and was looking at me as if I'd asked him a deep theological question. "Wait a minute," he said. "Come with me." He beckoned me away from the jerky and the Wheat Thins and the cases of flies, around a corner to another room entirely—one I would never have guessed was there. In this room a potbellied woodstove hissed and crackled. A family was seated around the stove: two brothers in red flannel shirts and jeans were cleaning their guns; a young woman, with cheeks flushed from the heat of the stove, was knitting; a baby, also red-faced, with its knitted cap fallen low over one eye, lay regal and stunned in its swaddling.

The proprietor seated himself at a round table piled high with yarn, feathers, fur and thread. "Here we go," he said. He wound red chenille around the shank of a hook, and burned both ends with a match. "I call it the Poor Man's San Juan Worm," he said. "It has no class, but when all else fails—"

I didn't leave right away. I held myself still, welcomed, if not into the life of the river, then a step closer to it. It was like falling into a fine old painting of peasant life, where there's a golden light coming from some window you can't see. The dog sleeps, the hunters pause over their guns, the baby lies amazed under the golden light. We are at the beginning again, with Rock Creek just outside, moving swiftly through its canyon as the dark comes on in earnest. Cocteau would approve, and so would my old mentor: by failing to catch trout, look at the gift you've been granted.

Never mind that on my next visit to Missoula, the owner of the fly shop will look at my San Juan Worm and say accusingly, "Where the hell did you get this? It's all wrong. Who made it?" My host at Rock Creek must have known this would happen, because as he handed me the finished fly, he smiled the brief, cramped smile of the failed artist, the wise teacher.

"Just a little present," he said. "Since you tried so hard. Just promise me you won't tell the guys in Missoula who made it. They'd have my head."

Mallory Burton

Mallory Burton writes from her home on the northern British Columbia
coast, where she teaches, writes, and fishes. In the summer she heads south to
Montana, where the weather is hot, the trout big, and the dry flies small. Like
Norman Maclean in *A River Runs Through It,* she explores family and
personal relationships in many of her fishing stories, including
this one, but from a woman's perspective. Her work has
appeared in various fishing magazines, and is collected in her
1995 book, *Reading the Water: Stories and Essays of Flyfishing and
Life.*

The Emerger

Several years ago, at the beginning of fishing season, I bought my eight-year-old son a light-action spinning rod and reel. Anthony was already a veteran fisherman by this time, having netted sizable bass and northerns at his grandparents' place back East. My father ran a guiding service in northern Ontario, and anyone who ventured out in a boat with him was guaranteed to have a successful trip. Members of the immediate family were not only guaranteed but obligated to catch fish.

"Mum," said Anthony as we drove away from the tackle shop. "Is this really my very own fishing rod?"

"Of course it's your rod," I said, slightly irritated that he would ask. I had become a confirmed fly fisher and hadn't touched a spinning rod since before he was born.

I hoped, of course, that my son would eventually develop an interest in fly fishing, but I wasn't going to push him. Fly fishing isn't like that. Either it calls you or it doesn't.

We fished many of the lakes and rivers between Prince Rupert and Terrace, British Columbia, that season, from the tiny Lost Lake with its doubtful rowboats to the fast-flowing Copper River. Anthony fished with worms and briny-smelling gobs of salmon roe, while I persisted in trying to raise trout to a floating fly.

Anthony enviously admired the stringers of cutthroat and Dolly Varden taken by the bait fishermen we encountered on rivers and lake shores. He had almost given up trying to persuade me to keep the fish I caught, watching incredulously as I removed the barbless hooks and slipped the fish back into the water.

"But that's a keeper," he'd protest. "Why do you have to put him back?"

Because he took the fly so deliberately. Because he was a wild trout, not a hatchery fish. Because the exhausted fish came to my feet so quietly, with none of the panicked, thrashing resistance that might have sparked some killing instinct in me. They were not the kinds of reasons that would have made sense to an eight-year-old.

Occasionally I took pictures of the fish I released, especially the dark-spotted cutts, with their scarlet slash below the gill cover, or the sleek, bright steelhead trout. Anthony kept all of his regulation-size fish. We had an agreement that I would fish for picture fish while he fished for food fish.

Fortunately, the wild stocks were in no danger from my fish-killing son, who wasn't patient enough to be very deadly. His tolerance was limited to one netted fish, one lost lure or one hopelessly tangled line, whichever came first. After that, he was content to build luxurious toad habitats or holding ponds, where he watched his captured sculpins swim until they found a hole between the rocks and darted away.

"They don't mind," he said of the imprisoned fish. "It's like a puzzle for them. It makes them smarter." At his age I'd constructed similar mazes, subjecting insects to treacherous obstacle courses and congratulating myself on their intelligent escapes.

He shared my childhood enthusiasm for collecting dragonfly nymphs and caddis-fly larvae, which he put into plastic bug boxes and scrutinized with a cracked magnifying glass. Occasionally he would extract a caddis worm from its cylinder and dissect the tube of gravel bits and bark, marveling at the strength of the silk that held the bits together.

Once he waded into the Lakelse River during a mayfly hatch to observe the wormlike nymphs floating up from the bottom of the river and emerging as winged adults. Together we watched the newly hatched adults drift across the surface to dry their wings for a few seconds before coming off the water. Later he sat beside me for hours as I tied nymph, emerger and adult insect imitations on small hooks, advising me on their correct size and color for the waters we were fishing.

"I'd like to try that," he announced one evening. He was disappointed when I suggested he start with a much larger hook and an easier pattern.

Eventually Anthony fished with a fly I had tied. After the Kloiya River closed for the season, I lost interest in fishing, but Anthony was still keen on visiting the lakes. Near the end of August, he decided to try his luck at a pair of tiny lakes outside Prince Rupert that were really better suited for picknicking than angling. There might have been some larger fish in their depths, but I secretly doubted that any really decent fish would live in lakes named Tweedledum and Tweedledee. Anthony fished while I picked berries nearby.

I could tell it was going to be a short expedition. Arriving on the marshy shore, Anthony promptly stepped into the bog, filling his gum boots with reeking slime. And he was rapidly using his supply of worms, winging them right off the hook with vigorous casts or losing them to the minnows that boiled around his bobber like a school of miniature piranhas.

"Are you ready to call it a day?" I asked him when the worms ran out.

"No," he called. "Look there." Several larger rings on the water's surface suggested better fish. I set down my berry pail and quickly knotted a trailing leader of six inches to a thumbnail spinner. I tied on a fly called a Muddler Minnow and handed it to him. He looked dubiously at the fly setup but recognized it as a sculpin imitation and clipped it on the swivel in place of the bobber.

His ferocious cast plunked the spinner well on the other side of the rising fish. Reeling in rapidly, he tried to jerk the tackle clear of a clump of reeds as it came within four feet of the bank, but the spinner caught in the rushes. As Anthony tugged on the snagged spinner, the trailing fly flopped wildly on the surface. Suddenly a fourteen-inch trout sailed through the air, nailing the Muddler with an angry splash. The force of its impact freed the snagged spinner, and the fish was airborne a second time. In moments, Anthony horsed it out of the water onto the shore. The cutthroat was legal size and therefore a goner. I thought.

To my surprise Anthony picked up the fish, carefully removed the hook and gently eased the trout back into the water. He watched it swim away and turned with an odd expression on his face.

"What an incredible fish! Did you see the way he hit that fly?" I nodded. "Do they always hit a floating fly like that?"

"They don't often sail through the air, but you usually see the take."

My son's hands trembled slightly as he picked up his rod and slowly reeled in the line. He took a deep breath and shook his head.

"Awesome," he said. I knew the feeling.

Kathleen Dean Moore

Kathleen Dean Moore's 1995 book, *Riverwalking*, which includes the chapter reprinted here, brings nature writing, rivers, and family life together in a new and important way. Moore's reflections on her young son Jonathan's growth into fishing and fly-tying suggest the hidden but powerful connections between the child's curiosity and the young man's life-direction, between the fisher, the fly, and the waters of life. Her new book, *Holdfast: At Home in the Natural World*, continues her explorations of nature in our lives. Kathleen Dean Moore is head of the philosophy department at Oregon State University.

The Deschutes River

In the cove at drift mile 17, the water is transparent and scarcely deep enough to float a boat. Wave action has carved the riverbed into a sculpture of the surface—lapping waves etched in sand. Close to shore, the driftboat swings on its anchor line and rocks in the wash of the swell. Frank's fly rod is hanging by its reel from a crook in the branches of a grand old juniper that arches over the cove, and his chest-waders dangle by their straps, flapping when the wind blows, kicking up their heels. Frank and I are eating lunch, sitting on the bank with our feet in the water. Jonathan, of course, is still out fishing.

Under a high sun, the surface of the water throws wavering nets of light across the riverbed, across our feet, across the sedges, the snail shells. Rows of caddisfly cases roll gently up and down in the line of bubbles where the water washes onshore. The cases are tubes made of tiny sticks and juniper scales and splinters, all stuck together every which way.

Like all insects, maybe like all of us, caddisflies move through a fixed sequence of changes in the course of their lives. Egg to larva. Larva to pupa. Pupa to adult. To protect themselves during their larval stage, they build hard cases, putting them together from whatever they find on the bottom of the river. They pass the months backed into the tubes with only their head and legs protruding and their soft caterpillar of a body encased in the shell, like a snail. If a larva is threatened, it withdraws entirely and becomes a juniper twig blown into the river by afternoon winds, a stick in a pile of sticks. But when the danger has passed, the stick will come to life, untangle itself from the little pile of debris, and walk along the bottom of the river.

After several months, the larvae leave their tubes and encase themselves in amber capsules as glossy as buds on a willow. There, the nymphs absorb their own soft bodies and recreate themselves as adults. They rise to the surface of the river, split their skins up the back, and crawl out onto the surface tension. Transformed into dun flies with lacy wings pitched like tents, they lift their wings, pull away from the draw of the water, and blow into the air.

Jonathan casts an elk-hair caddis onto the seam where the river current meets the slack water of the cove. He has tied his fly to imitate a winged adult struggling to escape the pull of the river. That fly has a frantic, disheveled look about it—a spray of hair and a tuft of white fur. Then Jonathan moves on upriver and I lose him behind a screen of junipers. But I can still hear the river piling against his legs, and I can hear the drag on his reel, a sound like ripping cloth, that tells me he is stripping out line to lengthen his reach, heaving line across the river, stripping line off his reel, heaving it out, stripping line, until he can set his fly down on the deep water where adult fish hold.

Two years ago, Jonathan would have been wading with me in the cove, turning rocks, picking up caddisfly cases. Last year he fished the edges of the river, always in Frank's sight, or mine. This year, he moves entirely beyond our view. His jacket rests on the bank beside me, along with his fly box, an aluminum box small enough to fit in a boy's hand. I open it like a storybook and find neat rows of hand-tied trout flies—dry flies, nymphs, streamers, muddlers—each tucked under its own little clip, each a tuft of feathers and a pellet of deer hair and maybe some tinsel or flashabou tied with his daydreams to the tiny hook. I hang the jacket in the juniper, away from the dampness, and close the little box of flies.

Drift mile 19. Skookum Creek. Frank drops anchor and the boat swings around next to a gravel bar. Jonathan steps out and walks upstream. Soon his line sails out over the river. The line curls back on itself and sails forward. Another curl behind, another forward, and his line leaps out, pauses, and drops onto the water.

When Jonathan wades back to the boat, he is cradling a gleaming rainbow trout in his hands. Golden light with a glow of pink, quicksilver light playing through the colors, so beautiful, so fluid, the fish may be nothing more than refracted light, the idea of a rainbow trout. Jonathan lowers the trout into the water. When I look again, it is gone.

Jonathan ties all his own trout flies, and many of his father's. An entire quadrant of his bedroom is taken up with a fly-tying table that spills over with animal parts and pill boxes and spools of thread on spindles. A rooster's neck, a pheasant's tail, a rabbit's ear, a calf's tail. Elk hair, bear hair, grouse breast, turkey quills. Brass hooks, gold thread, black thread, silver beads—materials tucked into the compartments of a complicated wooden suitcase and overflowing from shoeboxes that smell of mothballs and rabbit skins. The finished flies are on the floor, neatly organized in plastic boxes.

It's hard to watch Jonathan create trout flies, because the parts are so small, and his hands move so quickly, and maybe because the truth of the tying, the sense of the insect, is in the private place his mind wanders while he winds the threads, the expeditions he imagines, the swiftness of the current and the boldness of the strike. But even the visible acts of creation are magical—a spontaneous generation.

Jonathan holds a little #12 hook in the jaws of a vise and squeezes down the handle to keep it steady. With two quick turns, he attaches a thread to the hook. His left hand holds a golden cord against the shank while his right hand whips the thread around to hold it in place. He pulls a tuft of angora goat fur from a plastic bag and spins it with his fingers onto the thread, then whips the furry thread around the hook to make a body. The gold cord he winds diagonally up the body, pulling a bit so that the tension dents the body into segments. He makes the insect's head from a peacock herl, winding the iridescent barb around and around into a clump. With scissors that he wears on his fingers, he cuts fibers from a pheasant's tail and ties them in to look like legs. Standing behind Jonathan, I can see his hair, which spirals from a single point like a nebula, and the long, flat plane of his cheek. He cuts the thread, touches the end with a probe dabbed in glue, releases the hook, and holds in his hand the tiny imitation of a caddis fly larva.

The open palm extended to a parent. Look. Look what I have found. Look what I have made. Look what I have made of myself.

Trout flies are chimeras, insects built of feathers and fur, and this may be what draws Jonathan to them. As long ago as I can remember, he has drawn pictures of fabulous composite creatures, creating them from segments of animals that must float as freely in his imagination as foam on water. When he was little, he stood on a chair to draw, the same chair where he now sits to tie feathers to fur. He held his crayon in his right fist like a dagger and on big sheets of newsprint carved the shapes of slouching, starving panther-lizards, bears that spit flames, a saber-toothed, salamander-footed python with hair standing up on the back of its neck and its eyes shooting sparks, a flock of stilt-legged birds laying purple eggs in mid-flight, a tyrannosauric Trojan Horse with an entire army dead at its feet.

When Jonny was a toddler, his favorite toy was an aquarium net. He sat on his heels at the edge of every river and poked endlessly at the pebbles and floating weeds, turning rocks. When he found something that interested him, he carried it in his open hand to his father to learn its name—periwinkle, caddis case, agate—and then, satisfied, he carried it back and dumped it in the river. This same child, a tall teenager, stands now in swift, knee-deep water while the current raises waves against his calves and slaps the anchored boat around. Leaning down to hold a net in the current, he probes with a heavy boot to dislodge the invertebrates, then catches them as they float downriver. He dumps the contents of the net on the deck of the boat and, leaning over the pile, pushes it apart with one finger. Bits of twigs, skeletonized leaves, a snail shell, two fish eggs, the whole pile wriggling, alive with larval insects. The larvae in his net will tell him what the trout are eating, and so what imitation might lure them from behind the boulders.

Jonathan knows where to put the legs on his nymphs and what colors to mix in the dubbing. He senses the right pitch of the wings and how big the head should be. He knows which insects have wing pads and how to re-create the struggle in the wings of flying insects leaving the water.

He knows these things because he has paid attention. Ever since he could walk upright, he has been happiest to be the observer, unobserved. If you focused too closely on Jonny, he backed away and, as surely as a caddisfly larva, became only surface—the opaque details of a life. Better to stand beside him and look in the direction he was looking. Soon you would be drawn into his world, a place with hawks on posts and millipedes under rocks and, at the edge of the river, the smell of juniper, and tar on the railroad tracks. And then somehow you would feel closer to what is hidden, the unchanging center.

Stand now beside Jonathan at the edge of the Deschutes, and he will show you how to see through the surface of the river to trout holding behind rocks. He will snatch insects out of the air like a magician grabs nickels and open his hand to show you a golden stone fly as big as your thumb. But he will not tell you what he hopes and fears, or what he thinks about before he goes to sleep.

At drift mile 28, I sit in the boat and watch Jonathan watch the river, the corrugated hillsides, the flocks of blackbirds scattered and rising like ashes from a fire, the Hereford steers standing up to their knees in water. A northwest wind picks up. Cottonwoods turn silver and fall warblers tumble out, dun green. Nine miles of river so far today. Whiskey Dick. White Horse Rapids. The riffle at Two Springs Ranch. Above flat water by Red Birch Camp, swallows sail low over the river, haul up close to the wind, and cant into the air on set wings. Without taking his eyes off the river, Jonathan pulls his fly rod out of its case. He bends down to snip off the fly and tie on an elk-hair caddis. Light little insects flutter over the river. A flip of water, another, as trout rise to take flies off the surface.

Peter Patricelli

Peter Patricelli is a physician in Eugene, Oregon, and a longtime member and former president of the McKenzie Flyfishers. He has headed an adolescent drug treatment program in Eugene which used fly tying and fly fishing as part of the therapy. While editing the Flyfishers' newsletter, he began writing memoirs of his fishing experiences, like the one which appears below. This parent-son memoir compares interestingly with those by Mallory Burton and Kathleen Dean Moore. Other stories by Peter Patricelli have been published in *Gray's Sporting Journal* and *Flyfishing the West*.

The Lesson

Now just what, Matt," I said in my most stern and unflinching voice, "do you intend to do about the situation?"

My ten-year-old son stood, tears streaming down his face, in billowy adult-sized latex waders that exposed only a small neck and head, on a gravel bar in the Deschutes River. I could see his fine but forgetful mind spinning through the choices, small in number and poor as they were. He was trapped, and I knew it, and the tears showed he was rapidly reaching that same conclusion. The question and the tone in my voice removed one of his three options. That I would fix it for him. Inside though, I felt as tearful as he did. This was not going to be a fun day on the river.

The problem was that Matt's rod, Matt's new Orvis "Fine n' Far," 9'3" Christmas present, given as a blank at Christmas six months ago, finished by Matt the week before, was leaning against a tree somewhere in our last campsite two miles upriver. On a five-day, fifty-mile float trip, our party of six in two boats had quickly broken camp after breakfast to get on the river early to secure our next and most favored campsite.

After forty-five minutes of floating, I had pulled the McKenzie River boat to shore to fish and Matt had asked, "Where's my rod?"

When a thorough search of the boat yielded nothing, Matt thought it might be in the other boat, which was out of sight downstream. "You better be right," I said, with my stomach churning, knowing it was either going to be fine if the rod was in the other boat, or a lot worse as we slipped rapidly downstream in the current. I rowed hard trying to catch up as quickly as possible, and finally did after another mile. And thus two boats, four adults, and my older son waited on a sterile and fishless gravel bar in the Deschutes Canyon for Matt's decision.

Matt sobbed, wishing he could melt into an immobile puddle of tears as sometimes was his habit in such a situation. But such a meltdown here would still be three miles from his rod.

"I'm going to have to walk back and get the rod," he finally blurted, and sobbed harder now that his fate was sealed.

I knew he wanted to leave it, just write it off and wait for Santa's return trip, but I was not about to let that happen. Matt's forgetfulness, the result of an active and uncluttered mind merrily dancing along its merry way, needed a lesson. As a parent, I thought his recognition of responsibility sounded like The Solution. The Deschutes River in its canyon is as indifferent as it is beautiful, and definitely is a one-way experience. Those elements had now become Matt's adversary.

"O.K., now listen," I said, getting the worst out all at once. "Get out of your waders and put on your socks and tennis shoes. Just follow the railroad tracks upriver back to the old camp. You can't get lost. Take a Pepsi or two because it's going to be hot. We'll be camped at the bower. You know where that is, just below the long, diagonal riffle."

At this, I felt three adults and my older son's eyes turn on me. I had just added another two miles to his return, downstream walk. Silence. No one would say a word, I knew. It was my call as father. I was glad his mother wasn't there, and I hoped this would be funny by the time she heard of it.

"It should take you about three hours. If you get too hot, dunk your t-shirt in the river," I finished.

Matt climbed into the boat, still crying, and began searching through the camping gear for his tennis shoes. He threw things around, but warily. He changed into his shoes and I handed him a Pepsi. I carried him to the bank to keep his shoes dry. He struggled up through the brush, an invisible, moving noise, and emerged on the railroad tracks above us. Looking at his feet, he started upstream, still crying.

"See you in three hours," I called. We all watched him depart in silence.

When Matt was out of hearing, I finally faced the rest of the group.

"We would have waited," Larry, my brother-in-law, said. Bob, the oldest of the group and a grandfather several times over, said little but was visibly hurting. Don, who had never married and had no children, was the most shaken. I was the leader of this expedition but the youngest adult by ten years.

A calculated gamble. A gamble made possible by the unique structure of the situation: the enclosing canyon, the river, the railroad tracks, the solitude, and what I assumed to be my intimate knowledge of them. A gamble which perhaps not everyone would take. But ten years of multiple week-long float trips each summer made this MY territory. There was a lesson there for Matt, an experience, and he was just barely old enough to do it, which would make it that much more poignant and unforgettable. A parent's gamble.

"No," I said, "it would be ridiculous for the five of us to sit here and swelter for two hours, lose the campsite, and nearly a whole day's fishing. Matt forgot it, and he can get it. It's going to hurt, but there's no way he can get into trouble out here."

And before I could change my mind, trying to appear more certain than I really was, I raised the anchor and pushed off the bar.

At nine a.m. in mid-July it was hot, too hot in the boat to keep your waders up. The desert sun would be burning in another hour and the dark basalt canyon would be at full bake by afternoon, over 100 degrees. Walking the tracks on a hot day, I knew, was a special kind of hell: sweltering, unshaded exposure as you stepped off-stride from tie to tie, the tracks seeming to freeze you in place with their unchanging parallel convergence, without apparent progress. And the contrast with the river below the tracks, its green shade and cool, moist air, trapped only thirty feet below, lifted up now and then by a tantalizing zephyr. Matt might find a bisected and dehydrated rattlesnake or two, but that would likely be the sum total of his experience on the track that day. And the lesson he would never forget.

We fished on down the river. I subconsciously lingered, slowing our progress so badly that, when we finally pulled in, the Bower campsite was already taken. We had to settle for the sandy, exposed campsite just below. Hot and dusty, back too far from the river to get the river air, its only feature—a distinct negative in a sizzling mid-day sun—was a wide open view of the canyon. At least we could see the tracks for a quarter mile upriver. Under normal circumstances, missing the Bower site, I might have pushed on further and abandoned some of the best fishing water on the river just to avoid camping totally exposed to the sun for a full afternoon. But that now was out of the question.

So we pulled camp, box by box out of the boats, hauled it up the path between the streamside poison oak to the sand site, and set up. After lunch, everyone puttered around the hateful camp, setting up tents, fiddling with fishing gear, tying flies, drinking gallons of fluid and watching it disappear from one another's brow and lips, all with a cool river and spectacular fishing a mere hundred feet away, until it became perfectly obvious. Everyone was watching the tracks.

One o'clock, four hours, no Matt. We told fishing stories, played cards, soaked our shirts in riverwater and let them dry on our backs. I recalculated the distance, the walking time again in my mind. Seven miles by river, actually less by the tracks, since they cut across the inside turns. Three hours walk, four at the most.

Two o'clock, no Matt. I explained to the group the local fishing water upstream and down, mentally splitting it up between them for the evening's fishing. I told all the Sand campsite stories from previous trips, and started preparations for dinner so we could fish late.

Three o'clock, no Matt.

"He's late," Don said, to no one in particular, looking up at the tracks for the hundredth time. "Maybe I'll wander up the tracks and give him some company walking back."

"No. I'll go," I said. "I'm curious as to why he's so late."

I dunked my shirt, downed as much water as I could hold, and headed up the trail to intercept the tracks on the long straightaway. As I climbed onto the railbed itself, my heart sank. I could see at least a mile up the tracks in the shimmering heat and no small, reassuring blob broke their symmetry. I was in for a walk myself. At the end of the straight, I passed a farmhouse and a barking dog, notable as the only break in the monotony. I could gauge my progress up river by recognizing the structure of the better fishing stretches. Two miles and still no sign of Matt. I was puzzled. There was no way he could get lost, or out of the canyon even if he wanted to, no one else around except an occasional raft floating down the river, and nothing to do but walk.

At three miles I rounded a railroad bend, agonizingly slowly at walking speed because I could then look up another long straightaway. Nothing. Halfway through the straight, another quarter mile, I noticed movement at the bottom of a scree bank which dropped directly from the tracks into the river. A little kid, fishing, his rod surging down and away into the deep slow current, then the roll and wake of a large trout. I sat down to watch.

He landed and released the fish, then climbed the bank to the tracks and walked slowly downstream, peering intently down into the river from a thirty-foot height. He was oblivious to my presence downstream. He stopped and cupped his hands around his eyes and sunglasses, staring into the water, then walked quickly downriver another forty feet and slid down the bank to the water again. He picked his way upstream ten feet or so, stabilized himself on the rocks, and began casting. That made the identification, that incredible, high, impossibly flat backcast he had from the first day he ever held a fly rod at age six, beyond anything I could possibly have related to him in words. He rose but missed a fish, a sizeable splash visible even from my distance, slapped his rod down on the water in boyish anger, and climbed the bank again. The cycle repeated itself.

I shook my head in amazement, shedding whatever vestiges of anger I might have had. If anyone had earned this day, he had. The amazement was also that his fishing vest was in the boat at the new camp. He had ONE fly on the already rigged rod, tied on a light leader. And he had been doing this for hours.

On the third trip up to the tracks he spotted me and walked on down. I sat where I was until he reached me, then got up and dusted myself off. He had a big grin on his face.

"You found the rod, I see."

"Yeah, it was leaning against the tree behind where the tent was. I just forgot it." Then his speech gathered momentum as he remembered. "I was walking back and at one point where the tracks were just above the river I was looking down and I could see big fish rising along the bank."

"How many did you get?"

"About four or so, one of them a big hog. I lost two bigger ones, though."

"You didn't lose your fly?"

"No, it just pulled away. I had to really climb a bush and a tree or two to get it back when I snagged up." He was still grinning.

I let the picture of it all run through my mind. I knew just how it went.

"Well, we'd better get back. Don will be worried. Aren't you thirsty?"

"Well, sort of. But I found a full Coke in a back eddy and that helped." He giggled at his luck.

I shook my head, trying hard to remember there was supposed to have been a harsh lesson in all this. For HIM.

I tried a last cast toward the rapidly dissolving connection to what was supposed to have happened.

"Well, at least you got your rod back." And we started down the shimmering tracks.

It rolled right off his back. Matt nearly surged forward into a run in anticipation of telling HIS stories to the men waiting at Sand Camp.

Michael Baughman

Michael Baughman began fishing for trout at the age of five, on his great-grandfather's farm in western Pennsylvania. He moved to Hawaii at eleven and became a spear-fisherman until he came to Oregon with his wife Hilde in 1966. They fish regularly for steelhead on their beloved North Umpqua River, of which Michael has written in his 1995 book, *A River Seen Right.* He is also the author of *The Perfect Fishing Trip, Ocean Fishing,* and a number of fishing pieces in *Sports Illustrated.* The Baughmans live in Ashland, Oregon, with occasional trips to Baja California to fish for dorado. In the following piece, Michael gives new meaning to an old fishing term.

Skunked

The most common arguments that fly fishermen use to promote their sport are that fly-casting is esthetically superior to any other form of angling and, therefore, more enjoyable, and that when a fish is hooked in the lip—as opposed to having taken a bait hook into its stomach—it may easily be released to fight again another day. These are valid points, but, in my opinion, there is another good reason for switching from a spinning or bait rod to a fly rod, and that is the relative cheapness of fly-fishing. Though the sport is thought by many to be the preserve of wealthy gentlemen who take periodic jaunts to Norway or Iceland for Atlantic salmon and to New Zealand for huge trout, the truth is that the vast majority of us fly-fishermen angle in waters within driving distance of our homes and that casting flies saves us money. A dozen years ago I could afford to fish only once a week because on every trip I would leave as much as $10 worth of spoons and spinners snagged on rocks on the bottom of the river. Now, having learned to tie my own flies, I can fish every day if I choose to.

I keep my fly-tying expenses to a minimum by scavenging most of the materials I use. The sources are endless. Around the house I obtain strands from old burlap sacks, scraps from my wife's knitting, colored thread from her sewing box, hair clipped from our dog, cats or horse, and tinsel from Christmas and birthday packages. During hikes and runs through the woods, I've procured a wide variety of feathers and animal fur. The bird hunting I used to do has left me with a lifetime supply of pheasant, grouse, quail, and duck skins, and deer-hunting friends have given me plenty of bucktail. With a little time, and the skill that comes with practice and patience, I've been able to pursue a satisfying second hobby that allows me to fish cheaply and conveniently. Because of all this

I've considered myself a practical-minded conservationist, but a couple of years ago I learned that the conservation ethic can be stretched too far.

Driving home from a fishing trip on a cool day in early spring, I saw a dead skunk along the side of a two-lane country road. Though apparently a road kill, it looked to be in perfect shape, its winter coat thick and lustrous. The long, coarse hair from a skunk's tail is said to be better than bucktail for tying streamer flies, so I slowed the car, braked to a stop and backed up for a closer look and smell.

I had thought about salvaging skunk tails before, but every road kill I had ever passed was either messy or odorful, or both. When I rolled down the car window this time, I didn't smell a thing. The skunk lay on its side, facing away from me, looking more asleep than dead. But I took no chances. I used a trick that I remembered reading about in Hemingway's *Green Hills of Africa*. I climbed out of the car and found some pebbles on the shoulder of the road and, from a safe distance, tossed them at the skunk. When three or four had bounced off the animal and it hadn't moved, I was certain it was dead. (True, Hemingway's pebbles had been tossed at a lion that had just been shot, but otherwise the situations were similar.)

As I stepped up close to the skunk, pocketknife in hand, there was indeed an odor—not overpowering, but decidedly unpleasant. So I worked as quickly as I could, gripping the end of the tail in my left hand and using the knife in my right to saw through the tail's base. But it was a dull knife, and the work went slowly. The odor steadily increased. By the time I was about halfway through, I had to hold my breath as I hacked away, then sprint 15 or 20 yards down the road to take a gulp of fresh air and return to work again.

After about five minutes of this, my perseverance was wearing thin, but so was the base of the tail, and almost out of breath again, I decided that a quick hard yank would probably sever the tail from the skunk's body. Holding its rear legs down with the toe of my left boot, I grasped the tip of its tail and pulled upward—hard.

But the tail didn't come off. Instead, a spray of greenish-yellow liquid shot at me from the skunk. Rather, I think that it was greenish-yellow, that it came straight up at me and that there was a lot of it, but I'll never know for sure, because the odor that came with the spray was the most powerful natural force I've ever encountered. I've been tackled hard by huge linemen, punched in the jaw, and wiped out by enormous waves in Hawaii, but these experiences were truly pleasurable compared to the stench from that skunk.

I staggered back, temporarily blinded, gasping for breath. I ended up behind my car, hands on my knees, shaking my head to clear it. In 30 seconds I could see again, but my eyes were watering so badly that the car itself was nothing but a brown blur. I had the presence of mind to take my jacket off and toss it away. That helped some. When a couple of minutes had passed, my eyes had cleared and my breathing was back to normal, though inhaling certainly was no longer an involuntary act. I realized that I had dropped my knife, but I didn't care. In fact, I didn't even look toward the skunk as I abandoned my plan, climbed into the car and drove away.

It was still more than 100 miles to my house, and I soon knew I'd never make it unless I did something to drastically diminish the stench. As it had when I'd been cutting away at the tail, the odor grew steadily stronger, from simply objectionable to gaggingly repulsive. If you've ever been around skunks, you know what I mean. If you haven't, all I can tell you is that the smell is indescribable. It's as foul as anything you can imagine, and then some—and then a great deal, in fact.

I had all the car windows rolled down and even tried driving with my head out one of them, but that was tiring and dangerous and afforded no real relief anyway. I remembered that a couple of years before, my bird dog had been sprayed by a skunk. When we got him home we soaked him in tomato juice, the standard treatment for dogs under such circumstances. It certainly didn't eliminate the odor, but it seemed to help. If it worked on dogs, I reasoned, the same prescription should work on people. It seemed worth a shot. I stopped at the first grocery store I came to, a mom-and-pop establishment with a gas pump out front.

I parked at the pump, and when an elderly gentleman in overalls and a long white apron came out the front door, he sniffed curiously although he was still 20 feet from the car. Fifteen feet away he made a face and stopped.

"Skunk," I called out.

"Just one?" he said.

"Look, could you bring me out six large cans of tomato juice? I'll help myself to some gas while you get them."

"Only six?" he said.

"Six. And a can opener, too, please."

"They probably ain't going to help much."

"That's O.K. I want to try it."

He backed off a step. "Good idea, son."

It took a few minutes to complete the transaction. He left the juice and opener in a sack by the road, well away from the store, and I left his money there, including a tip. As I drove off I looked in the rear-view mirror and saw him approaching the money cautiously, like a soldier crossing a minefield.

A few miles farther along I came to a Forest Service campground, which at that time of the year was deserted. In the rest room I undressed, kicked my clothes into a pile in the corner, opened all six cans of tomato juice—twelve quarts—and bathed myself thoroughly, slowly emptying each can over my head, then rubbing the juice in carefully as it flowed down over my body. It was cool and rather thick. The sweetish smell certainly didn't eliminate the skunk odor, but at least it mixed with it to create something different and possibly a little less repulsive.

I wanted to give the juice a chance to do as much as it could, so I let it dry, hopping up and down on the tile floor to warm I myself. In a few minutes, when the juice had become a very uncomfortably sticky coating, I went to a sink to wash myself. There wasn't any water. I tried all the sinks, but there was nary a drop. Apparently the water was shut off, except during the summer camping season. So I dressed as I was and returned to the car, hoping above all— praying, in fact—that I wouldn't run into anybody. I must have looked like something from a Japanese horror movie, and the odor, though somewhat altered, hadn't really diminished at all.

It was a long drive home. I hit the freeway half an hour after my juice bath. By then the sun was down and the night air was so cool I had to roll the windows up and use the heater. That made the smell impossible to take, so I stopped at a deserted rest area, took everything off but my undershorts, and dropped my jeans, shirt and a $50 pair of boots into a garbage can. The boots smelled worse than anything else, I think. .

I was very careful to obey the speed limit after that, for Lord knows what summary action a state trooper might have taken if he had stopped a foul-smelling man coated from head to foot with tomato juice and wearing only undershorts.

Finally, about 20 minutes from my house, my right rear tire went flat and I coasted to the shoulder of the road. After a few seconds of hollow-stomached panic, I realized that I could wear my chest waders to change the tire.

A number of cars slowed as they went by. One large, brightly painted van nearly stopped beside me. It was full of teenagers. "Far out!" one of them yelled at me. "Weirdo!" screamed another. I heard them all laughing as the van sped away.

I changed the tire and made it home. My family was understanding, but it took a couple of days and more than a couple of baths before my life returned to normal. I could eat at the dinner table once again, and the dog stopped backing off at my approach.

If all this had happened to Aesop and he had wanted to write a fable about it, the moral would be clear enough: *When tying streamer flies, bucktail will surely do.*

Don Berry

Not yet thirty, Portlander Don Berry in 1960 published *Trask,* the definitive historical novel of the Oregon coast. *Trask* was shortly followed by Berry's novels *Moontrap* and *To Build a Ship,* and by his history of the Rocky Mountain fur trade, *A Majority of Scoundrels.* Don Berry has become, over the years accomplished in many creative arts as well as the crafter of a personal life that rivals in achievement and distinctiveness that of his onetime housemate and fellow student at Reed College, Gary Snyder. Although the following selection has nothing to do with the Northwest, Berry shows us what happens when a legendary Northwesterner takes an imaginative look at flyfishing from some new perspectives.

How to Dress a Nymph

Let us be straightforward here. This is an essay in praise of illusion. Between honesty and deception, we choose deception; between reality and mere appearance, our vote goes to appearance.

Outright, intentional, even joyful deceit is our game, and it places us in one of those gray areas of our culture where our ethical principles are put to the test. And fail.

In our society, deception is much practiced and little praised. To be sure, we have defined a few occasions where we will accept it—the sleight-of-hand artist, for example. But the condition there is that we know we are being deceived, and so can laugh with friends, admiring the deceiver's skill. For the most part, though, it makes us exceedingly nervous to know that a deceiver is about the premises, and not to know his/her intentions for us.

This is to say that readers of high ethical standards may find themselves fish out of water, so to speak, and prefer to turn elsewhere. Those who accept that all Art is illusion, that the Craft of Deception may be perfected like any other craft—read on.

To dress a nymph you will need an eyed feather from the tail of a male peacock, iridescent. You will need two tufts of soft fur from the base of a hare's ear.

But I have rushed ahead of myself, dear reader. You will first of all need Understanding

It has wisely been said that the only reason for counterfeit money is real money. To deceive correctly requires considerable knowledge of the Real.

Thus, to dress a nymph, it will first be necessary for you to understand her naked nature, the realities of her existence, the ways of her family. We will call her Hexagenia.

Her family is ancient beyond time. Their name in Greek is literal and to the point: and in classic Greek their name is also their tragic destiny.

They are the family Ephemeroptera, meaning "they-of-the-short-lived-wing."

Hexagenia is truly an ephemeral creature, not entirely of our world. Mortal eye has seen her only under the rarest of conditions. To see her truly requires that the desirous human transcend his own terrestrial existence and enter her world of sunlit riffles on the water, of deep shadowy pools where time is suspended, of swift, threatening currents.

Here she lives all her life, except for one brief, explosive moment of sunlit ecstasy, a burst of extravagant sexuality that makes the air itself shimmer. To consummate the uncontrollable fire of her sexuality, she risks everything, abandons her known universe of water to enter the brilliant and dizzying world of light and air. And there, inevitably, dies. It is her destiny, and the destiny of her family, from long before the time the ape-like creatures of land learned to use a tool.

The transition between universes is fraught with perils, which is probably why we undertake it so seldom. As the mystics inform us, a personal transformation is required, a death-in-life, a rebirth in ecstasy. And this is confirmed by the history of Hexagenia and her sisters, whose ecstatic transformations are fired by sexuality.

In the dreamy, drifting, underwater world of the nymphs, a tremor passes. An electric tremor, an incomprehensible frisson of desire in those who have never known desire. It cannot be understood, any more than the first tremblings of sexuality can be understood by an adolescent girl.

It grows in power. It seizes upon Hexagenia and all her sisters at the same time. It inflames their desire. The dark and comforting world they have known suddenly seems confined, a watery, sexless prison.

They become restless, dissatisfied. They conceive an inexplicable passion for that strange light that has hovered over them all their lives.

They begin to dance, slowly at first, swaying in the current, wrapping their cloaks about their naked bodies, now becoming mysteriously transformed.

Suddenly, one rips her cloak asunder and, intensely vulnerable in her nakedness, flies upward and upward to the edge of the universe. Then another, and another, and soon the full frenzy has spread to all the sisters. They rip away their garments in ecstasy and penetrate the fragile film that separates the Worlds.

Now, gasping in the unfamiliar air, blinded by the intensity of light, consumed by passion, they find that they have been transformed into winged creatures.

No longer innocent nymphs dreaming their watery dreams, they are in that phase of their life where they are known as "duns. " They struggle helplessly at the surface, wings too new and too wet to fly. And in their consuming passion they have thrown themselves into a realm of threatening monsters which arise from the depths to consume Hexagenia and her sisters by the thousands.

Hexagenia struggles, trying to move her wings, trying to escape this sudden, undreamed danger. Somehow, miraculously, she is able to fly a bit, then a bit more. With each perilous flight her wings dry a little, and she can fly a little farther. In a matter of moments, another transformation has occurred. Hexagenia is now a "spinner."

For a thousand days of life, she will spend one single day of ecstatic sexual maturity as a "spinner," breathing air for the first time, feeling the heat of the unaccustomed sun. In the world she now inhabits, love and death are equally balanced, equally inevitable.

Ah, but the dance, the dance of love. Above her in the air the intricate dance of thousands of passionate males is swirling. Their passion is equal to hers; they will die for it. Their last vital energy is expended in the explosive sexuality of the dance; and they fall, dead, in the hundreds, in the thousands, in the tens of thousands.

At last, her volcanic passions gratified, she reaches the shore, and falls exhausted.

But now her own death is near. She will have the shortest of times to fulfill her mission, to complete her circle of life's spiral.

Shortly she takes wing again, gliding out over the surface of the water where she arose. In her last act, she gives immortality to her family. She deposits her eggs in the water, where they sink into the green, mysterious depths to begin the circle again.

Then she falls, dead, to the surface, her wings so new now useless, flat, spent. It is her final transformation: She is known as a "spentwing."

That is the truth of the matter, the reality behind our deception.

From Nymph to Dun to Spinner to Spentwing is the life cycle of Ephemeroptera Hexagenia, the common may-fly.

Hexagenia is a principal source of food for the trout, and it is on the trout we will practice our deception.

The language of the angler is precise and ambivalent at the same time, and much of it is his alone. The entomologist, for example, knows nothing of nymphs and duns and spinners and spentwings. He speaks of larval shucks and sub-imagoes and imagoes.

And take the simple word "strike." It refers (1) to the moment the fish takes the hook, (2) to the action of the angler in setting the hook, and (3) to the whole gestalt in which the fish takes the hook and the angler sets it. Which of these is meant at any given moment is clear only to the angler.

It seems logical, or at least reasonable, that folk who invent their own vocabulary should come to devote themselves to graceful deception. And, indeed, they came to it rather quickly, as history goes.

About the year 200 A.D., the Roman naturalist Aelian reported:

> I have heard of a Macedonian way of catching fish: between Beroea and Thessalonica runs a river called the Astraeus, and in it there are fish with speckled skins.
>
> What they are called, you had best ask the Macedonians.
>
> These fish feed on a fly peculiar to the country. In boldness it is like a fly, in size you might call it a midge. It imitates the color of a wasp, and it hums like a bee. The natives generally call it Hippouros.
>
> When the fish observes a fly on the surface, it swims quietly up, afraid to stir the water above, lest it should scare away its prey.
>
> Then, coming up by its shadow, it opens its mouth gently and gulps down the fly, like a wolf carrying off a sheep from the fold, or an eagle a goose from the

farmyard; having done this, it goes below the rippling water.

Now, though the fishermen know of this, they do not use these flies at all for bait; for if a man's hand touch them, they lose their natural color, their wings wither, and they become unfit food for the fish.

But the fishermen have planned a snare for the fish, and get the better of them by their fisherman's craft.

They fasten red wool around a hook, and fix on to the wool two feathers of a waxy color which grow under a cock's wattles. Their rod is six feet long, and their line is the same length.

Then they throw their snare, and the fish, attracted and maddened by the color, comes straight at it, thinking from the pretty sight to get a dainty mouthful. When, however, it opens its jaws, it is caught by the hook and enjoys a bitter meal, a captive.

Let us now leap forward a millennium or so, to the year 1496, to be precise. A man named Columbus is still trying to convince the centers of capital that there is something of value over the water. But a canny woman of God named Dame Juliana Berners is revealing the treasures that lie beneath the waters, and how to acquire them.

Dame Juliana was Prioress of Sopwell, England. In 1496 she published "A Treatyse of Fysshynge with an Angle." In it she described twelve varieties of artificial fly, with complete instructions on how to dress them. A number of these flies are dressed today exactly as she described them.

I do not believe Dame Juliana was beatified by her Church. This oversight, as it must have been, has certainly been corrected by the church of the fly fisherman, where she is installed permanently as a presiding semi-deity.

Her Treatyse was incorporated into a new edition of the Boke of St. Albans, a kind of training manual for the young nobility. It treated, as well, the sportive arts of falconry, heraldry and hunting.

If this seems a limited publication, it was. However, it suited the purposes of Dame Juliana perfectly. It was definitely her aim to restrict her secret weapon to those of impeccable moral stature.

She wished to discourage the interest of idlers in the sport of fishing, "which they might destroy utterly by virtue of the skill acquired from this treatise."

Dame Juliana was death on the vice of Idleness, "which is the principal cause inciting a man to many other vices, as is right well known."

She was also an exponent of what we would call environmentalism today. Remember she is giving this counsel in 1496:

> I charge you, that you break no man's hedges in going about your sports, nor open any man's gates without shutting them again. Also, you must not use this aforesaid artful sport for covetousness, merely for the increasing or saving of your money, but mainly for your enjoyment and to procure the health of your body, and more especially of your soul.
>
> Also, you must not be too greedy in catching your said game [the fish is meant here], as in taking too much at one time, a thing which can easily happen if you do in every point as this present treatise shows you.
> That could easily be the occasion of destroying your own sport and other men's also.
> When you have a sufficient mess, you should covet no more at that time. Also you should busy yourself to nourish the game in everything that you can.
> And all those that do according to this rule, will have the blessing of God and St. Peter.

Fair enough. That seems to me a good bargain.

The classic tragedy of the Ephemeroptera is known by the angler (rather too prosaically, I think) as "the hatch." When the may-fly nymphs are transformed for their dazzling dance of sunlit sex, the air above the stream is a swirling cloud of translucent wings, vibrating at the frequency dictated by the Goddess of All.

The trout at these times become infected with the possibly more mundane frenzy of feeding. The surface of a stream can become almost invisible in the churning maelstrom of trout rising to take the duns as they emerge from the nymphal case. (The duns here are known as "emergers.") Sometimes the fish will leap out of the water entirely to gulp down a fluttering spinner.

The angler at this time is usually in a state of electric adrenaline excitement: he is "fishing the hatch," or "fishing the rise," a moment somewhat resembling orgasm in other areas of endeavor.

The angler knows that this magical moment, when his desires have intersected the desires of Hexagenia and the trout simultaneously, will not long endure. It may be a period of opportunity only a few moments long, or an hour. In the extraordinary event of a "multiple hatch," when several species come simultaneously to term, it can last a day. Not many have fished the rise for an entire day.

It is the angler's task now to "match the hatch." By studying the species and the size of insect, he tries to duplicate that exactly from his box of flies. With trembling hands he ties his best guess to his "tippet," the ultimate, hair-thin tip of his leader. (The breaking strength of his tippet is approximately that of two strands of white hair from a horse's tail, twisted together; as was Dame Juliana's. That of the modern angler is monofilament nylon, of course.)

In fishing the hatch, he will probably first attempt to deceive the trout with the simulacrum of a floating fly, which is to say, a dun that has fallen back to the water after becoming airborne, or one that has not yet escaped the surface tension. This is "fishing the dry fly," since the fly rests as lightly as possible on the surface of the water, and does not sink.

But sometimes, even when the hatch is on, this will prove fruitless. To the angler's frustrated eyes, the trout are rising to take everything that appears—except his tempting deception.

Then he may notice, if he is still capable of noticing anything, that the trout are not striking, but "bulging."

When a trout bulges, he does not actually break the surface, but causes a distinct hump in the water; he is rising and turning just below the surface.

To the practiced eye, bulging means only one thing—the trout are "nymphing." That is, they are ignoring the flies which have reached the surface, and are taking the emergers before they have cast off the nymphal case.

During the hatch, the insects are present in every stage from nymph to spinner. It is not known why trout will, by common agreement, choose to feed only on one stage, but they do. In the angler's lexicon, they are being "selective."

When the trout are nymphing, then clearly the angler must nymph as well. (Here is another case in which a single verb refers equally to what the fish is doing, what the angler is doing, and the two combined.) He will replace his dry fly with another illusion, this one suggesting the nymphal stage, or the emerger.

In recent years, fishing the nymph has almost entirely replaced the traditional (since Macedonian times) method of fishing the wet fly. The dry fly was a recent innovation anyway, as such things go, having appeared in the middle of the last century.

It is getting pretty sophisticated. The angler can find instructions on tying what are called "stillborn duns." This particular deception consists of imitating those duns which have been unable to free themselves completely from the nymphal case. Patterns are available with one wing free, both wings free, either wing free, the nymphal case almost entirely shucked off, the nymphal case barely shucked off at all, and so forth.

The verisimilitude of these deceptions is remarkable, particularly since the illusion is created by the crafty combination of feathers from birds, furs from mammals, and bits of tinsel from laboratories.

Many an angler owns certain flies which he admires so much for their aesthetics that he won't fish them, for fear of spoiling their artistic perfection. Most of them are a little embarrassed by this situation, but they do it anyway.

The art of tying a fly is a painterly craft rather than a draftsman's. It is more the art of a Manet than an Ingres.

For all the meticulous imitation of detail, everything is done by suggestion. A bit of tinsel properly placed suggests the flash of light from a segmented body; a lightly barred feather from a cock's neck suggests the delicate veining of Hexagenia's wings. All here is the aesthetics of illusion, not of mechanical duplication.

There are chicken farms exclusively devoted to raising chickens for the character of their feathers, and their special use in deceiving the trout. An excellent "grizzly" neck from a single cock may bring $60 in the marketplace. A "saddle hackle" (from the chicken's back) is less valued, but will still cost $20 or so. A single chicken may thus be worth well over a hundred dollars, as it is ultimately retailed.

There is, however, a fundamental contradiction in this gospel of perfect imitation. Because it is unquestionable fact that some of the greatest flies ever created (from the point of view of catching fish) resemble no insect ever seen on the face of the earth.

The angler's lexicon accommodates this puzzling anomaly by dividing artificial flies into two categories, the "Imitators" and the "Attractors." An Attractor, most simply put, is an artificial which catches fish but doesn't look like anything in particular.

The Royal Coachman, for example, one of the all-time great Attractors, resembles no known insect. It is so named because it is dressed in the colors of the Royal Coachman of the English Court, and was reputedly first tied by the Royal Coachman himself. I do not vouch for the latter part, as it was told to me by a fly fisherman.

I have promised to teach you how to dress a nymph, and so I shall: the Gold-ribbed Hare's Ear Nymph.

In addition to its obvious aesthetics, the Gold-Ribbed Hare's Ear is a proven fish taker. It is, in the angler's vocabulary, "deadly." Here are the materials you will need. If it seems like a listing of alchemical significance, you are correct. There is something a bit alchemical in all of this.

1. A #10 to #16 double length hook.

2. A medium brown feather from the breast of a partridge.

3. A tuft of fur from the base of a hare's ear.

4. Four inches of medium gold tinsel.

5. A dark brown feather from the wing of a turkey. A spool of tying thread.

6. Secure the hook, point down, in a small vise. With pliers, crush the barb of the hook flat. (This is so you may release your trout without harming him. You are correct in believing the Macedonians knew nothing of this...).

7. Wrap the shank of the hook with tying thread, moving from the eye back to the bend. Leave the thread hanging.

8. Select a few fibers from the tip of a partridge feather. A professional fly tyer can whip these out so rapidly you would find it difficult to believe.

This pattern, Attractor-like, has been slightly simplified for easier visualization by non-anglers. It is, in fact, the illusion of a Gold-ribbed Hare's Ear.

Now you have dressed, or visualized dressing, your first nymph—the illusion of an illusion. You have transcended mere actuality and entered into the very Heart of Illusion from which actuality is born.

Do not concern yourself with the opinion of other anglers on your nymph. In this art, they are the critics, long on opinion and short on insight. The only aesthetic authority here is the trout, he of the speckled skin.

And bear in mind that if your artful illusion prevails, it is not merely some brainless fish you have deceived. If you fool the trout, you have fooled Nature herself. Fortunately, She seems to like that, from time to time.

If you want to know more, you had best ask the Macedonians.

Dave Hughes

Because Dave Hughes is a contemporary of the other modern Northwestern fishing writers in this opening section, he belongs with them as a "new voice." But as an Astoria-born Oregonian who started writing early and has published a number of solid books on fishing, he is also something of an oldtimer. Thus, he links us to the second section of this book, Northwest Tradition, which follows his essay.

"Lost Lakes" is from one of Dave Hughes' early books, *An Angler's Astoria* (1982). Some of his other books are *Wet Flies, Fly Fishing Basics, Strategies For Stillwater, Reading the Water, Tactics For Trout,* and, with his entomologist friend and fishing companion Rick Hafele, *The Complete Book of Western Hatches.*

Lost Lakes

The lakes I fish in the hills around Astoria are called Lost Lakes. Some are so called because they are too small to have been named. Others have proper names, but are referred to as "lost" because those who refer to them desire to introduce the extreme of confusion into every reference. They hope the lakes will remain lost; fishermen who manage to extract directions to them usually wind up as lost as the lakes.

I fish these lakes at two times of the year. The first is during the earliest sunny days of spring, when warmth draws a hatch of mayflies to the surface, and the mayflies draw the trout upward. The second is in fall, when most people have quit fishing, and when the fish have put on a summer's worth of weight.

Few of the lakes in the hills here have feeder streams with sufficient gravel and flow for spawning. The fish in the lakes are plants, and in recent years all of the plants have been legal trout, eight to nine inches long. Planted fish are not considered desirable game by some fishermen, who look down their noses at them. But nature arranged it so trout only spawn in flowing water, and nature arranged most of our lakes without stream systems where trout can spawn, so I happily accept fishing for plants as an alternative to not fishing the lakes at all.

Planted fish have a rightful reputation as pushovers. As soon as they have recovered from the shock of being hauled away from the hatchery in a tank, and dumped into strange water, they start cruising and accepting nearly any bait or lure thrown in their way. They are hungry, and they do not know how to make their way without a daily ladling of pellets to sustain them. What we mistake for stupidity, however, is merely ignorance. When they find out what is safe to eat in their new environment the worm turns, and the turn of the worm is in favor of the fly fisherman, not the worm fisherman: One of the first things they find out is that worms are not safe to eat.

Most coastal mountain lakes are shallow and rich with insect life. It takes planted trout about three weeks to zero in on these insects. After that time they can be just as selective as natives. A selective snub is easier to take from native trout; when mere plants turn into snobs and refuse flies in the midst of a hatch it is an unexpected insult. It is, however, also an unexpected challenge, and fishing which lacks at least a trace of challenge will have more than a trace of boredom.

A fisherman can experiment during a hatch, and through trial and error, eventually find one or two standard patterns that take one or two of these newly finicky fish. The person who is willing to take a look—a close look—at the insect that is hatching will likely save himself hours, sometimes days or even seasons, of fruitless searching for the right fly.

For many years the insect hatches on lost lakes in spring seemed to me a simple affair: there were the blue dun mayflies, and that was that. These were observed from a few feet and matched with No. 12 Blue Duns, or Blue Uprights, or even an Adams. These flies always caught a few fish but I could cast over dozens, sometimes hundreds, of rises each day without barbing but a handful of fish.

One day I got adventurous and took a closer look at the insect. It was quite a surprise: the closer I looked at the blue dun the browner it got. Up close, at about the range a trout takes aim and strikes, it was dark slate-brown. I flipped the dun over to look at the same underside from which a trout makes its murdering approach, and found that I was imitating a tannish- olive belly with a muskrat-bodied fly.

Great improvement in my spring fishing attended this discovery. Similar close observation has helped elsewhere, and many blue duns have gone up in tan, olive, and brown smoke. But I still knocked on a lot of unanswered doors in my spring lake fishing, so I looked a little further.

A stomach sample was the next step. I killed a fish, sliced it open, and squeezed its stomach contents into a round white jar lid. After a few seconds of stirring, the mix started to separate, and another startling fact about this blue dun hatch became clear: the fish, though appearing to feed exclusively on hatching duns, were in fact feeding predominantly on nymphs.

A little knowledge of insects can go a long way. I learned the blue dun was a *Callibaetis* mayfly, which placed the nymph in the swimmer category, and meant its emergence required a long, lonely swim from the bottom of the lake to the top. Those planted fish, in the lake about a month, already knew it was more profitable to ambush ascendants than to cruise with eyes only for duns, already hatched and poised for flight on the surface above.

There still are times when the hatch is strong, and enough fish feed on the surface, to keep me fishing with dry flies. This is true especially on windy or wet days when duns have a hard time getting off the water. Trout take them consistently then. When fish are rising sporadically during a good hatch, however, I know that a Gold Ribbed Hare's Ear nymph fished under the surface will get down to interfere with the greater activity taking place below.

With all this knowledge about *Callibaetis* hatches I felt well armed to attack the lakes in spring. But if the truth were wrung out of me, I would still have been forced to admit that a lot of fish rose without paying any attention to my flies. The blue dun that turned brown was not the answer to all of my lost lake problems.

The next piece of the puzzle did not fit into place quickly or easily. It was probably delayed by complacence; my luck was a lot better than it had been. But I still missed more fish than I caught.

A hint came one day when a breeze piled a skiff of wind drift against the log from which I fished. Wind drift can include a record of what has hatched all day on any lake. I get snoopy whenever I see it. I got down on my hands and knees to take a closer look. Among the usual leaves and twigs and bits of bark were a lot of cast shucks from the immature stages of insects. The few *Callibaetis* shucks did not surprise me. The greatest number, however, were midge shucks. Midge is the common name for insects of the family Chironomidae, and in that sense these were midges. The term is also used for any tiny insect or fly pattern. In that respect these were not midges at all: they would be matched with flies tied on No. 12 hooks.

These shucks explained a certain number of mysterious rises that took place every year when no insect activity was apparent on the surface. I managed to catch a fish, and took another stomach sample. It contained two midge pupae, similar to the shucks, but with the insects still alive inside their cuticles. This was not overwhelming evidence that midges were the exclusive diet, but it was enough to indicate they were acceptable to the trout. It also gave me the size, form and color of the natural, for here I was holding in my hand two that had just been taken by a trout. Most importantly, it told me the stage on which the fish fed.

The fish took pupae, and the pupae were long, slender, and black. Armed with these facts, at home, I sat down to a tying table, and created all sorts of experimental patterns, based on different approaches to imitation. All worked a little; none worked well.

My problem was presentation. Midge pupae hang from the surface film momentarily before the adult is able to wriggle free of the pupal cuticle. A successful imitation would also have to suspend itself from the surface film. It is not enough to copy exactly the size, form, and color of the insect, because it is impossible to suspend a fly that is as slender as the natural. The hook is too heavy; the fly sinks below the zone in which fish expect to find it.

That is the way it stands right now. I tried several new patterns this spring. I ran out of midge hatches before I devised a consistent dressing. But I know the problem now, and sometimes it is more fun to have a problem than it is to solve it, so I am in no hurry to solve this one. I will work on it again next spring.

Trout planted in lakes put on weight all summer. I am usually fishing elsewhere in the warm mid-summer months, and pay my lost lakes scant attention. I get on them enough to know they are difficult in summer, especially on hot lazy days in late July and August, and to know that they present a whole new set of problems then. There are different aquatic hatches. There is a fall of flying ants that has completely frustrated my slight attempts to match it.

When nights turn chilly and water temperatures drop I start to visit the lakes more often. Fall is better not because fishing is better, but because the fish themselves are better. Those eight to nine inch plants are twelve to thirteen inches long. In lakes with a good crop of crayfish the fish have tiny heads and tiny tails, and look like blimps between. Their meat is firm and bright red. I admit a sincere temptation, often indulged, to save the fish from bitter winter.

Fall presents more unsolved problems. Fortunately the fish grow impatient as rations grow short; they sometimes take anything that looks good to eat. Fall also throws a lot of baffling days at me when the fish refuse to show at all. The more I fish the more I find myself content to not fish when trout are not rising. I know I should string up with a wet tip fine and a wet fly and cast in searching arcs to cover all of the water. I know, when that fails, that I should tie on a nymph and search the water again. Sometimes I do it the way I should. Other times I have patience for only about an hour of such fishing. If that goes unrewarded I am just as happy to prowl around looking for insects, flowers, birds, and all of the etceteras that we tend to overlook when we tend our fishing too closely. Whenever I tramp the lakeside looking for such peripheral pleasures, I keep one eye cocked for rising fish. If the lake is dead, but I expect it to come alive later in the day, there is some chance that I can be caught lying back on a log reading a book.

If fall offers some of the slowest days, for our contemplation, it also offers some of the fastest hours to make up for them.

One evening I was on the road home to Astoria from Portland. I stopped at one of my favorite lost lakes to fish the last hour of daylight. It was the last day of September. A group of deer hunters had already set up camp to do some pre-season scouting in the area. Their abandoned wives and children were tethered to bobbers that rested lifelessly on the quiet surface of the lake. They had, they said, been fishing for hours with no positive results. There were five of them, lined up on a log about seventy-five yards across the lake from the log on which I chose to fish.

There was no activity on the surface other than a rare and distant swirl of a large fish as it cruised the shoreline. I tied on a No. 8 wet Dark Cahill and began to cast, bringing it back with an absentminded wet fly stripping retrieve.

The first retrieve was almost at my feet when a fish yanked. I had the sense to turn things loose instantly, and the fish took off across the surface like a skipped rock. It must have known those frustrated bobberwatchers were gaping, because it headed their way and jumped twice and twice again for their benefit. There was so little light left that I could only see its silhouette in the air; it was as deep-bodied and thick as a bass.

My log was surrounded by submerged limbs, was steep and high sided, and I had no landing net. I led the trout across the surface to it, and stooped to get my hand under the fish, but it slid off the fingers that I cautiously slipped under its belly. It shot away from the log and into the air again. I let it wear itself out, out there, then led it back in and beached it after hopping off the log to the shore behind it. The fish was 15 inches long. It weighed two pounds: remarkarkable progress for a plant. I could hear the fishermen mumbling across the lake, but could not hear what they were saying. I gave them more to mumble about.

Another fish swirled near the log. I presented the wet fly into its rise-rings, and it was on before I could get the slack out of my line. This fish and its fight were mates to the first, I laid it alongside its fellow after about ten minutes.

In the next half hour I hooked five more, but my luck ran out with the light and I only landed two of them. These I released. The bait fishermen had abandoned their log in disgust by the time I lost my fly and could not see to tie on a new one.

When I cleaned the fish I checked their stomachs to see what had moved them to my fly, beyond plain hunger. Both were stuffed with crayfish from one-half inch to three inches long. Hunger was not their problem. Each also contained two or three dragonfly nymphs. These dragonfly nymphs were one-half to three-quarters of an inch long. slender, and dark grayish- brown. When I laid the Cahill next to them it was easy to see why the fish were eager to have it: the fly was exactly the size of the dragonfly nymphs. The color was the same. These nymphs take water into an anal cavity and expel it to jet themselves forward in three to four inch darts: Even my stripping retrieve was perfect.

Thinking that I had all of the answers to my fall problems, I returned with the Cahill a few days later. Fish were rising to take flying termites which descended winkingly in the sunlight from the hemlock trees, in confusing numbers, to the lake below. I had no flies to match them. The fish, conditioned by six months of lake living since their release from a tank, refused to accept anything that did not look exactly like a termite.

Now I have a lake problem for spring of next year: the midge pupa pattern that must float suspended from the surface film rather than sink through it or float on top of it. And I have a lake problem for fall: those evening termite flights. Solving problems is the cornerstone of a curious angler's happiness. I am curious. It looks like I will go back to my lost lakes next year with plenty of problems to be happy about.

Part Two: Northwest Tradition

I n the following pages are the writers who, taken as a group, shaped the history of sports angling literature in the Pacific Northwest. They are presented in chronological order.

There was, of course, a long tradition of orally told fishing stories during the thousands of years of Native American settlement in the Northwest. Such tales, found in books like Jarold Ramsey's *Coyote Was Going There* and Elizabeth D. Jacobs' *Nehalem Tillamook Tales*, reveal a close kinship between native peoples and Northwest plants and animals, especially the great runs of salmon which coursed through Northwest rivers. Fishing in the Northwest Indian culture was not a sport but a communal act of subsistence, invested with spiritual meaning.

Written literature on fishing, especially recreational angling, did not appear until a relatively late period of European-American settlement. The earliest stories and essays about angling for sport included here were written by famous visitors, on vacation. One of the first of these was the legendary Rudyard Kipling, making a fast-paced trip though the Pacific Northwest in 1889, on his way back to England from India. Kipling was a tourist just passing through, but as a writer, a keen fisherman, and an Englishman well-steeped in the sporting tradition of his native country, he treated fishing as an experience worth telling about in print. His fishing adventure on a river just outside Portland, featured in his book, *American Notes*, marked a regional turning-point from fishing for subsistence, or as an early commercial venture for white entrepreneurs, to fishing as a literary subject in the Northwest.

Zane Grey was another famous tourist-fisherman in the Northwest, a kind of American version of the English sporting gentleman. By the time he began fishing Northwest rivers in the late teens of the twentieth century, he was already a world-famous writer whose book sales would number over forty million. He fished in Washington and Oregon through the 1920s and 1930s, particularly on the Rogue and Umpqua rivers. With his fame and his entourage of servants, followers, and friends, he was always something of a bizarre presence, often resented by locals, so the story goes, for his practice of stationing a hireling in the pre-dawn darkness at his choice fishing spot to ward off any other would-be anglers, until he arrived to begin fishing at a gentlemanly hour.

After the famous tourists, Portlander Ben Hur Lampman began turning Northwesterners' eyes to the pleasures of nearby nature and fishing in his *Oregonian* essays and stories. Then there was Roderick Haig-Brown, who came in the late 1920s to the Northwest from England as a young man to fish, work in the woods, and otherwise scratch out a living while escaping the social restrictions which had chafed him at home. Haig-Brown was to crown the tradition of fishing writers deeply connected to the Northwest. He married, raised a family, and made a permanent home on Vancouver Island's Campbell River. He was eventually to author over thirty books, most of them centered upon Northwest angling.

Haig-Brown, Ben Hur Lampman, and all of the writers who follow them in this section of the book were either Northwest-born or were long-time residents of the region. They wrote from a sense of place formed by long associations. They knew the native plants and animals. They knew the weather and the waters and the fish. They had the country in their bones, and the fishing and the country were, for them, part of the same thing.

Rudyard Kipling

Every reader knows some poem or story by Rudyard Kipling (1865-1936), one of England's most famous writers. Kipling is the acknowledged great interpreter of British imperialism at the close of the nineteenth century, and the first English writer to win the Nobel Prize for literature. He also lived and wrote in Brattleboro, Vermont, for several years, and published *Captains Courageous*, which was concerned with the American scene.

Kipling made a whirlwind visit to the Pacific Northwest in 1889, part of a several-month journey across America described in a collection of his newspaper articles, *American Notes*. During his swing through the Northwest, he fished for salmon on the Clackamas River near Portland, with exciting results.

Salmon on the Clackamas

"The race is neither to the swift nor the battle to the
strong; but time and chance cometh to all."

1 have lived!
The American Continent may now sink under the sea, for I
have taken the best that it yields, and the best was neither
dollars, love, nor real estate.

Hear now, gentlemen of the Punjab Fishing Club, who whip the
reaches of the Tavi, and you who painfully import trout to
Ootacamund, and I will tell you how "old man California" and I
went fishing, and you shall envy....

We reached Portland, California and I , crying for salmon, and
the real-estate man, to whom we had been instructed by "Portland"
the insurance man, met us in the street saying that fifteen miles
away, across country, we should come upon a place called Clackamas
where we might perchance find what we desired. And California,
his coat-tails flying in the wind, ran to a livery stable and chartered
a wagon and team forthwith. I could push the wagon about with
one hand, so light was its structure. The team was purely American—
that is to say, almost human in its intelligence and docility. Some
one said that the roads were not good on the way to Clackamas
and warned us against smashing the springs. "Portland," who had
watched the preparations, finally reckoned "he'd come along too,"
and under heavenly skies we three companions of a day set forth;
California carefully lashing our rods into the carriage, and the
bystanders overwhelming us with directions as to the sawmills we
were to pass, the ferries we were to cross, and the sign- posts we
were to seek signs from. Half a mile from this city of fifty thousand
souls we struck (and this must be taken literally) a plank-road that
would have been a disgrace to an Irish village.

Then six miles of macadamized road showed us that the team could move. A railway ran between us and the banks of the Willamette, and another above us through the mountains. All the land was dotted with small townships, and the roads were full of farmers in their town wagons, bunches of tow-haired, boggle-eyed urchins sitting in the hay behind. The men generally looked like loafers, but their women were all well dressed. Brown hussar-braiding on a tailor-made jacket does not, however, consort with hay-wagons. Then we struck into the woods along what California called a *"camina reale,"*—a good road,—and Portland a "fair track." It wound in and out among fire-blackened stumps, under pine trees, along the corners of log-fences, through hollows which must be hopeless marsh in the winter, and up absurd gradients. But nowhere throughout its length did I see any evidence of road-making. There was a track,—you couldn't well get off it,—and it was all you could do to stay on it. The dust lay a foot thick in the blind ruts, and under the dust we found bits of planking and bundles of brushwood that sent the wagon bounding into the air. Sometimes we crashed through bracken; anon where the blackberries grew rankest we found a lonely little cemetery, the wooden rails all awry, and the pitiful stumpy headstones nodding drunkenly at the soft green mulleins. Then with oaths and the sound of rent underwood a yoke of mighty bulls would swing down a "skid" road, hauling a forty-foot log along a rudely made slide. A valley full of wheat and cherry trees succeeded, and halting at a house we bought ten pound weight of luscious black cherries for something less than a rupee and got a drink of icy-cold water for nothing, while the untended team browsed sagaciously by the roadside. Once we found a wayside camp of horse-dealers lounging by a pool, ready for a sale or a swap, and once two sun-tanned youngsters shot down a hill on Indian ponies, their full creels banging from the high-pommeled saddles. They had been fishing, and were our brethren therefore. We shouted aloud in chorus to scare a wild-cat; we squabbled over the reasons that had led a snake to cross a road; we heaved bits of bark at a venturesome chipmunk, who was really the little gray squirrel of India and had come to call on me; we lost our way and got the wagon so beautifully fixed on a steep road that we had to tie the two hind-wheels to get it down. Above all, California told tales of Nevada and Arizona, of lonely nights spent out prospecting, of the slaughter of deer and the chase of men, of woman, lovely woman, who is a firebrand in a Western city and leads to the popping of pistols and of the sudden changes and chances of Fortune, who delights in making the miner or the lumberman a quadruplicate millionaire, and in busting the railroad king. That was a day to be remembered, and it had only begun when we drew rein at a tiny farmhouse on the banks of the Clackamas and sought horse-feed and lodging ere we hastened to the river that broke over a weir not a quarter of a mile away.

Imagine a stream seventy yards broad divided by a pebbly island, running over seductive riffles and swirling into deep, quiet pools where the good salmon goes to smoke his pipe after meals. Set such a stream amid fields of breast-high crops surrounded by hills of pine, throw in where you please quiet water, log-fenced meadows, and a hundred-foot bluff just to keep the scenery from growing too monotonous, and you will get some faint notion of the Clackamas.

Portland had no rod. He held the gaff and the whisky. California sniffed, upstream and downstream across the racing water, chose his ground, and let the gaudy spoon drop in the tail of a riffle. I was getting my rod together when I heard the joyous shriek of the reel and the yells of California, and three feet of silver leaped into the air far across the water. The forces were engaged. The salmon tore up stream, the tense line cutting the water like a tide-rip behind him, and the light bamboo bowed to breaking. What happened after I cannot tell. California swore and prayed, and Portland shouted advice, and I did all three for what appeared to be half a day, but was in reality a little over a quarter of an hour, and sullenly our fish came home with spurts of temper, dashes head-on, and sarabands in the air; but home to the bank came he, and the remorseless reel gathered up the thread of his life inch by inch. We landed him in a little bay, and the spring weight checked at eleven and a half pounds. Eleven and one half pounds of fighting salmon! We danced a war-dance on the pebbles, and California caught me round the waist in a hug that went near to breaking my ribs while he shouted: "Partner! Partner! This is glory! Now you catch your fish! Twenty-four years I've waited for this!"

I went into that icy-cold river and made my cast just above a weir, and all but foul-hooked a blue and black water-snake with a coral mouth who coiled herself on a stone and hissed maledictions.

The next cast—ah, the pride of it, the regal splendor of it! the thrill that ran down from finger-tip to toe! The water boiled. He broke for the fly and got it! There remained enough sense in me to give him all he wanted when he jumped not once but twenty times before the upstream flight that ran my line out to the last half-dozen turns, and I saw the nickled reel-bar glitter under the thinning green coils. My thumb was burned deep when I strove to stopper the line, but I did not feel it till later, for my soul was out in the dancing water praying for him to turn ere he took my tackle away. The prayer was heard. As I bowed back, the butt of the rod on my left hip-bone and the top joint dipping like unto a weeping willow, he turned, and I accepted each inch of slack that I could by any means get in as a favor from on High. There be several sorts of success in this world that taste well in the moment of enjoyment, but I question whether the stealthy theft of line from an able-bodied salmon who knows exactly what you are doing and why you are doing it is not sweeter than any other victory within human scope. Like California's fish, he ran at me head-on and leaped against the line, but the Lord gave me two hundred and fifty pairs of fingers in that hour. The banks and the pine trees danced dizzily round me, but I only reeled—reeled as for life—reeled for hours, and at the end of the reeling continued to give him the butt while he sulked in a pool. California was farther up the reach, and with the corner of my eye I could see him casting with long casts and much skill. Then he struck, and my fish broke for the weir at the same instant, and down the reach we came, California and I; reel answering reel, even as the morning stars sung together.

The first wild enthusiasm of capture had died away. We were both at work now in deadly earnest to prevent the lines fouling, to stall off a downstream rush for deep water just above the weir, and at the same time to get the fish into the shallow bay downstream that gave the best practicable landing. Portland bade us both be of good heart, and volunteered to take the rod from my hands. I would rather have died among the pebbles than surrender my right to play and land my first salmon, weight unknown, on an eight-ounce rod. I heard California, at my ear it seemed, gasping: "He's a fighter from Fightersville, sure!" as his fish made a fresh break across the stream. I saw Portland fall off a log fence, break the overhanging bank, and clatter down to the pebbles, all sand and landing-net, and I dropped on a log to rest for a moment. As I drew breath the weary hands slackened their hold, and I forgot to give him the butt. A wild scutter in the water, a plunge and a break for the headwaters of the Clackamas was my reward, and the hot toil of reeling-in with one eye under the water and the other on the top joint of the rod, was renewed.. Worst of all, I was blocking California's path to the little landingbay aforesaid, and he had to halt and tire his prize where he was. "The Father of all Salmon!" he shouted. "For the love of Heaven, get your *trout* to bank, Johnny Bull." But I could no more. Even the insult failed to move me. The rest of the game was with the salmon. He suffered himself to be drawn, skipping with pretended delight at getting to the haven where I would fain have him. Yet no sooner did he feel shoal water under his ponderous belly than he backed like a torpedo-boat, and the snarl of the reel told me that my labor was in vain. A dozen times at least this happened ere the line hinted he had given up that battle and would be towed in. He was towed. The landing-net was useless for one of his size, and I would not have him gaffed. I stepped into the shallows and heaved him out with a respectful hand under the gill, for which kindness he battered me about the legs with his tail, and I felt the strength of him and was proud. California had taken my place in the shallows, his fish hard held. I was up the bank lying full length on the sweet-scented grass, and gasping in company with my first salmon caught, played and landed on an eight-ounce rod. My hands were cut and bleeding. I was dripping with sweat, spangled like harlequin with scales, wet from the waist down, nose peeled by the sun, but utterly, supremely, and consummately happy. He, the beauty, the darling, the daisy, my Salmon Bahadur, weighed twelve pounds, and I had been seven and thirty minutes bringing him to bank! He had been lightly hooked on the angle of the right jaw, and the hook had not wearied him. That hour I sat among princes and crowned heads—greater than them all. Below the bank we heard California scuffling with his salmon, and swearing Spanish oaths. Portland and I assisted at the capture, and the fish dragged the spring-balance out by the roots. It was only constructed to weigh up to fifteen pounds. We stretched the three fish on the grass, —the eleven and a half, the twelve, and the fifteen pounder,—and we swore an oath that all who came after should merely be weighed and put back again.

How shall I tell the glories of that day so that you may be interested? Again and again did California and I prance down that reach to the little bay, each with a salmon in tow, and land him in the shallows. Then Portland took my rod, and caught some ten-pounders, and my spoon was carried away by an unknown leviathan. Each fish, for the merits of the three that had died so gamely, was hastily hooked on the balance and flung back, Portland recording the weight in a pocket-book, for he was a real-estate man. Each fish fought for all he was worth, and none more savagely than the smallest—a game little six-pounder. At the end of six hours we added up the list. Total: sixteen fish, aggregate weight 142 lbs. The score in detail runs something like this—it is only interesting to those concerned: 15, $11^1/2$, 12, 10, $9^3/4$, 8, and so forth; as I have said, nothing under six pounds, and three ten-pounders.

Very solemnly and thankfully we put up our rods—it was glory enough for all time ...

Zane Grey

"My father was sure I would come to some bad end because I loved to fish,"
recalled Zane Grey (1872-1939). Grey became the twentieth century's
archetypal writer of westerns, with worldwide sales of his novels estimated at
over forty million. But he never lost his love for fishing. He frequently visited
Oregon's Umpqua and Rogue rivers, and had a cabin at Winkle
Bar on the Rogue. He also wrote nine fishing books,
including *Tales of Fresh-Water Fishing*, in which the following
chapter appears. Here Grey fishes for steelhead on a hard-to-
reach Deer Creek, a tributary of the Stillaguamish River, north of Seattle. A
few years later, a young Roderick Haig-Brown, recently arrived from England
and working in a logging camp near Deer Creek, would fish the same stream
and write about it in the opening chapter of *A River Never Sleeps*.

Deer Creek, Washington—1918

Two unlucky and futile trips after the famous and illusive steelhead trout had in no wise dampened R.C.'s ambition nor Lone Angler's infallible optimism nor my unquenchable ardor. Indeed I fear I have inoculated my comrades with the peculiar fever in my blood that makes me long for the unattainable. How often I find myself realizing more and more that though to catch fish is the motive of angling, it is not the all! The unattainable is not the fish. It is that beauty and spirit and life which Tagore felt when he saw the leaping fish of the Ganges River. It is what Hudson felt when he took his long, lonely, apparently objectless rides on the desert of Patagonia.

In August on our way to Vancouver we found ourselves in Seattle, with a week to devote to steelhead trout. Upon inquiring we learned that the run of steelhead was over. The recent rain was just what the fish had been waiting for. With the freshets the steelhead had gone up to the headwaters of the streams.

From several of the fishing-tackle dealers, who kindly lent us all the assistance in their power, we got vague information about the wonderful steelhead fishing in Deer Creek. Not one of them, however, had been there. They showed us Deer Creek on the map and claimed that it was almost inaccessible. But if we could get there!

R. C. and Lone Angler and I spent two days running that Deer Creek legend to earth. At length we met the best two steelhead anglers in Seattle—Hiller and Van Tassel. They vouched for the marvelous fishing we might find in Deer Creek—if we could get there. Neither of these fishermen had ever been near it. But one of their favorite steelhead pools was in the Stillaguamish at the mouth of Deer Creek. Just recently that pool had been full of steelhead. When the rains came and the creek rose these fish disappeared.

They had gone up the creek. This was logical, and I began to yield to my old weakness for pioneering.

Van Tassel rounded up an old G. A. R. man who fished Deer Creek and never went any other place. He showed us photographs of a mess of steelhead that made R. C. gasp, Lone Angler look queer, and me dizzy. Seventeen pounds, the smallest! Tackle-smashers! You had to have a heavy rod, line, leader, and hook to hold those Deer Creek fish. The water was deep, swift, full of rocks. In fact the old gentleman emphasized how full of rocks and fish this creek was. In about ten minutes he had us three musketeers in a state of mental aberration. Finally the practical Lone Angler asked how to get to Deer Creek.

"Wal, I ain't been thar for two years," replied our informant. "I'm gittin' too old to walk—an' you can't go any other way. Thar ain't no trail, nuther. What's wuss, them Finns have took to dynamitin' the creek."

This was like dashing a bucket of cold water in our eager faces. We thanked the old angler and repaired to a spot of seclusion where we could confer on the matter.

"Same old gag!" muttered R. C., darkly and regretfully.

"Bum steer!" added Lone Angler, tersely.

Both my comrades were for discarding the Deer Creek idea as a myth. But I was loath to give it up.

"Nothing ventured, nothing gained!" was my argument. "We miss our goal many times, but now and then we do hit it."

So again, as often before, I prevailed against the better judgment of my trail partners. Moreover, they became imbued with my enthusiasm. Over the range, far away, was something calling. We decided to motor to McMurray, a lumbering town somewhere near the headwaters of Deer Creek, and there see if we could not find some one to guide us.

Our acquaintances, Van Tassel and Hiller, were enthusiastic over this project, but they prevailed upon us to go fishing with them first. Arlington, where they wanted to take us, was on the road to McMurray.

So next morning we rode fifty miles to Arlington through country most of which was a hideous black slash left by lumbermen.

Before dawn the next morning we were on our way to the Stillaguamish River. Day broke, the sun came up, and our road led toward a great gap in a magnificent mountain range. It was a relief to get by the deforested areas and see something of Washington's thick and verdant forests. Before six o'clock we reached the Stillaguamish, a limpid little river, rushing and placid by turns. And the pool they selected to try lay at the mouth of Deer Creek.

It developed that these experts had a singular method of bait fishing. They used rather heavy fly rods with enameled silk lines, the same as those used for fly-casting; a short heavy gut leader, transparent in the water; a sinker that would roll on the bottom with the current; and very small hooks. For bait a small ball of fresh salmon eggs that hid the hook was essential. They strapped a wire or canvas basket, large as a small dishpan, to their waists. And from this strap depended also a bait box, and a long rag to do service as a towel. I was soon to learn what a mess salmon eggs make on the hands.

The use of the basket was unique. I was indeed curious about it. Van Tassel waded knee-deep into the water, put on a bait, and stripping off the reel a goodly length of line, which fell in coils into the basket, he gave his rod a long side sweep and flip and sent that bait clear across the stream. It was an admirable performance, and far from easy, as we anglers soon learned. After considerable practice I learned to master about sixty or seventy feet, which was half of Van Tassel's cast. Mostly I threw the bait off.

We fished, and our instructors fished, but not a steelhead did we raise. The fish must have left the river for the creek. We returned to Arlington, and had breakfast at noon, and afterward we drove about ten miles to McMurray. There was one street, rather forlorn and deserted; and a beautiful lake; a huge sawmill belching smoke; and all around hills denuded of trees, stark and bare.

After considerable inquiry we located a fellow named Sam Arnold. It was he who had taken the old G. A. R. angler to Deer Creek. Then we were to learn that no one else had ever fished this stream, that it was full of big rainbows and steelhead, that the distance was eleven miles over a bad trail up and down through forest.

"All right. We don't care how hard it is to get there or what it costs," I said, concisely. "We are going. Will you take us?"

It developed that scarcely a month had elapsed since Arnold had been operated upon for appendicitis, and he felt that he was hardly strong enough to undertake the trip. Furthermore, there was absolutely no one else whom we could discover that knew how to get to Deer Creek. It appeared we had come to an impasse. R. C. and Lone Angler made facetious remarks. If there was no one to take us we could not go—that was all there was to it. But I was thinking. Not for an instant did I abandon my idea of going. Deer Creek had become a haunting, compelling obstacle to overcome. Finally I suggested that he take charge of our little expedition and not do any of the work himself.

"You can ride and get some men to do the packing," I concluded.

"Ride! Say, friend, there are no horses or mules in this country. If you go to Deer Creek you'll have to walk and pack your own outfit on your back."

R. C. and Lone Angler hailed this information with ill-concealed delight. It nettled me a little. Apparently it pleased them when I encountered insurmountable difficulties.

"Very well, we will walk," I replied, without the slightest hesitation. "Arnold, will you take us?"

"Guess I'll have to, seein' your heart's so set on it," he replied, with a smile I liked. "How long will you want to stay?"

"Only a few days—a week at most. We'll go light as possible. I'll give you money to buy supplies. We'll get a tent and blankets at Arlington, and be back here tomorrow morning."

"Better make it about one o'clock," he replied. "We'll ride on the lumber train to the loggin' camp. That'll save a couple of miles. An' mebbe we can hire some lumberjacks to help pack the outfit in to Deer Creek."

So then and there it was settled, and we departed. My genial and effusive comrades could not fool me. Another wild-goose chase had I planned. Maybe! But despite their laments and misgivings I knew that deep down in their hearts, where the boy still lived, they were excited and thrilled. It could not have been otherwise.

Next day at noon we arrived at McMurray with as little equipment as we could persuade ourselves was absolutely necessary. We brought no tent because there was none at Arlington, and only a few blankets which a kindly merchant lent us. Van Tassel came with us.

Arnold was on hand to meet us, having with him four boys to pack the outfit. One of these was a sturdy fellow who carried an Alaskan pack-board to sling on his back. He had packed his own outfit over Chilcoot Pass.

While waiting for the lumber train we talked somewhat of the difficulties of getting to Deer Creek, but mostly of the alluring possibilities. It is that unknown element of chance, of adventure, of luck that makes wild expeditions so thrilling.

When I saw the lumber train I wondered where we would ride. The cars were merely frames on trucks, with huge iron spikes to hold the logs. It did not look at all safe. Lone Angler reversed his familiar speech. "We got here first, but I wish it'd been last and we'd missed this Pullman."

The train was long, and the longer it grew the more my doubts augmented. There was a caboose, however, and we threw our baggage into it and climbed aboard. Several other passengers were bound for the logging camp. This camp was about seven miles away, but we had to travel twice that distance to get there.

The moment I climbed aboard I knew things were going to happen. They did, and they began at once. The engineer of the train knew, of course, that he had some new passengers, and he undoubtedly intended that we should remember the ride. He started off smoothly and evenly. R. C. and I went out on the back platform of the caboose. I was facing the door, looking in, while holding on to the brake wheel with both hands. R. C., too, faced forward, but he did not have hold of anything. He was admiring the scenery. We were leaving McMurray and running rather fast, for a log train, when suddenly the engineer threw on the brakes. The caboose gave a terrific jerk. I thought there was a wreck. Every one inside went plunging head over heels. I saw Lone Angler Wiborn fall from the back end to the front end, and turn upside down in a corner, and drop like a sack of potatoes. Everybody howled. R. C. suffered a catapultic slam against the side of the caboose. His face appeared pasted against the wood, and as he drew it away, in rage and pain, I saw a big bruise appear high on his cheek. Then he furiously arraigned me for leading him on this log train. Really, the way some people's minds work is beyond comprehension. As it turned out, R.C.'s hurt could not be compared with Wiborn's, and with those of others inside the caboose.

The next happening was the advent of a loquacious brakeman who related hair-breadth escapes of the train crew while on duty. Never took a round trip without jumping the track, ditching a car, or piling up logs!

"Aw, we don't mind shake-ups, onless when we're crossin' trestles," he averred, nonchalantly. "Some of them trestles is high an' on curves."

The first trestle was bad enough for me. It was long and on a curve, and it rattled and creaked and shook under the log train. If it did this under an empty train what would it do under a loaded one? I could only conjecture. My Deer Creek enterprise began to lose something of its allurement. We passed over the lowlands, and climbed the foothills, and then began to cross trestles, some of which spanned the heads of canyons over a hundred feet deep. I saw deep cuts on the railroad ties and woodwork where cars had run off the track. Moreover, these high trestles wabbled so that my hair started to rise stiff on my head.

About half a dozen miles up in these foothills the sixth car in front of the caboose jumped the track. What a fearful lurch it gave us! The engineer stopped the train in less than a car-length. Dust rose in a cloud. We all climbed down to find the rear wheels of the derailed car two feet off the track.

"Huh! We started out on a walking tour and I reckon we'll walk back to McMurray," grunted R. C.

But it turned out presently that such accidents were trivial to the resourceful train crew. They placed a heavy triangular piece of iron against the wheels, and then the engineer, starting slowly ahead, pulled the dislodged car back on the track. The operation did not consume five minutes. We rode on without further mishap, around the slopes of denuded hills, and eventually arrived at the logging camp.

A great black and brown slash in the forest, a hideous clearing of stumps and burned tree trunks, surrounded a number of buildings, large and small, all constructed of new yellow lumber. Railroad tracks ran here and there. This logging camp was owned and operated by an English company, and we were told that it was a model up-to-date camp in every particular. Verily it did appear so. Store, restaurant, billiard hall, reading room, mess house, bunk houses, all were spick and span. These lumberjacks had a chef, electric lights, hot and cold water, a doctor, and all possible conveniences.

While Arnold was endeavoring to hire more men to pack us in to Deer Creek I climbed an adjacent hill where the lumbering was in progress. There were several crews of men at work in that vicinity. I saw an engine they called the "donkey," mounted upon a huge log sled, pull itself through the forest, over logs and stumps. I saw another in actual operation. By means of a thick wire cable this engine pulled huge logs eight feet thick and a hundred long fully a quarter of a mile uphill, to load them on the steel-spiked trucks. What they called the spar tree was most interesting of all to me. It was one that dominated a central point on a hill, and had been shorn of branches and top, and braced by wire cables on all sides. The running cable from the "donkey" was attached high up this spar tree on a pulley, and it swung monarchs of the forest with incredible ease. The most astounding feat was to see a lumberjack prepare one of these trees for a spar. He wore long spiked tree-climbers, and he had a rope looped round tree and himself. He gave the loop a hitch upward, and then holding the rope he jammed his spikes into the bark and walked up several steps. Ax and saw dangled below him on a cord. Arriving at the first branch, he leaned back in the loop of the rope, pulled up his ax, and in a few strokes chopped off the branch. Up and up he scaled, cutting branch after branch, and when perhaps two hundred feet from the ground he discarded ax for saw and sawed the tree through at that point. A fifth of the huge cedar fell with a crash. The trunk swayed to and fro under the shock. Yet the lumberjack held his position securely and safely.

Men like this lumberjack and the flag-pole painters on the city skyscrapers and the construction workers of steel buildings are all of the same breed, men, heroic and daring, forgetful of self.

All around me sounded the crash of the falling giants of the woods. In that sound I heard the death knell of the magnificent cedars of Washington, of the towering beautiful firs of Oregon, of the grand redwoods of California. The speed of the juggernaut appalled me.

Upon returning to the water tank where I had left my party I found them almost packed and ready to start. Arnold had succeeded in hiring four lumberjacks to help us. This made ten men, counting

Arnold and my chauffeur. Arnold insisted on carrying a pack. And as for R. C. and Wiborn and myself, we had a load that I grimly realized would grow heavy.

Our guide led off on an old abandoned railroad track that soon left the camp and wound into the forest. All of a sudden I strode out of a ghastly naked blot on the earth, out of the hot glaring sunlight, into what seemed long arched temples of green and amber, dark, shady, cool, and fragrant. The forest primeval! How high the towers of lacy fringed foliage! These cedars were huge, round, straight, smooth-barked, brownish-gray in hue, with branches far aloft.

We left the camp at four o'clock. With all our load we could not tarry and rest, and our guide kept up a good pace. Once Lone Angler remarked: "If that guide hadn't been operated on lately he'd be running through the woods. We're sure lucky."

Half a mile out the railroad ended and we took to a trail. It was one seldom used. For the most part it appeared so covered by the underbrush meeting overhead that we could scarcely see the forest trees, and nothing of the sky. Vines, ferns, flowers, grass, damp and luxuriant, with the fragrance of the forest, brushed us softly as we passed. The walking over a soft springy duff was easy, and for a mile or more it was level. Then we began to climb. Soon the trail opened into a forest like a park, and ground, logs, and trees appeared to take on an amber-green cast. Every fallen tree was a long mound of moss, fringed with exquisite tiny ferns. We labored up and down through this forest, and the sunlight began to fail. About six o'clock we descended another heavily wooded slope, and at the foot of it came upon a dark body of water—Cavanaugh Lake.

There was scarcely open space enough for a camp. But as darkness was not far away I thought we had better make a halt. Across the lake a big black mountain loomed up, forbidding in the dusk.

We pitched camp as best we could. There was no dry firewood, and the expected cheerful hour was here comfortless and gloomy. The day had been long and arduous. My comrades were tired and somewhat dejected. My usual spirit seemed ebbing. Sleep seemed the only solution.

We were up at dawn, in the cool dark dampness of the forest, packing before we had breakfast. And when we left that camp the sun was just silvering the fog over the lake. Fresh and rested, we did not feel daunted at the prospect of a six-mile tramp to Deer Creek. But right off we struck an uphill trail, and soon realized what it meant to pack heavy burdens. Our packers rested every quarter of a mile, but we seldom passed them. It took an hour to climb that wooded ridge.

Here we entered a denser forest, and one strikingly beautiful and strange. I looked as I trudged along, although there were many places where the trail led over windfalls and deep narrow gorges spanned by fallen trees, and here I needed my eyes for careful stepping. The great cedars predominated, some of which were apparently ten feet or more thick at the base and towered straight and true so high that I had to crane my neck to see their tips. And then these tips seemed lost in a green spreading canopy pierced by shafts of golden sunlight and flecked with spots of blue sky. Underbrush was scant and very low, in remarkable contrast with the Vancouver forests. The green mantle of moss covered the ground and everything upon it, as completely as a heavy snow might have. Not a speck of bare earth or stone revealed itself to my searching gaze. The trail was like many layers of the softest Persian rugs. It gave forth not the slightest sound. This made walking easy. In some of the huge fallen trees notches had been cut for steps. It was a novel experience to take five or six steps to get over one log. Walking the many logs over narrow gullies and ditches was thrilling, though not conducive to enjoyment. They were slippery with wet moss. The beauty of this forest consisted of gray somber tree trunks rising out of a wonderful dark green, to disappear in a spreading roof of lighter green, pierced by arrows of golden sunshine.

The reason for the strangeness of it, however, did not readily come to me. At last I analyzed it as a solemn dead silence and a total absence of life. Not a sound! Not a stir of leaf or rustle of brush! There was not a bird or a squirrel or an insect, or any living creature to cross my sight or utter sound to hear. Moreover, I could not find a single track in the trail. For that matter, there were but few places where any wild creature would have left tracks. Melancholy, lonely, silent as a grave, this forest began to have a depressing effect on me. What a damp, sodden green maze! I contrasted it most unfavorably with the dry, sweet open pine forests of Arizona, with their golden aspen glades and their flaming maple thickets, where the elk bugled and deer rustled the leaves, and turkeys called, and squirrels and birds chattered all day long.

At the end of two hours of climbing and plodding, packing more than I should have carried, I just about hated that forest. It developed, however, that I had no time for self-indulgence. At a fork in the trail the lumberjacks mutinied. Arnold could not change them. They wanted to quit then and there. By dint of persuasion and offer of extra money I got them to go on.

Soon after that we reached the brow of the mountain and started down. R.C.'s quick ear, keen as an Indian's, first caught the low mellow roar of running water. It came from deep down in that green-choked abyss, and gradually grew stronger. What a relief to start downhill, even if it was steep and falling and sliding seemed the order of travel!

Our guide evidently knew where he was heading, but he certainly got off the trail, if there was one. And he led us down places that filled me with vague distress. How would we ever climb back? But getting out was not yet the issue. Deer Creek sent up a deep roar of rushing waters. That was a spur. As we descended farther into this canyon, the underbrush, mostly maple, grew high and thick, shutting out the light. Windfalls were so intricate and immense that they simply had to be climbed over, and as all this was at an angle of forty-five degrees, our labor and hazard were considerable. Once R. C. slipped and fell into what appeared to be a green hole. I was much concerned and called lustily. No answer! I fell all over myself getting to this place, and looked down. He had slid into a hole under a windfall, and had found an easy exit below. The rascal did not answer me because he wanted me to think he had been killed. And I heard Lone Angler say to him: "Say, what's the Chief bawlin' about? Do you think he's just right in his head?"

At last we descended to a point where, from under the giant cedars, we could look down upon Deer Creek. A beautiful green-and-white stream, shining here, dark and gleaming there, wound through a steep-walled canyon. It was worth working for. What struck me at once was the wonderful transparency of the water and the multitude of boulders, some of them huge.

Here everyone except myself appeared to want to rest. The men wiped their moist red faces. Arnold, however, looked pale, despite his smile, and I feared he had overexerted himself.

"Deer Creek, all right," he said, "an' I just saw a jack-salmon going up the shallows. But the water looks pretty low—too low. This has been the dryest season for years."

"We got here first and no low water is going to queer us," averred Lone Angler.

"What bothers me, now we're here, is how'n h— we'll ever get out," replied the realistic, romance-killing R. C.

"Sufficient unto the day is the trouble thereof!" I exclaimed. "Let's get down to the creek, and across somehow."

The last descent into the bed of that canyon was performed with considerable rapidity and ease—we ran down a mossy incline, slid down a steep gravel bank, and fell the rest of the way in soft clay. Then we walked down to the rocks, and unpacking our rubber boots we waded after the men across to a sandy level on the opposite side. I paid the lumberjacks and dismissed them. Arnold and his boys I kept to do our camp work and help us get back. I calculated we would have considerably less to pack back, and in case we could not take all the outfit these boys could make another trip in. Indeed, I gave scant thought to our return trip. We were here on Deer Creek. Van Tassel, however, seemed immensely disappointed in Deer Creek. It was too low and the steelhead were not there. Incongruous indeed it seemed that this little creek could be full of big fish. But I refused to entertain any other idea.

We made camp with our limited outfit, as best we could, and then while the men busied themselves cooking a meal we anglers rigged up our tackles. Van Tassel found that the salmon eggs we had packed for bait had grown stale, and to him this appeared a grievous misfortune.

Right above camp there was a riffle and below that a deep pool. Arnold informed us he had seen fish in it, but could not be certain they were steelhead. R. C. fished it carefully, after our method of trout fishing, without getting a strike. Van Tassel had no better luck. Lone Angler slipped off up the creek by himself, and I went downstream. Pools appeared to be scarce. Half a mile below camp I came upon a jumble of immense boulders, some as large as houses, that blocked the whole canyon bed, and through the labyrinthine passages the creek foamed and eddied and babbled in a most bewildering network of waterways. I climbed up on boulders, and leaped fissures, and leisurely clambered this way and that, dropping my bait in likely places. Small trout took my bait off persistently, but that was all I had in the way of bites. I sat on one huge rock and then on another, content, absorbed in the music of the stream, the strange conformations of the smooth boulders, the color and current of the water, the sense of the overshadowing mighty cedars. Deer Creek was the most beautiful trout water I had ever seen. Clear as crystal, cold as ice, it spoke eloquently of the pure springs of the mountain fastnesses. Under the water the rocks were amber- colored, and along the banks they were green with moss and gray with lichen.

Van Tassel passed along the bank and worked on down the creek out of sight. In an hour or so he came back carrying a six-pound salmon. He had not seen a steelhead nor had a strike from one, and considered the fact most damaging to our hopes. He had found one large pool where steelhead should have been if they were anywhere in Deer Creek. We returned to camp. R. C. reported only numerous small trout. We hoped for better from Lone Angler. But about sunset, when we were ready for supper, he returned without a fish.

"Saw some thundering big fish up above. Wonderful pools up there," he said. "But I couldn't get a strike or class the fish."

"Reckon they're salmon an' steelhead," said Arnold. "You see, the creek is low an' these big fish are wary. They have enemies. You must keep out of sight. Every pool ought to give you one strike a day. Mornin' is best. You'll ketch some steelhead an' hook some big ones.'"

His assurance was cheering and satisfying, and I replied that we were not difficult to please. A little went a long way with us.

After supper I was tired, and enjoyed a rest. Likewise did Wiborn. But R. C. took his rod and slipped off downstream to the pool just above the jumble of huge boulders. A big cedar tree had fallen across the creek and lay a few feet above the water. The current had cut a deep long narrow hole close to the right bank, and it shoaled gradually almost to where the tree crossed. I had fished it and remarked what a likely place it looked.

Presently we were all roused by a ringing yell from R. C. Jumping up, I looked to see him hanging on to a bent wagging rod. We all started to run to see the fun, and I, having on light rubber shoes, made better time over the boulder-strewn shore. I reached the fallen tree and, leaping upon it, ran out over the shoal water.

"What—you—got?" I queried, out of breath, as I looked at R. C.

He stood over to my left, nearly fifty yards, and judging from his face and the way he was working that tackle I anticipated much.

"Don't know what he is," he replied, "but I never had a fish nail a bait so hard. He went like a flash, down there. Thought it sure was good night. He's got most of my line, but think he's coming back."

I had seen R. C. reeling frantically, and next I made the astonishing discovery that his line ran right under the log upon which I was standing. Suddenly a fish swam into my sight—a trout—gray-green, and of gamy shape, two feet long. For an instant I did not connect him with R. C. Then I saw the leader curved in front of him. I yelled and waved. The trout shot into deep water out of sight. By this time the rest of our contingent had arrived, to become interested spectators of the fight. I saw the fish twice after that, once when he leaped, and again when he flashed rose and silver at the lower end of the pool. Van Tassel saw him too and assured R. C. that he was a steelhead, and advised very gentle handling. Eventually R. C. led the tired fish out of deep water, through the little channels among the rocks, and slipped him into a safe place where he lay gasping.

Not only was this the first steelhead we had ever captured, but the first we had ever seen. It was a strikingly beautiful fish, graceful, symmetrical, powerfully built, with great broad tail and blunt, pugnacious nose. The faint pinkish color, almost a glow, shone from a background of silver and green.

R. C. was very proud of his first steelhead. "You never could have made me believe he didn't weigh twice four pounds. Some fish!"

Then, wetting his hands, R. C. carefully unhooked the steelhead and gently slipped him back into the stream, which action greatly pleased Lone Angler and myself.

That night round a real camp fire Arnold told us some interesting facts about fish. One of them particularly struck me as worthy of recording.

"Both Chinook salmon an' steelhead have gone up the creek," he said. "I know, because the jack-salmon, the kind Mr. Van caught, always follow them. They eat the salmon eggs. I've watched a big fat salmon spawning in shallow water, an' I've seen a jack ram her— bump her in the side hard an' bust out her eggs. Then that jack would drop back in the current an' eat the eggs. I've seen it done."

The reward of all watchers of the trails and streams is that sometime they see a rare and marvelous phenomenon of nature. All observers do not see the same, for nature is vast and inexhaustibly rich in its strange habits of self- preservation and evolution.

We went to bed, to discover that away from the camp fire the air was full of tiny invisible gnats. They annoyed us, bit severely, but in spite of them we fell asleep and had a restful night. R. C. was the first of us up. He fished the pool in front of camp before he washed his face. While the others were dallying over a bountiful breakfast I made off upstream as fast as I could travel over the slippery rocks.

How cool and fresh and shady and redolent of cedar that deep canyon! How melodious with murmur and gurgle and roar of water! Then the beauty of this Deer Creek and its environment gave me a sense of sheer, wild, exquisite joy.

I passed a number of likely looking pools that I left for my comrades. But presently I came to one that resembled the pool of an angler's dream. Above rushed a narrow fast rapid, white and foamy, and it ended in a deep dark lane between two rocks, and below widened out, and at last shoaled to a sand bar on the left and a shallow channel of rocks on the right.

I kept out of sight, and going round this pool, I came down behind the big rock on my side, and dropped my bait into the swift water. As it sank and floated down I certainly trembled. And scarcely had it gotten beyond the rock when a fish took it with a violent jerk and ran. What a thrill tingled along my veins! The days of my boyhood danced in my very bones. I hooked that fish.

Then came a solid pull, a screech of the reel, and a heavy splash. The fish had leaped behind the rock. As I ran up on this boulder my line was going out so fast that I wished for anything but a fly reel. Besides, there were only forty yards of line.

A dark gleam shot into the shallow water. How swift! Then it changed to a silver flash with glints of red. I saw a big fish swoop up and then come clear out into the air—a steelhead, savage and beautiful, fight in every line of his curved body. Then he plunged back to dart toward me. Slack line! There were yards of it. I could not reel it in, and he ran past me, pulling a bagged line after him, and ran up into the white swift water. Instantly he turned back and ran the length of the pool. But I did not see him then. On his second run upstream, which was slower, I got the line tight and kept it so. He repeated his dash into the swift water and then darted again for the end of the pool. Evidently this time he meant to go down into the rapids below, but he miscalculated and got into the shallow water and over the sand bar.

At this juncture I leaped off the rock and ran along the pool, beyond the shoal Place, and then I had him at a disadvantage. He made surges here and there, stirring up the mud, and splashing like a crippled duck, but when he essayed to cross the bar back into the pool I held him. And so we fought it out there until he was vanquished. I put him on a string before I weighed him. Six and one half pounds! Then I tied the string to a root and let him recover and swim around, as I used to do with sunfish and bass when I was a boy. Van Tassel came along and warmly congratulated me on my good fortune. R. C. and Wiborn next hove in sight, slipping over the boulders, and they had lots to say. We saw a dozen long gray wavering fish shapes deep in the lower end of that pool—big steelhead—but we could not induce them to bite. Then we separated.

I wandered off up the creek, passing on my way the most wonderful pool I ever saw in my life. Heroically I left that for my comrades and departed upstream. In the next mile and a half I found some likely places and saw some fish, but did not have another strike. The water was too low and clear. Perhaps I was gone several hours, and when, on my return, I reached the wonderful pool, my three companions were there, talking across the creek, rods idle, lazily sunning themselves.

"Some whales in here," said R. C. "No good. They won't bite. Come over and look. Make you sick!"

"If we had fresh bait we'd catch one," added Van Tassel, who was on my side of the creek. R. C. and Lone Angler sat perched upon an enormous boulder, fully twenty feet above the pool. I made facetious remarks anent their lack of persistence and skill, and I looked for a place to cross. At the head of this pool ran a wide rapid of white water difficult to ford. I made it just by an inch. Then I scrambled down the shore, and climbed a bank, and labored over a huge pile of driftwood, and at last reached a point where I could jump on to the rock. Joining my comrades, I looked down where they pointed.

Deep in the limpid eddying water I saw many fish shapes, some of them so large as to seem in that comparatively small stream an exaggeration of the sight. But this particular pool could have harbored a swordfish. It held a great deal of water. And these fish were steelhead. I wondered why they would not bite. Then in a sort of helpless exasperated admiration I gazed from fish to pool. What a place for fish!

The enormous boulder projected far out into the pool. Just at the point where I stood it was narrowest, and the water appeared fifteen feet deep, gradually shoaling below, and widening into a broad space full of rocks and channels. But for thirty yards it was the tail end of a quiet pool, and I could see the amber bottom and little trout with startling clearness. In front where the steelhead lay the deep part began and ran up into the other half of the pool, black and swirling, with rock-lined banks, constricting to the swift water where I had crossed. What futile and thrilling conjecture as to how many fish lay unseen in that shadowy depth! Overhead towered the giant firs and cedars, so that only at this hour of noon did the sun shine here.

My brain conjured up days and tricks of my boyhood. Surely one of these steelhead could be caught, by hook or crook. R. C. and Lone Angler were talking about Santa Cruz Island, from which the latest mail had brought them news of a run of swordfish. They did not pay any attention to me. And on the other shore Van Tassel appeared asleep.

At the last pool above I had put on a little spinner to try, and it occurred to me now to twist off the small shiny spoon, leaving the tiny triangular gang of three hooks. Above this I slipped on a heavier lead, and then, half in earnest and half to deceive my comrades, I put on a small lump of salmon eggs. Thus equipped I stepped to the brink of the rock and cast out over the shadowy steelhead, and let my lead go to the bottom. My comrades took my move as an insult to their skill.

"Say, what're you going to do?" testily queried R. C.

When I did not vouchsafe any reply Lone Angler spoke up, "We fished this hole."

They both looked at me with lazy supreme scorn. But I paid little heed. I had an idea that, unless I had forgotten the skill of my boyhood, presently something would happen. When I saw the big steelhead paid no attention to my line, I knew positively there would be a startling surprise for my lofty companions.

Very cautiously I drew my line toward me. I could feel the lead dragging on the bottom. I could see my line stretching down and beyond the big steelhead on the outside. I expected to have a little fun, yet instinctively there was more than that in my thrill. You never can tell! Then I jerked hard.

My hooks caught. My rod bent. It quivered. Then suddenly sped upstream and off my reel. The screech of that reel galvanized my comrades. It did more to me. Actually I had hooked that big steelhead. I yelled with the sheer fun of it. The boys sprang up, amazed, open-mouthed, to watch my rod and line. Such a run! That fish took all the line off, and up there in the fast white water he leaped into the air.

R. C. saw that greyhound leap. So did Lone Angler. They yelled lustily. The steelhead looked enormous. As for me, that fierce run, and then the great size of the fish—these were my undoing. From jest I passed to dreadful earnest. A flash of reason crossed my mind— I would get just what I deserved. But that never changed me one whit. I was charged with uttermost longing and determination.

The steelhead hung up in the white water. I thought he had fouled my line. No! I felt the wavering of him to and fro. He had every inch of the line out, and it stretched as tight as a wire. I went to the extreme edge of the rock and extended the rod as far as possible. Suddenly the fish turned and came back, not swiftly, so that I was able to reel in the slack line. Slowly he swam toward me, deep, about in the middle of the channel. He passed the rock, out of the dark water, into plain sight.

"Oh! Oh!" exclaimed R. C. in mingled amaze, consternation, and delight.

"Look at that trout!" added Lone Angler.

I saw, but I could not express my feelings. I felt like a lost man. Retribution had overtaken me! Yet—it was possible to land this fish. He swam easily, then made a run that for sheer speed and vigor completely dazzled me. I thumbed the reel—the line. But he came to the surface and smashed the water white. Then he bored in three feet of water, and knocked his head against the rocks, and scared me stiff. If he kept on downstream all was over! But he came back upstream, holding along the bottom. Slowly he passed out of sight, and steadily my line went up the pool, to its deepest, blackest center, and there it stopped as if snagged.

For a long time he sulked on the bottom, during which I worked all I dared. Next he swam to and fro, and around, up and down, and then ran up into the swift water to hang there as if anchored. He stayed there what seemed a long time. But the steady strain I put on him gradually drew him out of the current. Down he came.

This time he headed for the dark shelving hole under the rock. I saw the dim shapes of snags and sunken logs. How he plugged! But I risked losing him and held hard. The rod bent under the rock in my effort to pull and lead him. There was a bad snag on the surface of the water, lodged against the rock. R. C. tried to climb down to move it while Wiborn went ashore, and by dint of strenuous work they pulled it out of the way.

My fish went down into the shoal place below us, and there in plain sight he swam two feet under the surface. R. C. and I gloated over that sight. He was getting tired. There was indeed a chance of vanquishing him. He swam around directly under us, and then we had our clearest sight of him. How long, thick, heavy! He had shoulders like a bonefish. His back was dark green, covered with black dots. When I pulled hard enough he turned on his side, and that moment was indescribable. Half a foot broad! A wide flare of deep rose color and silver! His fins waved like aspen leaves in a gentle wind. His huge mouth gaped, and then shut.

"What'll—he—weigh?" I panted.

"Twelve pounds—oh, maybe more," replied my brother. "This is awful. But you'll get him."

"Look at him, R. C.," I burst out. "Just look—so you'll never—forget. He'll go all of fifteen pounds. And I'll never hold him."

All this while I heard Van Tassel yelling at me, advice no doubt, but I never distinguished a word. My fish worked around the rock, and up the pool again.

"Can't you get across, on the other side?" queried R. C. "Then you could keep him away from these snags under the rock."

It was fully a ten-foot jump down to a log behind the rock, and more than that to the ground. When the steelhead got well up stream I essayed to go around with him. When Wiborn saw my intention he yelled. "Don't try it. That's how I broke my leg!"

Nevertheless I made the bank in two jumps, holding my rod up in both hands. Then as luck would have it the steelhead took a notion to go back, and this time he went fast. My line went round and over the rock. I had to get back. How I accomplished it I never knew, but I climbed straight up to R.C.'s outstretched hands. The contrary steelhead fooled around, swam back, and suddenly, without giving Wiborn any chance to get ready to photograph a leap, he came up and out, fully six feet into the air, a most prodigious performance, something unequaled in my experience of a beautiful and wonderful sight. But Wiborn was not ready. The steelhead plunged back. I believed that last effort had used him up.

Accordingly, when he headed slowly up the pool toward the swift water I jumped down on to the log, thence to the ground again, and ran over the rocks, reeling as fast as I could; and I all but fell several times.

I passed Wiborn and got even with where the steelhead hung. I could see him in the foamy water, wagging wearily. I leaped from the shore to a submerged rock, and then I was so close over the fish I could have kicked him. My rod described a circle. I plunged in ahead of him and waded in swift water up to my waist across a place I never would have dared in a calm moment. When I got across the boys whooped.

Whereupon I led my fish downstream, through the deep water of the pool, below to the place where the shoal began. Here I got his head under control, and half led, half dragged him into six inches of water. He was almost spent. Lazily he flopped.

"Scoop him out!" yelled R. C. to Van Tassel.

"Yes, yes," I joined in. "Get behind him—pitch him out on the sand."

"Aw no, you'll lose him," replied Van Tassel, in consternation. That was a trying situation for him. He was afraid to take the risk. But I knew as my fish began to slip and work out of that favorable place that we had lost our opportunity.

"Try it again," shouted R. C. "Then hand your rod to Van—and take the chance yourself."

This appeared the best of advice. I attempted it. The steelhead got his head and swam away, very wearily and ponderously. He could just wag his tail. But he was so heavy that I dared not check him entirely. I eased up, let him go a little, then pulled carefully to turn him. More than once I had his head coming round. I reeled in the line he had taken. Slowly he floated, tail toward us, gradually yielding. His broad tail waved. His great mouth gaped. He turned on his side, flashing pink and silver in the sunlight, and just when I realized he was a vanquished fish, most beautiful and desirable in the moment of surrender, the hooks tore out. For another moment he did not realize he was free. Then he righted himself and swam off very slowly, his great shape gradually growing dim, until he vanished in the depths of the pool.

Ben Hur Lampman

Ben Hur Lampman (1886-1954) began his writing as a boy working in his father's print shop in North Dakota. He came west to Gold Hill, Oregon, where he managed a weekly newspaper until 1916, when he moved to the Portland *Oregonian*. He remained on that newspaper's staff for thirty-five years, best known for his essays and stories on fishing and the pleasures of outdoor life. His writings are collected in books like *The Coming of the Pond Fishes, At the End of the Car Line,* and *A Leaf From French Eddy,* from which the following essay is taken.

Almost Time for Trout

There are reasons for this and for that, and we hear much of their openings, but really there is only one season that matters to many men at this time of the year. Looking out of office windows. Driving along in trucks. Handling freight down at the yards. Or walking a beat in the rain. There is one season that is best of all. That, of course, is the trout season, which is to open very soon. It is good to live in a land where there is plenty of trout fishing. You never tire of it, and never does the season open without the old tingling, the old response.

People try to explain it, although this is unnecessary, but nobody ever has been quite able to do so, not even Walton. But most fishermen are agreed there is a quality in trout fishing that approaches the ideal. It is like the pursuit and realization of a pleasing dream. The trout is its symbol of abundant reward. It is something like this: we know, of necessity, that we can never have all to which we aspire, and we realize, too, that the dreams of aspiration have a way of fading, and yielding, until they are gone beyond recovery, and we have but memories of them. Is it sad? No. That isn't it. This is the common experience of mankind. We are reconciled to it, or nearly so. Yet men must dream of a time, if it be no more than a single day, when their dreams shall come true, even as they dreamed them. Now the virtue of trout fishing is that it, of all pursuits, rewards the dreamer with realization of his dream. The trout are more beautiful than he remembered them as being, and the day, the scene and the occupation are at harmony. That is why men go trout fishing.

It has often been remarked by trout fishermen that when they are about the affairs of stream and rod, the events of yesterday and the necessities of tomorrow are singularly dwarfed in importance. They seem somehow to lack for real significance. The beauty of stream and forest, the beauty of the fish, the agreeable nature of the employment—these are real. All else appears to be of little moment, and to wear an aspect of trickery, as though men were both betrayed into and by it. It is for this reason that men go trout fishing, vowing that they prefer it to other recreations. Physically weary as they are before the sun is high, the truth is they are resting. They have rediscovered the escape. The stream they fish is running through their hearts to bear away the frets and worries of yesterday and tomorrow. All fishermen will know how it is, though it is uncommonly difficult to explain.

If any city dweller could enumerate at this moment the citizens, working and dwelling within a dozen miles of him, whose thoughts are fixed upon the opening of the trout season, he would be astonished at the number of them. And if he might, at the same time, appraise the gentleness and innocence of their reflections, he must be even more astonished by the essential boyishness of their natures. A recreation which sets aside the usual desires, and banishes the common thought of gain and selfishness—as any true recreation should—must be of important benefit to the people that practice it, and therefore to the commonwealth. The state could make no sounder investment than in trout. Such fishing is beneficial to the nature of the citizen. Anything that will persuade a great number of people to think sanely, and decently, and happily, though it be but of a favorite recreation, is of great importance to society.

But no trout fisherman is thinking of this, and small blame to him. He has more important matters to ponder. He must think of his flies and his tackle. He must speculate upon the probable condition of the water. He must recall, and this effortlessly, the very look and laughter of the stream to which he will be going. Mr. Coolidge says that fishing improves the republic, and Mr. Hoover holds the same view. But though we applaud their discernment, we submit that they have told us nothing not already known. There's a stream down toward the coast that should be right, as trout fishermen say, just right, in a day or so.

Roderick Haig-Brown

English-born Roderick Haig-Brown (1908-1976) came to the Northwest as a young man, settled along the Campbell River on Vancouver Island, and became the dean not just of Northwest angling writers, but of all North American angling writers. He is the author of such classics as *The Western Angler, Return to the River, A River Never Sleeps,* and *Fisherman's Fall* (1964), the opening chapter of which appears below. He closes this essay with a powerful appeal for the saving of the salmon, which now face tragic extinction in our waters. Haig-Brown, more than any other writer, brought an angling tradition in writing to the Pacific Northwest and shaped it to our own region.

Fall Defined

Fall comes quite gradually on the Pacific Coast of Canada, so gradually that one scarcely knows when or whether it has arrived. Sometimes a storm blows up from the south early in August, with a cold, wet rain that brings a subtle change. Yet it is certain the sun and the hot days will come again and perhaps hold on through most of September. If they do, there will be early frosts to turn the leaves and insist that fall is here. More often a storm around Labor Day brings the change. Again, the dry hot days may return after it, perhaps bringing woods' closure and forest fires; but the change will be clear; fogs will force in from the ocean and the morning dew will be everywhere. With or without frost, the leaves will turn and begin to fall.

Fall is also in the return of the salmon to their rivers—not, of course, in the early king salmon runs that come to a few rivers in May or the early running races of sockeye, but in the typical pink salmon runs that come in towards the end of July. With their coming the great fall movement to the coastal rivers begins. The big kings follow quickly, in August and September. A few cutthroat trout may have begun their movement even a little before the humpbacks. The cohos come in with the rains of September and October, the chum salmon are close behind them, and often with them, in October and November. Well before the last of the salmon is dead, it is December and unquestionably winter.

Fall fishing is a revival after the quieter times of summer. Cooler nights and the melt of early snowfall in the mountains bring falling water temperatures and rains freshen the streams. Shadows are longer, shielding the pools. The fish are more active and there is a touch of urgency about it all, a feeling that it cannot last very long so one had better get out and be doing. After all, there have been falls when the heavy rains came early and suddenly, the streams flooded and everything was over before it had started. Occasionally such memories trick me into going out and searching for runs before they have come in, using up fishing time that might have been better spent a week or two later. But I am not at all sure this is ever a matter for real regret, because there is always something around in the fall and one can come upon surprises—a few migrant fish running ahead of their time, an unexpected hatch that brings resident fish on the feed or even some phase of movement wholly unsuspected in other years. Few movements of wild creatures run to an exact timetable, year in, year out, and few are without their aberrant individuals; and few of us know our own familiar waters quite so well as we think we do.

Fall is almost everywhere a prime fishing time. In early fall the arctic grayling reaches his peak of fatness and condition and the lake trout move towards shallower water and their spawning. Brown trout and eastern brook trout are fall spawners, the cutthroat is chiefly a winter spawner; all three take on a special beauty of coloration as maturity approaches, echoing the reds and golds of the falling leaves. One may look for the bright and silvery immature fish among these and even prefer him, but his beauty is less vivid and he is not set apart as a sign of the season.

There is much pleasure in fall fishing, especially on streams where salmon run. But one does not have to fish to make the most of it. Of all times of the year on the Pacific watershed, fall is the most exciting. Spring is the most beautiful time, summer perhaps the most delightful, winter the most testing, at least physically, but fall is the time of movement. Anyone who passes along the streams may see it and feel it. Even when I am hunting ruffed grouse or Wilson's snipe, I find myself pushing out to the stream edges, following them where I can, looking down into the fall-dark water to search for the salmon's movements among the drifting leaves. Traveling fish roll up in the heavy water, spawners splash and work and struggle on the shallows, exhausted fish shelter in the eddies. Bear trails are worn and muddy along the banks, prints of coon and mink show up on sand bars and other soft places. Mallards, mergansers and goldeneyes start up from the quieter reaches where they have been feeding on salmon already dead. Being a fisherman, one looks for trout among the salmon or checks the brightness of the cohos to see if any are still worth taking, one studies the pools and runs and, when they are unfamiliar, promises oneself to come back some other time to test them. But none of this is necessary. It is enough to be on hand at this solemn, untidy time when the woods are wet and quiet and the salmon are completing their cycle.

To some people, the thought that the salmon, all Pacific salmon of all species, die very soon after spawning is a depressing one. They see in it only decay and waste, a sort of pathetic frustration of life. This is a natural view, but it does not question deeply enough; the end of the salmon is not death and corruption, but only fall, the autumn of their cycle. They come to the spawning gravels in all their brilliant colors—reds, browns, greens, gray and black and golden. Like the autumn leaves above them, they have their time of fierce glory. Then the frosts and the rains and the winds come. The leaves become torn and sodden and dulled and in their time they fall, covering the ground, drifting with the stream currents, piling against the rocks and shallows. But within the trees life is still strong and self-renewing.

As the winds stir and drift the dying leaves, so the waters drift and stir the dying salmon against the gray-brown gravels of the stream beds. But under those gravels life is strong and secret and protected in the buried eggs, the real life of the race. Fungus grows on the emptied bodies, as it grows among the fallen leaves; they collect in the eddies and strand on the gravel bars and the bacteria of change work in them to make a new fertility. In spring life will burst from the gravel as it bursts again from the trees, into the massive yield of the new cycle. Death is seldom more fleeting or more fertile than this.

The salmon runs are not the whole story of fall on the Pacific Coast streams, but no one can fish there and not be aware of them and no fisherman can fail to be curious about them and concerned for them. A great commercial fishery depends on them. Tens of thousands of anglers go out each year to catch them in the salt water and every angler who fishes a migratory stream sees them and finds his sport, directly or indirectly, through them, for the power of the runs persists through the year and affects all other fish.

But the salmon runs are more than this. They are a last true sample of the immense natural abundances of the North American continent. They have been damaged and reduced in many places, it is true, and in some places, especially the Columbia River, the damage is great and permanent. But they remain a massive abundance, complex and wonderful, throughout most of their range, and throughout much of it their potential of natural abundance is as great as ever, while new understanding of their ways and needs suggests that increase over the natural abundance may well be possible through man-made assistance.

I feel this as a special challenge to mankind in general and to North Americans in particular. Is there one wild thing on the face of the earth that we can use and live with in reasonable harmony, preserving and even enhancing its natural magnificence? The record to date suggests there is not, that our own demanding and untidy living habits must always destroy, if not the creature itself, then certainly the living space it depends upon. Yet for the salmon it would seem there is some hope. It is a valuable creature, fundamentally and irreplaceably valuable as a source of food in a hungry world. Much of its living space is the sea, an area of the globe that we have not so far found it possible or necessary to change or damage very greatly. The rest is in the streams, which our own interests demand that we keep as clean and pure as possible. Unhappily, we often consider it convenient to obstruct, divert or otherwise abuse them, but there is at least a possibility that we may develop beyond these primitive practices in time to save a good deal for the salmon.

This, I admit, is a rather special viewpoint in an age of relentless change and destruction. It reflects intangible values and instinctive, even primitive, sympathies that are not much in favor today. But when I come to write of a fisherman's autumn I am bound to think first of the salmon and then, remembering the sense of wonder they have stirred in me through nearly forty seasons, I am bound to plead their case and tell what little I know of them. I hope they will long be here, in the waters of California, Oregon, Washington, British Columbia and Alaska, to stir fresh wonder in the hearts and minds of later human generations.

H. L. Davis

H. L. (Harold Lenoir) Davis (1894-1960) won the Pulitzer Prize for fiction
with his 1935 novel, *Honey in the Horn,* one of a handful of truly great
Northwest novels. He was also a fine poet, short-story writer, and essayist. He
knew the Oregon and Washington country well, having spent his early years
in western Oregon and along the Columbia River, where he
graduated from high school in The Dalles. Later, he sang
folk songs on a Seattle radio station, before making his
reputation as a writer. "Fishing Fever" (1953) reveals Davis's rich
knowledge of Northwest history and folklore, as well as his love for trout
fishing and storytelling.

Fishing Fever

One thing about fishing that most fishermen are not conscious of and most non-fishermen are uninformed about is that it gives its devotees a slightly peculiar set of values—not distorted, exactly, but a little transfigured and elevated and outside what ordinary people might expect. The case of a friend of mine who works in the Government atomic-energy plant at Hanford in the State of Washington may illustrate how it sometimes works. He came back this spring from a fishing trip along a small creek that empties into the Yakima River a few miles from where he is employed, and reported various details about the state of the water and what flies the trout were rising to and how they had to be handled. He also mentioned that while he was fishing some of the downstream holes late one forenoon, he had happened on a couple or three buffalo grazing a strip of dead bunch grass between the county road and the creek. It struck him as unusual to find buffalo wandering loose along a main county road within picnicking distance of so modern a development as an atomic- energy plant— actually they must have been almost in sight of it—and he had thought for a moment of going back to his car and bringing a camera to photograph them, to prove that such things could happen.

It was too bad he changed his mind. The buffalo were not strays from some circus or carnival company, as might have been supposed. They were real native wild buffalo, from a small and scattered herd that had inhabited the broken country called the Rattlesnake Hills in the Big Bend of the Columbia River since long before any white men had ever seen it. Washington Irving's *Adventures of Captain Bonneville* mentions their being there in 1833, though even then they were so wild and cautious that the Indians never hunted them, and seldom even saw them. Two or three loose specimens from the only completely untamed buffalo herd in the

United States might have been worth a photograph or two, at least. My friend admitted that he should have got his camera and tried it. The trouble was that they were between him and his car, and he couldn't get to it without herding them down toward the creek. If they waded into it, they would muddy the water and spoil the fishing the rest of the way downstream, and he couldn't bring himself to risk that. Fishing, after all, was what he had come out there for. Photographing buffalo was all very well, but he was not prepared for it, physically, emotionally or temperamentally. He even regretted having a camera along to feel tempted by. Next time, he had decided, he would leave it at home so he could feel free to concentrate on essentials.

Fishing fever can do that to a man's sense of proportion. It can also color his judgment in matters that have nothing to do with nature or wild life at all. In the Pacific Northwest, where I was born and brought up, it once reached far enough to have a permanent effect on the country's history. Back in the 1840s when the Oregon boundary question was in controversy between the United States and Great Britain, a British admiral was sent out by his government to report on whether the disputed territory was worth holding onto. His report went into considerable detail about its worthlessness and savagery and remoteness, and added, as a final clincher, that the salmon in the streams and coastal waters were the most worthless part of it, because the blasted things wouldn't rise to a fly. In the light of all the evidence, he recommended handing the territory over to the United States, hide, hair, horns and fins, and good riddance, which was done. There is no record that his government ever gave evidence of displeasure over his recommendation. He had reported according to his lights as an officer, a patriot and an angler. No government could have asked more.

He was a little sweeping in stating that West Coast salmon wouldn't rise to a fly, though the oversight was not very important. There are times during the spring spawning run when they will rise to a fly, or to anything else within reach that is moving, but that phase only lasts a few days out of the year, and since nobody can ever tell when it will occur, it is hardly worth counting. The Indian system of seining or dipnetting at the foot of a rapid is still the most reliable way of catching them, and it bears much the same relation to sporting fishing as the Chinese method of catching fish with a trained cormorant, or the practice among the Nevada Paiutes of circling a river- shallow and clubbing them to death. The admiral was right in disdaining such low business, and in feeling that any region where it had to be resorted to was unworthy of membership in the Empire. His moral rigidity not only changed international boundaries and shunted a good many people into United States citizenship who might otherwise have been subjects of the Crown, but it may also have laid down a tradition of picayunishness in Northwestern angling. People who acquire their first experience of fishing in the Pacific Northwest are always a little sniffish about fishing techniques elsewhere, and about any kind of fishing that does not involve either trout, steelhead or salmon. Fishing for anything outside those three species is not really fishing at all, but merely something for school kids to piddle at with a bent pin and a switch and a length of string.

It is true that there are not many other species of edible fish in Northwestern streams—a few sturgeon in the Columbia River sometimes and an annual run of eels, which used to be dipnetted and dried by Indians for their winter food supply and shunned vigorously by everybody else—but even when some other edible species turns up it is likely to be viewed with suspicion, merely because it is outside any of the accepted categories. Once I dropped in on a sheep camp on the Upper Columbia River and found the two herders arguing acrimoniously over a tin bucket half-full of some largish high-keeled fish with heavy scales, which they had snagged out of a nearby slough and were having trouble identifying. One held that they were chubs, the other insisted that they were squawfish. It was not a point that could be easily compromised, so they had got down to personalities, which was not settling anything.

One thing they had managed to agree on. The fish, whatever they were, were mud eaters and unfit for human consumption, and they would have to be got rid of when the argument was over. I took a close look at the bucket, not being quite sure what either chubs or squawfish looked like, but being willing to learn. The fish were neither one nor the other. They were small-mouth bass. There were a dozen or fifteen of them, and some must have weighed close to a pound and a half. I explained to the herders what they were and that they were considered highly edible in many parts of the country where nothing better was available, but they were not much impressed. They seemed to suspect that I was trying to stay neutral by siding against both of them, and they went on with their argument as if I hadn't said anything. I left them building up a fire to burn the fish so their herd dogs couldn't get at them, and still arguing, sometimes changing sides on each other for the sake of variety. The argument mattered more than the fish, seemingly. Sheep herding is a draggy life, and anything that will make red-hot conversation is always welcome.

Even among the three categories to which fishermen in the Northwest are restricted by tradition and prejudice, there's room for individual preferences. A really confirmed salmon fisherman will hardly ever consider any other form of fishing worth talking about. My grandfather, a Hard-Shell Baptist clergyman, was of that stripe, and once flogged one of his sons for reminding him that it was Sunday when he was stringing up his tackle to head for the creek where the chinooks were cavorting like squirrels in a brush fire. When salmon fishing is good, it is lively enough to suit anybody. Nothing gets around faster or fights harder than a chinook, once he is hooked, and a man's glands would have to be down pretty low to resist the waves of varying emotions called into action in getting him worn down and landed. Still, the skill required is only in landing him, not in hooking him to begin with. No amount of art or guile can induce a salmon to take a lure unless he feels like it, and if he does feel like it, nothing can stop him. It is the same with steelhead. A steelhead will strike anything that moves at the depth where he happens to be feeding. If you can figure out what the depth is and sink your bait exactly to it, the rest is merely a matter of hanging on and praying that the tackle will hold.

By trout-fishing standards, this is missing out on two thirds of the fun. The best part of fishing, to a trout addict, is in figuring out a lure that the trout will fall for when they are not especially interested, or in some technique of casting or handling that will get a bait past the swarm of eager fingerlings near the surface to reach the big ones on the bottom, or some similar refinement that will make use of some idiosyncrasy of nature to circumvent the trout's sluggishness or cussedness. To such people, there is a more genuine sense of accomplishment in casting a Number Twelve fly thirty feet against a cross wind through a two-foot gap in the underbrush and hooking a reluctant trout than there is in landing a thirty-pound salmon after a fight lasting an hour and a half.

Even in trout fishing there are distinctions. Rainbow trout, because of their unusual hardiness and ability to stand transplanting, are almost the only species to be found in the Coast streams now, besides being common in the Andean lakes of South America, in New Zealand and even in some parts of Africa. They are a beautiful fish, resilient and high-spirited and adaptable almost anywhere, with a peculiar habit of changing coloration to suit their environment. In a sunlit stream with a varicolored bottom they will develop streaks and splashes of vivid scarlet against a ground of blackish-green, while in shaded mountain lakes with a heavy snow cast they breed to a pale leaf- gray with no markings at all. They are used almost exclusively in restocking Western streams, replacing the earlier speckled mountain trout, which have long since been crowded out by competition from livestock, irrigation projects, sawmills, chlorinating plants and people.

The speckled mountain trout was the species I knew earliest. There used to be nothing else in the small lakes and snow creeks of the high mountains. They were also in the upland streams of the Great Basin, where, since there was no such thing as trout transplanting then, they must have been ever since the post-glacial period. In spite of their touchiness about being crowded—or maybe because of it—I still think they were the finest trout to fish for that ever existed. They were not large: the biggest ones were from twelve to fifteen inches, and the average was less, but they had fire and dash and spirit, and when they came after a fly they put the whole works into it. A rainbow or a golden trout will sometimes fritter around for an hour making feints and passes at a floating object, out of mere curiosity or idle-mindedness. A speckled trout never moves till his mind is made up, and when he does move he means it. He grabs a fly before it is even in the water and is halfway to the next county before the astonished angler recovers enough presence of mind to take up slack. There is nothing shilly-shally about a speckled trout. Whatever he does, he does for all he is worth.

Rainbow trout are more adaptable and easier to handle, and they afford healthful recreation for thousands of weekend sportsmen who catch them out of every creek within range of a main highway as fast as the trucks from the State hatcheries can pour them in, but there is not the same feeling about them, or about that kind of fishing, for that matter. It lacks something; you can tell it by the grim, set-featured expressions of the anglers.

This tank-truck system of delivering trout to anglers is a highly practical and efficient one, though the people who run the tourist accommodations don't always seem as appreciative about it as one might expect. In a roadside lunchroom on the Chelan River in Central Washington this past summer, I remarked something to the waitress about some fishermen who had been flycasting across a long riffle near some tourist cabins for half an hour without any noticeable result except to get their lines tangled together a few times. She said she supposed they were practicing: the truck from the hatchery was not due till the end of the week, and there wouldn't be any fish in the river till it showed up.

"It only puts in enough to last through the weekend," she said. "Sometimes they don't last even that long. These hatchery trout are half-tame anyway, and you could catch them with your hands if it wasn't for all those tourists splashing around squabbling over them."

It didn't sound very absorbing. "You'd think they'd try out some of the creeks back in the mountains, instead of just waiting around like that," I said. "It would be less crowded, and they'd get away from traffic and see some new country."

"They don't want new country," she said. "They've got what they want, right here, traffic and all. They like it."

And still, this shift from the old outdoor spirit of self-reliance and exploration to a dependence on weekly fish deliveries by truck has a bright side to it. There are a lot of small back-country creeks where the hatchery trucks never come, because of their remoteness or inaccessibility or something. In the old days, when fishing meant going where the fish were, even the smallest of them got fished out thoroughly before the season had been open a week—sometimes sooner. Under the new system of trucking fish where the fishermen are, the wilder and smaller streams are left alone, and some of them that were once hardly worth fishing at all have come back surprisingly.

There was one where I stopped for a day last spring, out in the sagebrush country in Central Oregon; a little string of rain pools at the bottom of a rimrock canyon, called Buck Creek, which joins the Deschutes River a mile or so below the old Indian salmon-fishing ground at Sherar Rapids. It is very small and shallow; a man could step across it almost anywhere, and in the old days it was not considered worth bothering with except as a source of minnows and crawfish to use for bait in the big whirlpool below the rapids. I had walked upstream along it for a few hundred yards to look at an old Indian burying ground where a few beautifully made arrowheads sometimes got washed into sight by the spring rains. There were no arrowheads, but when I tossed a cigarette butt into the creek, the shallow pool churned and came alive with trout rushing to strike at it. I had no flies, only a few small bait hooks that I had got down the Coast and nothing to bait them with, and it was too early for grasshoppers; so as an experiment I tried baiting with a catkin from some willows along the bank. They grabbed at it as if it were money from home. They would probably have grabbed another cigarette butt as readily if I had wanted to insult them with one. I caught a couple of dozen from the one small pool in twenty minutes, and could have run it up to a hundred from the pools farther up the canyon if there had been anything to do with them.

One such place could have been an accident, but there were others. There was a creek back in the desert country a few weeks later where I sat for an hour watching a pair of hawks at work picking ten-inch trout out of a hole at the edge of an old hay meadow and carrying them away to a rimrock cliff a mile or so distant where they evidently had a nest. I don't know how much of a brood they had to provide for, but in the hour I spent watching them they lugged away enough trout to have foundered three or four full-grown men, and they were still at it when I left. Shooting at them would have scared them off, maybe, but it wouldn't have helped the trout much. The creek went dry in its lower reaches every summer, and saving them to dry up with it didn't seem any more humane than leaving them for the hawks, and considerably less picturesque.

There was still another small mountain creek out in the sagebrush near the Nevada line where an elderly Polish couple used to run an overnight station for travelers, with broiled trout as the staple item on their bill of fare. The old Polish woman had never managed to learn English in the forty years she had been living there, but she could go out back of the barn at any hour and in any season, with a cane pole and a dilapidated black-gnat fly with no leader, and come back in fifteen minutes with half a dozen trout running three-quarters of a pound apiece. Nobody else could catch anything out of the creek except water dogs in those days, but when I tried it this past summer there were trout in every hole, and they rose to almost anything that was thrown at them. Some of the sheep herders around the neighborhood thought the old woman had cast a spell on the creek while she lived there, and that it wore off after she moved away. But they were also prepared to argue that killing a spider would bring on rain and that food cooked by electricity introduced harmful electrons into the digestive system, so the theory didn't count for much except to give life in that part of the country a slight added interest, which it could stand. There were fish in the creek and they were biting, and it was more than they had ever done when the old Polish woman lived there, anyway.

Shifts of population have wiped out fishing in many places, but that also can work two ways. There used to be a wild stretch of burned-over hill country up the Oregon coast adjoining the Siuslaw National Forest where I went deer hunting sometimes in the fall. The only road into it then was a crooked wagon track down the open beach, with a few loose planks strung out across the worst places to keep cars from losing traction and miring down. There were small creeks every few miles that had to be forded with a rush and a prayer because of quicksand, and anybody rash enough to risk being overtaken by an incoming tide could catch a horseload of fish out of them in a morning—trout, salmon trout, steelhead, salmon, candle smelt—depending on the season. A new main highway has gone in since then, the whole coast country has filled up with people and towns, and the creeks have been converted into logging ponds and spillways for municipal sewer systems. There is an embarrassed feeling about going back to country like that, trying to figure out old landmarks that have been built over by glass-fronted residences and realty offices, buying color film and the latest magazines in a supermarket and remembering having killed an eight-point buck deer between its front entrance and the garden-supply emporium across the street. It really was not so long ago as it sounds—twenty years, maybe. If any of the townspeople were told about it now, they would undoubtedly conclude that it must have been done with a flintlock rifle, back around the time of Lewis and Clark. Anything that happened in the country before they moved in is all lumped together as pioneering, whether it happened in the administration of Jefferson or Hoover.

Back of one of the new towns there was an old pack trail that wound up into the hills, following an almost-dry watercourse for a couple of miles and ending at a little clearing and a clump of empty cabins where a man I knew had taken up a homestead back in the early 1920s. He was middle-aged then, with a good many years of assembly-line work behind him, and he had picked the place as a peaceful and uncompetitive location where he could live out the rest of his days, untroubled by urban pressures and work schedules and hurry and people. He had put in several years of hard work clearing the place and making it livable: felling trees, grubbing stumps, clearing brush, splitting rails and shingles, building fences and cabins and sheds and lugging furniture up the trail from the road, mostly on his back. I don't know whether he ever got it completely arranged to suit him or not; the population boom along the highway drew him away from it, as it drew all the people from those little back-country homesteads, and he was running a logging-camp commissary and lunch counter somewhere down the coast and doing very well at it.

The work he had done on the place was being taken back by the wilderness. Mountain laurel had overgrown his fence and garden, the sheds and cabins were sagging and half unroofed, and his beehives had all been tipped over and ripped apart by bears. Most of the things he had carried up the two miles of trail on his back were still there, though dilapidated—the cast-iron kitchen stove, the heavy old oak dresser, some walnut rocking chairs, a big nickel-plated kerosene lamp, a set of old-fashioned steelyards for weighing deer, a wheelbarrow: all things that represented hard work and hopefulness and illusion, all thrown away, rusting and falling apart in the bracken and dwarf alder and wild huckleberry that were beginning to push up even between the floor boards of the cabin.

The one thing that kept the feeling of futility and disappointment from being unbearable was the pond he had built for his water supply. It was merely a dammed-up spring that spread back into a pool about twenty feet across, mud-bottomed and overgrown with alders, and so shallow in most places that leaves fallen into it stuck half out of the water. But there were big speckled trout in it. I counted half a dozen that must have been fifteen inches long, lying close to the surface and paying not the slightest attention to me, though I could have knocked two or three of them out with a stick if there had been one handy. They couldn't have been planted there, because none of the hatcheries cultivated speckled trout, and they couldn't have come in from anywhere else, because the pond was completely landlocked, with no intake or outlet that they could have come by. It lightened the oppressive feeling about the place to have them there, wherever they had come from, and to know that Nature, instead of merely wiping out and burying man's errors of judgment, was turning some of them to use for her own purposes. Nature is more ingenious than we sometimes imagine, and she is accustomed to working over our mistakes from having worked over plenty of her own.

The problem of how fish get into waters that are completely landlocked is always fascinating to speculate on—the native trout that were in the upland streams of the Great Basin when the first whites came to the country, the annual run of huge indigenous suckers up the Truckee River in Nevada, unlike any other suckers in the world and with no point of origin except where they are now; the tiny little semisardines in the half-alkaline Lake Texcoco in the Valley of Mexico, the golden trout in the glacial lakes of the California High Sierras, the whitefish of the lovely little Lake Zirahuen in Michoacan: none of those waters have any outlet anywhere. There is no way that fish could have got into them from anywhere else. Could they have hatched out of the rocks all by themselves, or might it have been the mud? Neither seems altogether satisfying as an explanation, and still, they had to start somewhere. Did the pre-Columbian Indians know about fish planting?

I have never been able to work out any reasonable answer for it, and I never stop trying. Once, out pigeon hunting at the edge of a small village in the desert country of Northern Mexico, I got so absorbed in studying a swarm of odd-looking little yellow-and-black-spotted fish in an irrigation ditch that I forgot all about the pigeons in the nut palms overhead. Since pigeons were a regional delicacy and the fish weren't, I ruined the reputation of Americans as a practical-minded race for the entire village. The ditch was nothing but a small desert seep; it came out of the ground in one place, wandered through some gardens for half a mile, and went back into the ground again. None of the people in the village had any idea where the fish had come from or how long they had been there: always, they were inclined to think, though the subject didn't interest them much. The village was not especially interesting either, I thought. It is only because of the fish in the irrigation ditch that I remember it now. An interest in fish or fishing can communicate itself to things around it sometimes, and sometimes they need it.

Sometimes such an interest can get itself mixed into a man's individuality until it is hard to tell where he stops and it starts. I was staying for a few days at a run-down old hotel in one of the little Northern California hill towns last fall, and was sitting on the whittling bench outside the front entrance talking with the proprietor about some of the Indian reservations in the neighborhood when a man came riding down the street toward us on horseback. He was somewhere past middle age, gray-haired, trim and stately looking, dressed in store clothes and a white shirt, with a crutch laid across his saddle pommel like the long rifle in a Frederic Remington painting of a typical frontiersman. When he got close, I saw that he had a fishing rod strapped to the crutch. The hotel man nodded to him as he rode past, and said he lived in some old mining cabin a mile or two out of town, and had been a schoolteacher until he got too old and crotchety for it. Now he didn't do much of anything: drew a small pension, trapped a little in the winter, drafted legal documents that were not important enough to hire a lawyer for, wrote letters to the county newspaper for people who liked to pop off in public and wanted some big words thrown in for style—odds and ends like that. He managed to make out. The country didn't offer much of a field for him, what with his lameness and his education.

"There's places that might," I said. "He don't have to stay here, does he?"

"He thinks he does, I guess," the hotel man said. "He's at work lining out some old mining road that hits a little creek back in the hills. He alms to have it put back in shape and start some kind of a sportsmen's resort along the creek somewhere—charge a dollar a day for fishing and camping, or something like that. He thinks there'll be money in it. It might work. He claims there's trout up there so thick you can write your name in 'em with a stick, and I guess there are. He brings out plenty of 'em."

"Patching up one of those old mountain roads can run into money," I said. I had tried it once myself. A helicopter would have been cheaper; so would a monorail railroad, or a ski run, or almost anything. "It's a long trip in here from any of the main highways too. He might not get customers enough to pay himself out on it."

"Hell, he'll never do it anyway," the hotel man said. "He gets too much fun out of keeping his damned creek to himself. There ain't a week goes by that he don't come swaggering in with a big string of trout to slap people in the face with. He gets a lot out of it. A man's got to have something to be proud of, I guess."

"It's a wonder somebody don't try to find out where this road into his creek is," I said. "You could trail him."

"I don't care where it is," the hotel man said. "Let him keep it to himself, if it's any satisfaction to him. I've got a creek of my own back in the breaks that'll beat hell out of anything he's got."

There really is a sort of sustaining feeling about having a creek somewhere that other people don't know about, or in knowing something about it that they have missed. Mine is not a creek, exactly, but the backwater of an old hydroelectric dam across a small river that runs into the Columbia from the snowfields of the high Cascade Mountains in Southern Washington. The backwater forms a lake eight or ten miles long, though there are only two or three places in it where the fishing amounts to much. The country on both sides is logged-off stump land grown back to small second-growth timber and underbrush, the old sawmill sheds and bunkhouses are buried in rhododendron and wild blackberry vines, and there are the remains of a few old orchards that were bought out by the hydroelectric company and vacated when the dam went in. The water in the lake is deep and inhumanly cold, with an odd ash-green cast that makes it look opaque, though it is clear and colorless in the shallow places or when dipped out in a bucket. It seems odd to associate age with anything as contemporary as a hydroelectric installation, but it has been there a good many years: long enough for the vegetation and wild life to have become completely adapted to it—from the marten and wood ducks nesting along the shallows and deer and ruffed grouse in the old orchards to the trout that were originally rainbow-colored and have changed to the pale gray-green of the lake water in the deep places.

The trout stay deep and out of sight during the morning low water in the lake, and it is impossible to sink a spinner far enough down to reach them without fouling it in the tangled boughs of some old orchard that got flooded under when the dam went in. Around mid-afternoon, the floodgates are closed to build up the water level for the peak load that comes in the towns down the river after sundown—the quitting-time rush, the show windows and electric signs lighting up, the electric ranges and water heaters being turned on for dinner. The water rising somehow changes the afternoon light to a luminous white glare and strikes the air over it into a silence that feels as if something had stunned it. In the middle of the hush, in an expanse of smooth water where the reflection of light is so intense it hurts your eyes, the trout begin rising, breaking the glare and the silence with little rainbows of water drops as they come out of the water and slap back into it. It is like being suspended between two separate worlds, one among the drowned cabins and dead orchards at the bottom of the lake, the other of the towns down the river with their quitting-time rushes and electric ranges being turned on and show windows lighting up, feeling and knowing them both without being touched by either.

Silence and passion.... The trout work best on a Number Eight stonefly trailed about an inch below the surface on a long line. Some of them run two or three pounds apiece.

Enos Bradner

Enos Bradner (1892-1984) was outdoor editor of the *Seattle Times* from 1943 to 1969. He was one of the founders of the Washington Fly Fishing Club and was its first president. As a fly tier he created some of the Northwest's favorite flies, like the Brad's Brat. The selection which follows, from his book *Northwest Angling* (1969), describes one kind of Northwest fishing which remains fresh and adventuresome over the years.

Mountain Lake Fishing

When the God of the Outdoors created Washington's Cascade Range and the wilderness of the Olympics, he scattered hundreds of mountain lakes amid their towering peaks. These crystal-clear basins of water set like sapphires and emeralds amid the snow fields and tree-clad rocks were known only to the mountain goats for hundreds of years. But as the fisherman crept ever northward up through the river valleys of the coast, he cast longing eyes at the lofty mountain ranges and wondered what lakes could be hidden in the valleys and the upper benches. And as time went on, this curious human species, emulating the mountain goat, built trails into the hills and later with back-pack and pack train carried trout into virtually every one of the barren upper lakes. The trout flourished in the cold clear waters, and today are there awaiting the hardy hiker who desires virgin angling combined with unsurpassed scenery.

Mountain trails that reach like twisting lengths of rope from the lowlands up into the hills are to be found thickly threaded all through the mountain ranges of Washington. You find them starting off from modern four-lane highways, from government camp sites, from railroad crossings, and from swinging bridges over rushing rivers. They meander across the flats and then, carefully weaving along contour lines and around cliffs, gradually work right into the hills. The most famous are those belonging to the Pacific Crest Trail System, triangular white and green signs of which can take a hiker all along the entire summit of the Cascades from Canada to California.

Fishing in Lake Isobel. The mountain angler is most interested in his own particular trail, the one that takes him up to his chosen lake. On a June morning you and your hiking partner may have decided to climb in to Lake Isobel, which lies a short 54 miles northeast of Seattle. You not only hope to pick up a few large fat brookies, rainbows and maybe even some mackinaws, but you are also anxious to see if the lake is as entrancingly beautiful as you remembered it from the year before. You park your car at the end of the old tote road, shoulder your Trapper Nelson packs, one of which holds the rubber boat, and with metal rod case in hand to use as a cane, turn your steps into the narrow path that leads up to the lake.

The pink fingers of dawn are reaching into the eastern sky. The air is cool and moist, and the thick ferns lining the trail drip heavy dew onto your clothes. You switch back around a jutting cliff, and the trail heads steeply up through spindly alder brush.

Thimbleberry bushes studded with pale white blossoms grow in thick clumps and in the open the salal brush is all in bloom. You find an occasional salmonberry bush and you pop one of the tart reddish yellow berries into your mouth. The remembered flavor is still there. The brush gives way to second growth as you switch to the left, and now you can look out over the valley below, where the Skykomish River twists its way into the distance, unfolding a scene of breath-taking beauty before your eyes.

Small firs and hemlocks, perfectly formed, crowd close along the trail, their branches all candle-tipped with new growths of brilliant green. You are really climbing now, bracing your feet against each protruding rock to prevent back-slipping. Then you plunge into a shadowed tunnel of taller trees where the mountain walls are closing in on both sides.

In places such as this, mountain trails are apt to show signs of age. In the shade of tall conifers the path is spongy soft with moss and the turf is thickly blanketed with old needles that swallow up silently the scraping sound of your hobnailed boots.

You are now going up steeply again. On every side tree trunks, ramrod straight, reach up a hundred feet toward the sun. There are firs and hemlocks and now and then a growth of cedar—gnarled giants, many of them four to eight feet through at the base, with striated trunks and occasionally with tops wind-twisted or broken off in a jagged gash.

You glimpse a thread of white water weaving down the steep hill on your right and you stop to have an ice-cold drink from a noisy brook. The trail gets steeper and more deeply rock pitted—evidence that torrents from the melting snows of spring, using it as a watercourse, had plunged recklessly down its center. The slopes on each side of the trail turn into sheer cliffs, and the walls close in ahead of you in a blind draw. Then the trail turns into an old puncheon pathway made of rudely split cedar boards that, in a series of twelve switchbacks, scales the cliff. To your left, a veil of water is washing down the same wall of rock, spilling out of the lake above. You push through thick, seemingly impenetrable huckleberry brush, take another step, and—without warning— there's your lake!

Barely twenty feet away, its clear waters are lapping against a huge cedar log. You realize with a start that the cliff you have just scaled is a natural dam that holds Lake Isobel in its vast hollow in the hills. You look up to see the mountain sides, tree-clad and rock-girt, rimming the lake, and reaching up to snow-capped summits.

You dump the rubber boat out of the pack, and start pumping it up. Your partner lines up the rods, threads on line and ties on a tiny bucktail coachman fly. Part of the lake is still in shadow and you paddle the small boat to that side. Partner flips his fly toward the shore. It floats a second or two, sinks, and has twitched along hardly a foot when there is a swift flash through the crystal-clear water. He has hooked into a fat 14-inch rainbow that shoots out of the water in a silvery arc and drops back with a swirl of foam.

You work slowly up the lake, taking turns to cover the shoreline or the few submerged rocks or logs. Isobel is an extremely deep lake with only a narrow shelf along the shore where a fly will work at all effectively.

After several hours you have traveled half way up the lake and have taken rainbows, brook trout, silvers and a couple of 20-inch mackinaws that struggle deep and are only brought to net after a great deal of head shaking.

You come at noon to a camp site and brew a pot of tea with a party of four who have hiked in the night before. Then you stretch out in the bright hot sun and soak in the clean wine-like air. As you watch a fleecy cloud drift past one of the mountain tops, you wonder why all of us spend so much time down in the valleys. Life is so intense and hurried down there in the smoky man-made cities. But everything is so quiet, so clean, so fresh, so peaceful up here in the mountains. You forget your daily frustrations and troubles and come down that evening refreshed and ready to tackle with new vigor the problems of the coming week.

A Virgin Lake Country. There are literally hundreds of lakes in the high country of Washington that call the hiker and the angler. Through the efforts of the Game Department, pack strings have distributed trout in the more accessible altitude lakes and, since the war, the Department has acquired an airplane which is utilized to drop trout fry into lakes "way back in."

In addition, that unselfish hard-working tribe of fishermen, the Trailblazers, have been planting lakes for the past decade. This band of sportsmen, though small in number, explore the Cascades for new barren lakes, and when they have found them, stock them with trout they have backpacked in. With fry furnished by the Game Department, they successfully put the lakes into production. It is due to them that many of these remote lakes are now good fishing spots.

Unless one has made a study of contour maps of this region, one will be utterly astounded at the vast number of altitude lakes open to a weekend angler out of the metropolitan district of Seattle. The mountains are full of them. Many of the valleys and watersheds are as thickly studded with sparkling lakes as if they had been dropped from a Paul Bunyan sprinkler. Although the majority of these "high-up" lakes remain untouched by civilization, they are at the same time easily accessible from the Seattle district in a week-end trip. Many of them can be fished in a single day, while others, a few miles further back, are better suited to an overnight hike. The fisherman can drive forty miles out of Seattle's city limits, park alongside a trunk highway, and by the time he has hiked over the first ridge, he is in back country that has remained unchanged since the days of Lewis and Clark.

These hike-in lakes of the Cascades and the Olympics have not yet been commercialized. There may be a few Forest Service shelters or cleared camp sites at some of the better known spots. There is usually a raft or two hidden away along the shore line, and in a few isolated cases rowboats or dugouts are available. However, at some of the more popular lakes that can be reached in a two or three hours' walk, it is likely, during the summer, that a party of anglers will have come in Friday night or Saturday morning. In these circumstances the rafts will be in use. For this reason, a portable rubber boat is almost a necessity for the Sunday angler.

But the lakes are never crowded. You do not find empty tin cans or paper bags scattered about, the usual signs of the auto tourist. A short walk along the shore line, and you can always find a secluded camp site. It may have a nearly vertical slant and have to be cleared of rocks or brush, but you will find yourself as aloof from other humans as if you were in the middle of the Klondike.

Fishing After the Spring Break-up. The unofficial opening for the "high-up" lake addict has traditionally been the Fourth of July. All of the lower altitude lakes should be open at this time, but some of the higher lakes, mainly those above 5,000 feet that are situated deep in steep valleys, may still be frozen over. Between the two extremes, you may find some that may be only half free of ice or be ice-rimmed along one shore. Fishing can be excellent under such conditions.

If the angler can hit a lake just after the ice has gone off he is apt to find the trout furiously hungry after their long imprisonment beneath the blanket of ice. At these times, the fishing can be so fast it takes your breath away, as the trout are inclined to hit any lure offered them.

I remember one spring when Jack Litsey and I hiked into Cottonwood Lake around June 20th. It is about a six- mile hike. The trail winds up around Lost Lake and then follows the contour line through the open park-like pine slopes of Eastern Washington. As we got up to the 3,000-foot elevation snow patches appeared under the trees and soon the trail was hidden by several feet of hard-packed winter snow. We managed to stick with the almost obliterated path and topping the 4,200-foot contour we dropped into the narrow valley that holds the very small lake. The south shore, where grows the single huge cottonwood tree, was free of snow but the north side was rimmed with ice and two feet of snow lay beneath the trees. By the time we had blown up the rubber boat, it was after ten o'clock. In slightly over an hour we were through fishing as there were two limits of brook trout resting in the creels. They had hit with abandon, taking any fly that was flipped out to them: bucktail coachman, gray hackles with yellow bodies, queen of the waters or carot nymphs. None of the fish were large—they ran uniformly between 10 and 12 inches—but they were fast as lightning. Their flesh was deep pink, firm as marble and, fried crisp and brown for the next day's breakfast, they were as delicious a morsel as any mortal could ever desire.

Brook trout do very well in mountain lakes and, although they do not attain great size, they are always firm-meated and excellent eating. They will usually hit readily for two to four weeks after the lakes open up, but seem to taper off during the bright hot days of August due, probably, to sluggishness induced by warmer water.

In the old days, a great many cutthroats, of both the native and the black-spotted Montana varieties, were planted in the mountain lakes. In some of the lakes they were able to reproduce naturally in the inlet creeks and have provided steady fishing. In others, they have not propagated but have grown to good size—twenty to twenty-six inches.

Along with the state-wide emphasis on planting of rainbow trout, a program for the hatching of 22,000,000 rainbow eggs in 1950 has been announced. The mountain lakes are receiving, at present, more rainbows than any other variety of trout. These fish evidently do well in the clear lakes, and while, like the brook trout, they do not often grow to the enormous size that they attain in the lowland waters, they are fast-jumping, furious fighters.

A few golden trout were planted by the Department and the Trailblazers several years ago and they may still be taken in a few lakes. During the past two summers, grayling trout from Montana have been planted as fry in mountain lakes in Skagit and King counties. There is no information up to this time how they have taken hold.

The altitude lakes of Washington and Oregon carry virtually the same varieties of trout and will respond to the same fishing technique. British Columbian waters differ because of the presence of Kamloops in lakes around the 4,000- to 5,00-foot levels. California has a few cutthroats, some introduced brook trout and brown trout, and many resident rainbow. In addition, California is famed for its golden trout, which are eagerly sought for each year by the hardy anglers who make summer climbs into the high Sierras.

Fishing Mountain Lakes with Bait or Spoon. Although the mountain lakes may be regarded as well-nigh virgin waters, their trout are, at times, as hard to catch as their more sophisticated relatives in the lowlands. The high-up lakes are invariably "gin clear" and under a bright sun objects can be picked out clearly on the bottom at thirty feet. Many of them are rock-lined and offer very sparse plant growth, and few hiding spots except in the deeper water. A cruising trout in the shallows near shore can be easily put down or frightened away by a clumsy angler making sudden motions or undue noise.

In such lakes, under the bright sun of July and August, fishing during midday is an almost fruitless undertaking. But if the sky is overcast or if there is a breeze to riffle the surface, you can fish successfully throughout the day. Otherwise the most productive periods are apt to be in early morning or late afternoon when the sun has dipped behind a ridge and part of the lake is in shadow.

Many of the "high-up" fishermen use bait or spoon in taking trout. When still-fishing they will anchor just at the edge of a drop-off or near deep water and use single eggs or worms, as they do in the lowland waters. As feed or fresh eggs are not legal in most of the upper lakes, the angler must depend on deception. Most of them use a whippy trout rod and very light tippets for their leaders. A weight test for the tippets of one or two pounds is usual, and it takes a light touch to land heavy trout on such tackle.

Trolling from a raft is hardly practical, so that the spoon anglers seldom use this type of fishing. However, a small spoon in sizes one or two, with a split shot for weight, may be cast a good distance off a raft with a fly rod. If it is then allowed to sink and retrieved with slow, easy jerks, it will often take good trout when they are not rising or not feeding near the surface.

High-up Trout on the Fly. The main problem in mountain lakes for the fly fisherman is—how to cover the water? Most altitude lakes of the Cascades do not permit offshore casting because of the nature of the terrain. However, in a few lakes set near or above timber line, the angler can fish from shore without interference for his backcast. There maybe a rock slide or section of shore line where you can walk along and whip out a fly. At other lakes there may be a flat surrounding the inlet and, if the lake is not too shallow at this point, it should be an excellent spot to try a fly. Or if the creek does not enter the lake by a waterfall or steep cascade the inlet itself may show good results.

In some lakes there may be a stream that rushes down the steep mountain side to enter the lake in a small bay. Often a fly cast out into the riffle where the creek enters the lake and allowed to float out with the current until it gradually sinks will take fish. Trout like to lie along this riffle waiting for food to float down and will strike at a fly drifted without drag. ...

One of the fascinations of mountain lake fishing in the Northwest lies in the fact that the angler can be his own explorer and plan a trip into a lake without the aid of guide or pack horse. All that he needs is a geological survey contour map and the urge to climb over the next ridge and find a "lost lake." At the better known lakes he will find a path that a blind man could follow. But before getting into other spots he may have to consult his map and a compass most of the way. He may have to fight brush at the start and then clamber up rock slides and steep cliffs with no trail to guide him. But when he does find the lake, he has the satisfaction of having pioneered the way in all by himself.

Washington's "High-up" Lake Country. Although it takes a bit of studying to locate these seldom-visited spots, there are many mountain valleys that can be fished on a week-day where other anglers will infrequently be found. The following list, which attempts to enumerate only a few of the better-known mountain lake districts, can be used as a basis on which to plan either a Sunday trip or a whole summer vacation.

Western Washington: the Snoqualmie Pass District. In the Snoqualmie Pass area, after starting up the highway out of North Bend, you can branch off up the Middle Fork of the Snoqualmie and head either for Pratt Lake, which contains rainbows and eastern brooks, for Thompson for rainbows and Montana black-spots, or for Myrtle for rainbows. Going further up the Pass you can strike into Tuscohatchee for brookies and rainbows. The Mountain Cabin Memorial Association has, with the co-operation of the U. S. Forest Service, just erected a shelter cabin there for the use of the public. From there you can go into Blue for brookies, Mason for rainbows, Melakwa for brooks and rainbows, Snow for rainbows and black-spots, or Derrick for cutthroats.

Over the hump on the open pine slopes of eastern Washington the angler will find good country back of Keechelus Lake. Lakes in this section include Lost for brooks and rainbows, Cottonwood and Twin for brooks, and Stirrup for rainbows and brooks. Then up the Salmon Lasac country north of Cle Elum there lie a number of scenic lakes, including Pete for rainbows and brooks, Spectacle for brooks, Hyas for rainbows and brooks, and Waptus for brooks and rainbows.

The Skykomish District. Perhaps the most prolifically lake-studded section near Seattle, if not in the Northwest, is that found up the South Fork of the Skykomish River. Here the lakes are clustered as thick as raisins in a fruit cake, ranging in size from bodies of water two miles long to small pot-holes in an alpine meadow. A few of the more easily accessible spots will be sure to have several parties of fishermen every Sunday while the more remote will be visited on only a couple of week-ends each summer.

This is a region of breath-taking grandeur. The peaks run up to 8,000 feet, many of them snow-capped. There are slopes of virgin timber never touched by man extending in every direction as far as the eye can see, there are whole hillsides covered with heather and alpine flowers, and of course there are the lakes. Many of these lie in chains with the lower lake sending its outlet cascading down over a thousand-foot-high ridge. From these vantage points the fisherman can feast his eyes on scenery that, if it were in Switzerland, would have a funicular railway heading into it and a high-priced hotel placed in the center. But the only charge to fish these "sky" lakes is that expended by a good pair of lungs and legs used to hiking.

I remember once hiking into Copper Lake and in the dark of a warm August night spreading the bed roll on the ground next to the open shelter. It was the first time we had been in this spot and it was too late to see anything of the mountain scenery. But when I awoke at early dawn the next morning, the sight was such that I lay in the bed roll for half an hour just soaking in the beauty of the rugged surroundings. Here lay the blue waters of Copper Lake unruffled and darkly mysterious in the early half light. Across the lake, the sun was turning pink the summit of the 6,000-foot ridge that rose steeply from the further edge of the lake. Snow was still hanging in the upper gullies. All the trees and rocks were fresh and new in the dew of morning. A camp robber was teetering on a branch overhead waiting for us to start breakfast. The stiff hike in had already been repaid by a satisfaction we could never buy in the city and the fish we caught afterwards were just the extra dividend for a trip already made worth while.

This section along the South Fork of the Skykomish River includes the watershed of the Miller River. Lakes in this district include Dorothy Lake for brooks and rainbows; and Snoqualmie for cutthroats and black-spots. Then over to the Foss River chain which we have just described, where you find Malachite Lake for black-spots and rainbows; Copper Lake for the same; Hart Lake for rainbows; Angeline and Chetwood for rainbows and golden trout; and Delta for rainbows. Another trip leads into entrancing Necklace Valley, that holds a series of beautiful small lakes stocked with rainbows by the Trailblazers. Going east over the ridge, you come to Marmot for rainbows and goldens; Square for cutthroats; Surprise for rainbows and brooks; and Josephine for rainbows and black-spots. The area north of the Skykomish contains fewer lakes but most of them show extra good fishing. Two of them, Eagle for cutthroats and rainbows and Sims for cutthroats, are unusually good.

Other districts in western Washington that will appeal to the hiker-angler include the Skagit Valley that reaches up into Canada, and the wild, seldom-explored district around Glacier Peak. One of the noted lakes of this section is Byrne Lake north of Kennedy Hot Springs, a long hike in but a grand lake for large rainbows, brooks and cutthroats.

Eastern Washington: Chelan—Bumping River—Mount Adams. South and east of this district lies the Lake Chelan country.

Its main interest is Lake Chelan itself, which is 52 miles long. It is situated in a precipitous gash in the mountains 6,000 feet deep and possesses unparalleled beauty. It is virtually untouched by the tourist. It holds cutthroats, rainbows, silver trout, and Dolly Varden and there are many fine fishing lakes in the surrounding hills. The starting point for these spots and best place to secure information is at the town of Chelan.

Over towering Chinook Pass into eastern Washington, south of Chelan, one may digress up Bumping River to tap a plateau dotted with mountain lakes, each teeming with trout. To list a few, there are Twin Sister for rainbows and brooks; Pear for rainbows; Apple for brooks; Dumbell, Frying Pan, and Jug for brooks; and Cramer and Dog for rainbows.

In the southern part of the state, north of the Columbia in the Mount Adams district, you will find a very beautiful alpine country, open for easy hiking. Mount Adams and Mount St. Helens loom up in sight much of the way along the Forest Service road from Carson to Randle. From this road that winds along at 4,000-foot elevation you sight lakes and odd lava formations from now-extinct volcanoes. From here you can reach Mosquito Lake for brooks, black-spots and rainbows; Council for brooks and black-spots; Goose for brooks; and Steamboat, Placid and Blue for brooks and rainbows.

The Virgin Lakes of the Olympics. Another paradise for the "high-up" angler is the Olympic Peninsula with its little-known Olympic National Park. This territory— the last untouched virgin wilderness in the United States,—is crisscrossed thickly with trails but contains no highways to attract the tin-can tourist. With a timberline at about 5,000 feet one can easily tap many isolated mountain lakes, the majority of them now within the boundaries of Olympic Park.

The best known of all the lakes in this region is the unbelievably beautiful Lake Crescent, which is nine miles long and circled, along one shore, by the highway. This lake of a deep blue color is set down amid surrounding peaks that rise directly from the lake's shores. It has the distinction of holding two species of trout—the Beardsley and the Crescenti—not found anywhere else in the world.

You can spend a week or a month hiking through the park either from north to south, up the Elwha River and then down the Quinault, which takes you from the Strait of Juan de Fuca to the Pacific, or from east to west going up any of the numerous river valleys. Although firearms cannot be carried in the Park, the hiker will sight bands of Roosevelt elk, many deer and occasionally a cougar.

Here are several suggested pack trips.

First, one can start up from the Hamma Hamma River and then take the short stiff climb to Lower Lena, which contains rainbows, some of large size. Proceed to Scout Lake, at an altitude of 4,300 feet, with rainbows, some of them lunkers. Then around Mount Stone to Hagen Lake at 5,400 feet with rainbows weighing up to five pounds, and from there to the top of the ridge and along it to the Stoneway Trail and the First Divide. From here you can make several choices as to how you will get back to a highway. One route would be over to the Duckabush River, visiting Heart Lake, which holds rainbows, and Marmot, also holding rainbows. Then you can circle back to Hood Canal, from where you started, either by way of the Duckabush or Dosewallips watersheds. Alternatively you can turn south west down the East Fork of the Quinault and through Enchanted Valley to the highway at Lake Quinault.

Another way to get to a highway would be to go back to Hood Canal by way of the North Fork of the Skokomish River by the

Hammer Way Trail. You could, on this route, go to Smith Lake, 3,700 feet high, containing brooks, rainbows, and black-spots; Flapjack Lakes, 3,500 feet with rainbows; and then out to Lake Cushman via the Staircase Trail.

A second trip would involve going in from the ocean side and. heading up the Quinault, striking Margaret and Mary lakes at the Low Divide. These two lakes, situated at an altitude of 3,606 feet, are $17^1/_2$ miles in by trail or 27 miles from the end of the road up the Elwha. They hold brooks, rainbows, and black-spots. Two miles away behind Mount Christie are the Martins Lakes, the larger of which holds some lunker blackspots. The Seven Lakes Basin lakes, which hold brooks and black-spots, lie in a beautiful scenic setting and may be reached from Sol Duc Hot Springs.

The Lakes of Rainier National Park. Although Washington's other National Park owes its fame to towering Mount Rainier, it holds as well some interesting alpine lakes. Most of these lakes are tapped either from Chinook Pass or from the Mowich or Yakima Park entrances. The Crystal Lakes are a short stiff hike from Chinook Pass, but they contain some lunker black-spots. Mowich Lake, one of the most beautiful lakes in the Park, may be reached by an easy grade from the Mowich entrance. It holds brooks, rainbows, and black-spots. Through the Carbon River Gate one can take the long hike into Lakes Ethel, James and Marjorie, which formerly put out wonderful catches of black-spots but which now hold mostly rainbows.

Through the Nisqually entrance one can make an easy hike into George Lake—4,232 feet elevation—where on July the Fourth you can see masses of avalanche lilies in a park-like meadow at one end. It produces fine brook and rainbow fishing. Following up the contour from Lake George one goes about three miles up over a ridge to drop down into Goat Lake. During the first week in July the hiker will tramp through hillside after hillside carpeted with bright alpine flowers. Goat Lake at one time provided excellent brook-trout fishing.

The Yakima Park entrance gives access to several small lakes and potholes many of which contain trout, mostly brooks. This district is a fine one in which to do some exploring against the backdrop of

Mount Rainier, fondly called "the Mountain" by Washington alpine hikers.

For the fisherman who does not wish to make back-pack trips into the "high-up lakes," pack horses may be rented that will take him into virtually any one of the districts of the Cascades or Olympics. For information write to the U. S. Forest Service.

Ken Kesey

Oregonian Ken Kesey launched himself into fame in 1962 with the publication of *One Flew Over the Cuckoo's Nest,* from which the selection below is taken. *Sometimes A Great Notion* followed in 1964. Both books were later made into memorable films, *Cuckoo's Nest* winning five Academy Awards. Tom Wolfe's *Electric Cool Aid Acid Test,* in 1968, established Kesey's reputation as the 1960s representative cult figure, but he has continued to evolve in new directions since then, in his personal life, and in books like *Sailor Song.*

In what follows, Kesey's characters, inmates in a mental asylum (the Cuckoo's Nest of the title) experience a rare episode of freedom on a salmon-fishing trip off the Oregon coast.

Salmon Party

A mile or so out George cut the speed to what he called a trolling idle, put four guys to the four poles in the back of the boat, and the rest of us sprawled in the sun on top of the cabin or up on the bow and took off our shirts and watched the guys trying to rig their poles. Harding said the rule was a guy got to hold a pole till he got one strike, then he had to change off with a man who hadn't had a chance. George stood at the wheel, squinting out through the salt-caked windshield, and hollered instructions back how to fix up the reels and lines and how to tie a herring into the herring harness and how far back to fish and how deep:

"And take that number *four* pole and you put you twelve ounces on him on a rope with a breakaway rig—I show you how in joost a minute—and we go after that *big* fella down on the bottom with that pole, by golly!"

Martini ran to the edge and leaned over the side and stared down into the water in the direction of his line. "Oh. Oh, my God," he said, but whatever he saw was too deep down for the rest of us.

There were other sports boats trolling up and down the coast, but George didn't make any attempt to join them; he kept pushing steadily straight on out past them, toward the open sea. "You bet," he said. "We go out with the commercial boats, where the real *fish* is."

The swells slid by, deep emerald on one side, chrome on the other. The only noise was the engine sputtering and humming, off and on, as the swells dipped the exhaust in and out of the water, and the funny, lost cry of the raggedy little black birds swimming around asking one another directions. Everything else was quiet. Some of the guys slept, and the others watched the water. We'd been trolling close to an hour when the tip of Sefelt's pole arched and dived into the water.

"George! Jesus, George, give us a hand!"

George wouldn't have a thing to do with the pole; he grinned and told Sefelt to ease up on the star drag, keep the tip pointed up, *up*, and work hell outa that fella!

"But what if I have a seizure?" Sefelt hollered.

"Why, we'll simply put hook and line on you and use you for a lure," Harding said. "Now work that fella, as the captain ordered, and quit worrying about a seizure."

Thirty yards back of the boat the fish broke into the sun in a shower of silver scales, and Sefelt's eyes popped and he got so excited watching the fish he let the end of his pole go down, and the line snapped into the boat like a rubber band.

"*Up*, I told you! You let him get a straight pull, don't you see? Keep that tip *up...up*! You had you one big silver there, by golly."

Sefelt's jaw was white and shaking when he finally gave up the pole to Fredrickson. "Okay—but if you get a fish with a hook in his mouth, that's my godblessed fish!"

I was as excited as the rest. I hadn't planned on fishing, but after seeing that steel power a salmon has at the end of a line I got off the cabin top and put on my shirt to wait my turn at a pole.

Scanlon got up a pool for the biggest fish and another for the first fish landed, four bits from everybody that wanted in it, and he'd no more'n got his money in his pocket than Billy drug in some awful thing that looked like a ten-pound toad with spines on it like a porcupine.

"That's no fish," Scanlon said. "You can't win on that."

"It isn't a b-b-bird.

"That there, he's a *ling* cod," George told us. "He's one good eating fish you get all his warts off."

"See there. He is too a fish. P-p-pay up."

Billy gave me his pole and took his money and went to sit up close to the cabin where McMurphy and the girl were, looking at the closed door forlornly. "I wu-wu-wu-wish we had enough poles to go around," he said, leaning back against the side of the cabin.

I sat down and held the pole and watched the line swoop out into the wake. I smelt the air and felt the four cans of beer I'd drunk shorting out dozens of control leads down inside me: all around, the chrome sides of the swells flickered and flashed in the sun.

George sang out for us to look up ahead, that here come just what we been looking for. I leaned around to look, but all I saw was a big drifting log and those black seagulls circling and diving around the log, like black leaves caught up in a dust devil. George speeded up some, heading into the place where the birds circled, and the speed of the boat dragged my line until I couldn't see how you'd be able to tell if you did get a bite.

"Those fellas, those cormorants, they go after a school of *candle* fishes," George told us as he drove. "Little white fishes the size of your finger. You dry them and they burn joost like a candle. They are *food* fish, chum fish. And you bet where there's a big school of them candle fish you find the silver salmon feeding."

He drove into the birds, missing the floating log, and suddenly all around me the smooth slopes of chrome were shattered by diving birds and churning minnows, and the sleek silver-blue torpedo backs of the salmon slicing through it all. I saw one of the backs check its direction and turn and set course for a spot thirty yards behind the end of my pole, where my herring would be. I braced, my heart ringing, and then felt a jolt up both arms as if somebody'd hit the pole with a ball bat, and my line went burning off the reel from under my thumb, red as blood. "Use the star drag!" George yelled at me, but what I knew about star drags you could put in your eye so I just mashed harder with my thumb until the line turned back to yellow, then slowed and stopped. I looked around, and there were all three of the other poles whipping around just like mine, and the rest of the guys scrambling down off the cabin at the excitement and doing everything in their power to get underfoot.

"Up! Up! Keep the tip up!" George was yelling.

"McMurphy! Get out here and look at this."

"Godbless you, Fred, you got my blessed fish!"

"McMurphy, we need some help!"

I heard McMurphy laughing and saw him out of the comer of my eye, just standing at the cabin door, not even making a move to do anything, and I was too busy cranking at my fish to ask him for help. Everyone was shouting at him to do something, but he wasn't moving. Even the doctor, who had the deep pole, was asking McMurphy for assistance. And McMurphy was just laughing. Harding finally saw McMurphy wasn't going to do anything, so he got the gaff and jerked my fish into the boat with a clean, graceful motion like he's been boating fish all his life. He's big as my leg, I thought, big as a fence post! I thought, He's bigger'n any fish we ever got at the falls. He's springing all over the bottom of the boat like a rainbow gone wild! Smearing blood and scattering scales like little silver dimes, and I'm scared he's gonna flop overboard. McMurphy won't make a move to help. Scanlon grabs the fish and wrestles it down to keep it from flopping over the side. The girl comes running up from below, yelling it's her turn, dang it, grabs my pole, and jerks the hook into me three times while I'm trying to tie on a herring for her.

"Chief, I'll be damned if I ever saw anything so slow! Ugh, your thumb's bleeding. Did that monster bite you? Somebody fix the Chief's thumb—hurry!"

"Here we go into them again," George yells, and I drop the line off the back of the boat and see the flash of the herring vanish in the dark blue-gray charge of a salmon and the line go sizzling down into the water. The girl wraps both arms around the pole and grits her teeth. "*Oh* no you don't, dang you! *Oh* no...!"

She's on her feet, got the butt of the pole scissored in her crotch and both arms wrapped below the reel and the reel crank knocking against her as the line spins out: "*Oh* no you don't!" She's still got on Billy's green jacket but that reel's whipped it open and everybody on board sees the T-shirt she had on is gone—everybody gawking, trying to play his own fish, dodge mine slamming around the boat bottom, with the crank of that reel fluttering her breast at such a speed the nipple's just a red blur!

Billy jumps to help. All he can think to do is reach around from behind and help her squeeze the pole tighter in between her breasts until the reel's finally stopped by nothing more than the pressure of her flesh. By this time she's flexed so taut and her breasts look so firm I think she and Billy could both turn loose with their hands and arms and she'd *still* keep hold of that pole.

This scramble of action holds for a space, a second there on the sea—the men yammering and struggling and cussing and trying to tend their poles while watching the girl; the bleeding, crashing battle between Scanlon and my fish at everybody's feet; the lines all tangled and shooting every which way with the doctor's glasses-on-a-string tangled and dangling from one line ten feet off the back of the boat, fish striking at the flash of the lens, and the girl cussing for all she's worth and looking now at her bare breasts, one white and one smarting red—and George takes his eye off where he's going and runs the boat into that log and kills the engine.

While McMurphy laughs. Rocking farther and farther backward against the cabin top, spreading his laugh out across the water—laughing at the girl, at the guys, at George, at me sucking my bleeding thumb, at the captain back at the pier and the bicycle rider and the service-station guys and the five thousand houses and the Big Nurse and all of it. Because he knows you have to laugh at the things that hurt you just to keep yourself in balance, just to keep the world from running you plumb crazy. He knows there's a painful side; he knows my thumb smarts and his girl friend has a bruised breast and the doctor is losing his glasses, but he won't let the pain blot out the humor no more'n he'll let the humor blot out the pain.

I notice Harding is collapsed beside McMurphy and is laughing too. And Scanlon from the bottom of the boat. At their own selves as well as at the rest of us. And the girl, with her eyes still smarting as she looks from her white breast to her red one, she starts laughing. And Sefelt and the doctor, and all.

It started slow and pumped itself full, swelling the men bigger and bigger. I watched, part of them, laughing with them—and somehow not with them. I was off the boat, blown up off the water and skating the wind with those black birds, high above myself, and I could look down and see myself and the rest of the guys, see the boat rocking there in the middle of those diving birds, see McMurphy surrounded by his dozen people, and watch them, us, swinging a laughter that rang out on the water in ever-widening circles, farther and farther, until it crashed up on beaches all over the coast, on beaches all over all coasts, in wave after wave after wave.

Norman Maclean

A revered teacher and English professor at the University of Chicago, Montana-born Norman Maclean (1902-1990) didn't begin writing stories about fishing and his family until after his retirement. He was seventy-three when *A River Runs Through It* was published in 1976. Norman Maclean's second book, *Young Men and Fire,* was published posthumously in 1992. More than any other work, *A River Runs Through It* and the film made from it have inspired a widening circle of flyfishers. In the following selection, Maclean tells of his last time fishing with his doomed brother, Paul.

Fishing with Paul

aul said, "Let's fish together today." I knew then that he was still taking care of me, because we almost always split up when we fished. "That's fine," I said. "I'll wade across and fish the other side," he said. I said, "Fine," again, and was doubly touched. On the other side you were backed against cliffs and trees, so it was mostly a roll-casting job, never my specialty. Besides, the river was powerful here with no good place to wade, and next to fishing Paul liked swimming in rivers with his rod in hand. It turned out he didn't have to swim here, but as he waded sometimes the wall of water rose to his upstream shoulder while it would be no higher than his hip behind him. He stumbled to shore from the weight of water in his clothes, and gave me a big wave.

I came down the bank to catch fish. Cool wind had blown in from Canada without causing any electric storms, so the fish should be off the bottom and feeding again. When a deer comes to water, his head shoots in and out of his shoulders to see what's ahead, and I was looking all around to see what fly to put on. But I didn't have to look further than my neck or my nose. Big, clumsy flies bumped into my face, swarmed on my neck and wiggled in my underwear. Blundering and soft- bellied, they had been born before they had brains. They had spent a year under water on legs, had crawled out on a rock, had become flies and copulated with the ninth and tenth segments of their abdomens, and then had died as the first light wind blew them into the water where the fish circled excitedly. They were a fish's dream come true—stupid, succulent, and exhausted from copulation. Still, it would be hard to know what gigantic portion of human life is spent in this same ratio of years under water on legs to one premature, exhausted moment on wings.

I sat on a log and opened my fly box. I knew I had to get a fly that would match these flies exactly, because when a big hatch like this or the salmon fly is out, the fish won't touch anything else. As proof, Paul hadn't had a strike yet, so far as I could see.

I figured he wouldn't have the right fly, and I knew I had it. As I explained earlier, he carried all his flies in his hat-band. He thought that with four or five generals in different sizes he could imitate the action of nearly any aquatic or terrestrial insect in any stage from larval to winged. He was always kidding me because I carried so many flies. "My, my," he would say, peering into my fly box, "wouldn't it be wonderful if a guy knew how to use ten of all those flies." But I've already told you about the Bee, and I'm still sure that there are times when a general won't turn a fish over. The fly that would work now had to be a big fly, it had to have a yellow, black-banded body, and it had to ride high in the water with extended wings, something like a butterfly that has had an accident and can't dry its wings by fluttering in the water.

It was so big and flashy it was the first fly I saw when I opened my box. It was called a Bunyan Bug, tied by a fly tyer in Missoula named Norman Means, who ties a line of big flashy flies all called Bunyan Bugs. They are tied on big hooks, No. 2's and No. 4's, have cork bodies with stiff horsehair tied crosswise so they ride high in the water like dragonflies on their backs. The cork bodies are painted different colors and then are shellacked. Probably the biggest and flashiest of the hundred flies my brother made fun of was the Bunyan Bug No. 2 Yellow Stone Fly.

I took one look at it and felt perfect. My wife, my mother-in-law, and my sister-in-law, each in her somewhat obscure style, had recently redeclared their love for me. I, in my somewhat obscure style, had returned their love. I might never see my brother-in-law again. My mother had found my father's old tackle and once more he was fishing with us. My brother was taking tender care of me, and not catching any fish. I was about to make a killing.

It is hard to cast Bunyan Bugs into the wind because the cork and horsehair make them light for their bulk. But, though the wind shortens the cast, it acts at the same time to lower the fly slowly and almost vertically to the water with no telltale splash. My Stone Fly was still hanging over the water when what seemed like a speedboat went by it, knocked it high into the air, circled, opened the throttle wide on the returning straight away, and roared over the spot marked X where the Stone Fly had settled. Then the speedboat turned into a submarine, disappearing with all on board including my fly, and headed for deep water. I couldn't throw line into the rod fast enough to keep up with what was disappearing and I couldn't change its course. Not being as fast as what was under water, I literally forced it into the air. From where I was I suppose I couldn't see what happened, but my heart was at the end of the line and telegraphed back its impressions as it went by. My general impression was that marine life had turned into a rodeo. My particular information was that a large Rainbow had gone sunfishing, turning over twice in the air, hitting my line each time and tearing loose from the fly which went sailing out into space. My distinct information was that it never looked around to see. My only close-at-hand information was that when the line was reeled in, there was nothing on the end of it but some cork and some hairs from a horse's tail.

The stone flies were just as thick as ever, fish still swirled in quiet water, and I was a little smarter. I don't care much about taking instructions, even from myself, but before I made the next cast I underlined the fact that big Rainbows sometimes come into quiet waters because aquatic insects hatch in or near quiet waters. "Be prepared," I said to myself, remembering an old war song. I also accepted my own advice to have some extra coils of line in my left hand to take some of the tension off the first run of the next big Rainbow swirling in quiet water.

So on this wonderful afternoon when all things came together it took me one cast, one fish, and some reluctantly accepted advice to attain perfection. I did not miss another.

From then on I let them run so far that sometimes they surged clear across the river and jumped right in front of Paul.

When I was young, a teacher had forbidden me to say "more perfect" because she said if a thing is perfect it can't be more so. But by now I had seen enough of life to have regained my confidence in it. Twenty minutes ago I had felt perfect, but by now my brother was taking off his hat and changing flies every few casts. I knew he didn't carry any such special as a Bunyan Bug No. 2 Yellow Stone Fly. I had five or six big Rainbows in my basket which began to hurt my shoulder so I left it behind on shore. Once in a while I looked back and smiled at the basket. I could hear it thumping on the rocks and falling on its side. However I may have violated grammar, I was feeling more perfect with every Rainbow.

Just after my basket gave an extra large thump there was an enormous splash in the water to the left of where I was casting. "My God," I thought before I could look, "there's nothing that big that swims in the Blackfoot," and, when I dared look, there was nothing but a large circle that got bigger and bigger. Finally the first wave went by my knees. "It must be a beaver," I thought. I was waiting for him to surface when something splashed behind me. "My God," I said again, "I would have seen a beaver swim by me under water. " While I was wrenching my neck backwards, the thing splashed right in front of me, too close for comfort but close enough so I could watch what was happening under water. The silt was rising from the bottom like smoke from the spot where lightning had struck. A fair-sized rock was sitting in the spot where the smoke was rising.

While I was relating my past to the present rock, there was another big splash in front of me, but this time I didn't bother to jump.

Beaver, hell! Without looking, I knew it was my brother. It didn't happen often in this life, only when his fishing partner was catching fish and he couldn't. It was a sight, however rare, that he could not bear to watch. So he would spoil his partner's hole, even if it was his brother's. I looked up just in time to see a fair-sized boulder come out of the sky and I ducked too late to keep it from splashing all over me.

He had his hat off and he shook his fist at me. I knew he had fished around his hat band before he threw the rocks. I shook my fist back at him, and waded to shore, where my basket was still thumping. In all my life, I had got the rock treatment only a couple of times before. I was feeling more perfect than ever.

I didn't mind that he spoiled the hole before I had filled my basket, because there was another big hole between us and father. It was a beautiful stretch of water, against cliffs and in shadows. The hole I had just fished was mostly in sunlight—the weather had become cooler, but was still warm enough so that the hole ahead in shadows should be even better than the one in sunlight and I

should have no trouble finishing off my basket with a Bunyan No.
2 Yellow Stone Fly.

Paul and I walked nearly the length of the first hole before we
could hear each other yell across the river. I knew he hated to be
heard yelling, "What were they biting on?" The last two words,
"biting on," kept echoing across the water and pleased me.

When the echoes ceased, I yelled back, "Yellow stone flies." These
words kept saying themselves until they subsided into the sounds
of the river. He kept turning his hat round and round in his hands.

I possibly began to get a little ashamed of myself. "I caught them
on a Bunyan Bug," I yelled. "Do you want one?"

"No," he yelled before "want one" had time to echo. Then "want
one" and "no" passed each other on the back turns.

"I'll wade across with one," I said through the cup of my hands.
That's a lot to say across a river, and the first part of it returning
met the last part of it just starting. I didn't know whether he had
understood what I had said, but the river still answered, "No."

While I was standing in quiet, shady water, I half noticed that
no stone flies were hatching, and I should have thought longer
about what I saw but instead I found myself thinking about
character. It seems somehow natural to start thinking about
character when you get ahead of somebody, especially about the
character of the one who is behind. I was thinking of how, when
things got tough, my brother looked to himself to get himself out
of trouble. He never looked for any flies from me. I had a whole
round of thoughts on this subject before I returned to reality and
yellow stone flies. I started by thinking that, though he was my
brother, he was sometimes knot-headed. I pursued this line of
thought back to the Greeks who believed that not wanting any
help might even get you killed. Then I suddenly remembered that
my brother was almost always a winner and often because he didn't
borrow flies. So I decided that the response we make to character
on any given day depends largely on the response fish are making
to character on the same day. And thinking of the response of fish,
I shifted rapidly back to reality, and said to myself, "I still have one
more hole to go."

I didn't get a strike and I didn't see a stone fly and it was the
same river as the one above, where I could have caught my limit a
few minutes before if my brother hadn't thrown rocks in it. My

prize Bunyan Bug began to look like a fake to me as well as to the fish. To me, it looked like a floating mattress. I cast it upstream and let it drift down naturally as if it had died. Then I popped it into the water as if it had been blown there. Then I made it zigzag while retrieving it, as if it were trying to launch itself into flight. But it evidently retained the appearance of a floating mattress. I took it off, and tried several other flies. There were no flies in the water for me to match, and by the same token there were no fish jumping.

I began to cast glances across the river under my hat brim. Paul wasn't doing much either. I saw him catch one, and he just turned and walked to shore with it, so it couldn't have been much of a fish. I was feeling a little less than more perfect.

Then Paul started doing something he practically never did, at least not since he had been old enough to be cocky. He suddenly started fishing upstream, back over the water he had just fished. That's more like me when I feel I haven't fished the hole right or from the right angle, but, when my brother fished a hole, he assumed nothing was left behind that could be induced to change its mind.

I was so startled I leaned against a big rock to watch.

Almost immediately he started hauling them in. Big ones, and he didn't spend much time landing them either. I thought he gave them too little line and took them in too fast, but I knew what he was up to. He expected to make a killing in this hole, and he wasn't going to let any one fish thrash around in the water until it scared the rest off. He had one on now and he held the line on it so tight he was forcing it high in the air. When it jumped, he leaned back on his rod and knocked the fish into the water again. Full of air now, it streaked across the top of the water with its tail like the propeller of a seaplane until it could get its submarine chambers adjusted and submerge again.

He lost a couple but he must have had ten by the time he got back to the head of the hole.

Then he looked across the river and saw me sitting beside my rod. He started fishing again, stopped, and took another look. He cupped his hands and yelled, "Do you have George's No. 2 Yellow Hackle with a feather not a horsehair wing?" It was fast water and I didn't get all the words immediately. "No. 2" I caught first, because it is a hell of a big hook, and then "George," because he was our fishing pal, and then "Yellow." With that much information I started to look in my box, and let the other words settle into a sentence later.

One bad thing about carrying a box loaded with flies, as I do, is that nearly half the time I still don't have the right one.

"No," I admitted across the water, and water keeps repeating your admissions.

"I'll be there," he called back and waded upstream.

"No," I yelled after him, meaning don't stop fishing on my account. You can't convey an implied meaning across a river, or, if you can, it is easy to ignore. My brother walked to the lower end of the first hole where the water was shallow and waded across.

By the time he got to me, I had recovered most of the pieces he must have used to figure out what the fish were biting. From the moment he had started fishing upstream his rod was at such a slant and there was so much slack in his line that he must have been fishing with a wet fly and letting it sink. In fact, the slack was such that he must have been letting the fly sink five or six inches. So when I was fishing this hole as I did the last one—with a cork-body fly that rides on top of the water—I was fighting the last war. "No. 2" hook told me of course it was a hell of a big insect, but "yellow" could mean a lot of things. My big question by the time he got to me was, "Are they biting on some aquatic insect in a larval or nymph stage or are they biting on a drowned fly?"

He gave me a pat on the back and one of George's No. 2 Yellow Hackles with a feather wing. He said, "They are feeding on drowned yellow stone flies."

I asked him, "How did you think that out?"

He thought back on what had happened like a reporter. He started to answer, shook his head when he found he was wrong, and then started out again. "All there is to thinking," he said, "is seeing something noticeable which makes you see something you weren't noticing which makes you see something that isn't even visible."

I said to my brother, "Give me a cigarette and say what you mean."

"Well," he said, "the first thing I noticed about this hole was that my brother wasn't catching any. There's nothing more noticeable to a fisherman than that his partner isn't catching any.

"This made me see that I hadn't seen any stone flies flying around this hole."

Then he asked me, "What's more obvious on earth than sunshine and shadow, but until I really saw that there were no stone flies hatching here I didn't notice that the upper hole where they were hatching was mostly in sunshine and this hole was in shadow."

I was thirsty to start with, and the cigarette made my mouth drier so I flipped the cigarette into the water.

"Then I knew," he said, "if there were flies in this hole they had to come from the hole above that's in the sunlight where there's enough heat to make them hatch.

"After that, I should have seen them dead in the water. Since I couldn't see them dead in the water, I knew they had to be at least six or seven inches under the water where I couldn't see them. So that's where I fished."

He leaned against a big rock with his hands behind his head to make the rock soft. "Wade out there and try George's No. 2," he said, pointing at the fly he had given me.

I didn't catch one right away, and I didn't expect to. My side of the river was the quiet water, the right side to be on in the hole above where the stone flies were hatching, but the drowned stone flies were washed down in the powerful water on the other side of this hole. After seven or eight casts, though, a small ring appeared on the surface. A small ring usually means that a small fish has risen to the surface, but it can also mean a big fish has rolled under water. If it is a big fish under water, he won't look so much like a fish as an arch of a rainbow that has appeared and disappeared.

Paul didn't even wait to see if I landed him. He waded out to talk to me. He went on talking as if I had time to listen to him and land a big fish. He said, "I'm going to wade back again and fish the rest of the hole." Sometimes I said, "Yes," and when the fish went out of the water, speech failed me, and when the fish made a long run I said at the end of it, "You'll have to say that over again."

Finally, we understood each other. He was going to wade the river again and fish the other side. We both should fish fairly fast, because Father probably was already waiting for us. Paul threw his cigarette in the water and was gone without seeing whether I landed the fish.

Not only was I on the wrong side of the river to fish with drowned stone flies, but Paul was a good enough roll caster to have already fished most of my side from his own. But I caught two more. They also started as little circles that looked like little fish feeding on the surface but were broken arches of big rainbows under water. After I caught these two, I quit. They made ten, and the last three were the finest fish I ever caught. They weren't the biggest or most spectacular fish I ever caught, but they were the three fish I caught because my brother waded across the river to give me the fly that would catch them and because they were the last fish I ever caught fishing with him.

Steve Raymond

Bellingham-born Steve Raymond has written some of the best books on fishing the Northwest and other waters. Although he has written recently enough to belong with the writers in the first section of this anthology, his work and life also reach back to embrace the Northwest tradition of Roderick Haig-Brown, Enos Bradner, and others. His first book, *Kamloops*, has become the definitive work on British Columbia's Kamloops trout. As a journalist and editor with the *Seattle Times* for almost thirty years, he received a Pulitzer Prize for feature writing in 1984. His *The Year of the Angler* has won wide praise, and his other fishing books are all highly regarded. The following selection closes his *The Year of the Trout* (1985), as it also closes this book.

The End of the Year

The year ebbs. The blush of autumn fades quickly from the hills and the first fall storms come sweeping in from the Pacific to drop their heavy freight of rain. The days give up on their warmth and the darkness lasts well into morning and comes again before the afternoon is done. High on the hillsides the snowfields start to grow; next year they will become the rivers.

All the quick life of the long warm months of spring and summer has gone to rest and the hills and valleys turn dark and drab in the gray late-autumn light. The days flow past as swiftly as the current in the streams and the prospect of winter hovers like a darkening storm on the near horizon. The season is late; the old familiar cycle once more is drawing to an end.

The years rest easily on the earth, which has seen so many come and go, but they weigh heavily on men. Inevitably their toll is felt: the trails begin to seem a little longer, the current in the rivers feels a little stronger and a dry fly floating at the end of a long cast becomes a much harder thing to see. There is a reminder of all these things in the passage of a year, and perhaps that is one reason why a trout fisherman seems determined to take advantage of every last remaining day. He plans one final trip, and then perhaps one more, even though the harsh breath of early winter already is blowing through the land.

I remember one such late-season trip. It still seemed too early to think of winter, though it was cold and wet when Pat Kirkpatrick and I left the city in early-morning darkness, and when we reached the Cascades summit the first light of dawn revealed fresh snow along the road. We agreed that was not unusual in the high country, but the snow persisted all through our long descent of the eastern slope. There was even snow around the Columbia Basin lake that was our destination, and we left the only tracks on the trail leading in. The air was as cold as the blade of a knife and the lake was dark and still as we launched our boats and began to fish alone.

After a while it grew even colder and crusts of ice began forming in our fly-rod guides. No trout took hold, nor did we even see a sign of one, and there was nothing to relieve the freezing monotony of the dark morning. The cold numbed our faces and fingers until finally we could tolerate it no longer; we went ashore, shook the snow from broken sagebrush limbs and built a reluctant fire. Its pale flame was a welcome sight, but though we huddled close we could feel little of its heat; the air was so bitter that even the fire seemed cold.

But we persevered, and early in the afternoon the air warmed a little and at last the trout began to stir. First there was a solitary rise far out in the center of the shallow lake; it was followed by another, then several at a time. Pat hit a fish and then I had one and before the afternoon was done each of us had caught a half dozen or more—all big, bright, hard-fighting rainbows. That night we drove to town and treated ourselves to a big steak dinner in a warm restaurant and decided the day had been well spent despite the discomfort we had been through.

Another time Ed Foss and I set out on a dark late-November day to fish for sea-run cutthroat. A cold wind drove mixed rain and snow into our faces and whipped the water to a froth so that we were forced to seek shelter along a lee shore. Late in the day, when we were thoroughly wet and chilled, we returned to the boat ramp and found a game warden in a warm car, waiting to check our licenses. His greeting was abrupt: "I've been all over this county and you two are the only damn fools I could find outdoors on a day like this." But he was surprised to learn we had both caught fish despite the weather, and by the standards of estuary fishing it had been a most successful day.

Yet there have been other days that were not so successful, days when we pushed the season or the weather or our luck a little too far, when wind or rain or snow or uncooperative trout forced a quick retreat indoors. And though such days tend to be soon forgotten, I suspect there have been more of them than any other kind.

What magic quality does the trout possess that compels men to search for it in such dark and desperate weather? What virtue does it offer to command such unwavering devotion? I can answer only for myself: I love trout because they are among the most beautiful and graceful of all creatures and because they dwell in some of the most beautiful and graceful of all places. I love them because I am a fly fisherman and trout inspired the invention of my sport; without them it would be a very different sport, if indeed it existed at all.

The trout has a way of rising to a floating fly that takes your breath away, and I love it for that and for what it will do after the fly is firmly taken. I love trout because they are honest and uncompromising creatures; no man was ever cheated by a trout. I love them because they have inspired me to seek a wider knowledge of the natural world, and such knowledge brings immense satisfaction and pleasure. And I love trout because they have led me into friendships with others who feel about them as I do, and such friendships make a man's life immeasurably richer.

A trout, by its very nature, is a thing that can only be touched and briefly held; an angler can never truly capture one or call a trout his own. If a trout is killed it becomes a lump of cold flesh, bereft of all the virtues that make it worth seeking; if it is returned to the stream, then the angler who caught it is left with only his fragile memory for a keepsake. Yet those are the only choices, and in that mysterious ephemeral quality of trout is the very magic that makes it something larger than itself: For us it becomes the fleeting fulfillment of a dream, a symbol that a man's hopes are sometimes realized—if only for a moment. That is why the trout commands such devotion from so many, why catching one sometimes is a mystical experience that strikes sparks in a fisherman's soul.

The bond between men and trout runs deep, though it is not ordinarily a thing that fishermen acknowledge or discuss. But it is always there, and sometimes it is revealed in unexpected ways.

One such display remains vivid in my mind. I was fishing the North Fork of the Stillaguamish and had hiked upstream from my cabin to a point where I could see the Deer Creek Riffle was empty, with no other anglers in sight. The empty stream was inviting and I hurried forward, but I had taken only a few steps when two fishermen emerged from the woods near the top of the run; they were much closer to it than I was, and my heart sank when I saw them.

But there was something unusual about the pair. They were moving at a painfully slow pace, and as I got closer I could see that although both wore waders and fishing vests and carried fly rods, one was on crutches and the other was helping him swing his legs over the scattered boulders. I stood aside and watched their slow progress toward the stream; when they finally reached it, the lame man leaned on his friend and together they inched their way out until they were knee-deep in the river. Then the helper took a crutch away, leaving his companion with only one to lean on, and gently placed a fly rod in his free hand. With the remaining crutch tucked under one arm, the lame man began to cast.

It was a touching sight and my heart went out to the young man leaning on the single crutch while the river curled around him. I learned from his friend that a bulldozer had crushed his legs and this was his first outing after many months in the hospital. Chances were he might never walk again, but even such a tragic infirmity was not enough to keep him from returning to the pursuit he loved. As I watched him there, standing unsteadily in the pool, I could not help but admire his quiet courage, and I said a silent prayer that a steelhead soon would come and take his fly.

The great sorrow is that all men do not love the trout as much. For a creature that has given men so much pleasure, inspiration and reward, the trout has suffered grievously from the activities of man. Too often it has been the victim of human ignorance, shortsightedness, or greed; the evidence lies everywhere in ruined rivers, defoliated slopes, impassable dams, and polluting industries. The truth is that man has nothing so important or urgent to do that he needs to sacrifice the trout or its habitat in order or do it— but truth is something that often is difficult for men to see while there is yet a chance to profit from the sight.

That the trout has been able to survive at the hands of man is a tribute to the toughness of its breed and to the efforts of those who have worked to preserve it. But it is late in The Year of the Trout and the future is far from assured.

November falls from the calendar like a last lonely stubborn leaf. Along the rivers the trees stand bare and bleak and dripping from the rain. In the limbs of some the eagles sit and wait, watching for the current to bring them the last of the spawned-out salmon.

The rain clatters heavily on the dead leaves that clad the forest floor and soaks down through them to the soil; soon it will re-emerge in far-off springs. Rain fills the swamps and beaver ponds in the deep woods and collects in little brooks and rivulets that mutter on the hillsides. Day after day it rains until all the springs and swamps and rivulets and brooks begin pouring their swollen discharge into the rivers. The rivers grow fat and gray and reach out to reclaim the gravel bars and empty sloughs that have been left to dry since spring. Sometimes it rains so long and hard that the rivers cannot carry the full weight of water pressing down on them; hour by hour they edge upward until suddenly they are out of their banks and running through the fields, breaking roads and threatening the transient works of men. People curse them, but the rivers are only doing what rivers have always done.

The swollen December flow brings up the first big run of winter steelhead, though their passage may be hidden by the glut of water. But late in the month, when the weather turns colder and the rivers begin to subside, there may be a chance to fish for them.

Such fishing, when and if it comes, has an unmistakable air of finality about it. There is the certain knowledge that it is the very last fishing of the year, that the steelhead—so bright and lively now—will soon be spent from spawning as their own cycle nears an end. Even the rivers seem to grow old before our eyes: We cast into the present, which exists only for the instant it takes for it to pass; then it flows downstream, forever beyond our reach, and becomes the past. Looking downstream is like looking backward from December at all the vanished moments of the year.

Some of those moments we will long remember—good times spent in pleasant places, the company of friends around the campfire, the thrill of large trout won or lost, and all the host of happy things that only a trout fisherman can know or feel or understand. These are rewards that we alone can share.

Now the winter dusk fades into darkness and the darkness brings more rain. Soon the rain becomes snow, heavy and wet and melting at its first touch upon the soil. But then it grows colder and the snow turns thick and fine and begins to stay; it collects first upon the foothill slopes, then reaches down into the valleys and finally settles slowly on the anglers' trails and empty campfire rings along the rivers.

In the softness of the snowy night the year at last steals quietly away. But time and the rivers continue flowing—and below the surface of the silent streams, the trout are always there.

Acknowledgments

Special thanks are extended to Ted Leeson and Jessica Maxwell for their suggestions, and for their help in securing permissions for this book. I also wish to thank Jo Alexander of OSU Press for her very helpful editorial assistance, and Bob Frank, Warren Slesinger, and others at OSU Press for their encouragement and support of this project.

"The Farthest Distance Between Two Points," from **The Habit of Rivers** by Ted Leeson. © 1994 by Ted Leeson. Reprinted by special arrangement with the Lyons Press (www.lyonspress.com).

"Building With Bones," from **North Bank** by Robin Carey. © 1998 by Robin Carey. Reprinted with permission of Oregon State University Press.

"River Deep, Mountain High," from **I Don't Know Why I Swallowed the Fly** by Jessica Maxwell. © 1997 by Jessica Maxwell. Reprinted with permission of Jessica Maxwell.

"Obituary With Bamboo Fly Rod," from **Bamboo Fly Rod Suite** by Frank Soos. © 1999 by Frank Soos. Reprinted with permission of The University of Georgia Press.

"Walk on Water For Me," © 1995 by Lorian Hemingway. Reprinted with permission of Lorian Hemingway.

"Where I Lived and What I Lived For," from **The River Why** by David James Duncan. © 1983 by David James Duncan. Reprinted with permission of Sierra Club Books.

"The Novitiate's Tale," from **The Night Gardener** by Marjorie Sandor. © 1996 by Marjorie Sandor. Reprinted by special arrangement with the Lyons Press.

"The Emerger," © 1991 by Mallory Burton. Reprinted from **Uncommon Waters: Women Write About Fishing**, edited by Holly Morris and published by Seal Press.

"The Deschutes River," from **Riverwalking** by Kathleen Dean Moore. © 1995 by Kathleen Dean Moore. Reprinted with special arragement with the Lyons Press.

"The Lesson," by Peter Patricelli. Printed with permission of Peter Patricelli.